HISTORY AND READING

Tocqueville, Foucault, French Studies

DOMINICK LACAPRA
Green College Lectures
Green College, University of British Columbia

UNIVERSITY OF TORONTO PRESS
Toronto Buffalo London

© University of Toronto Press Incorporated 2000
Toronto Buffalo London
Printed in Canada

ISBN 0-8020-4394-1 (cloth)
ISBN 0-8020-8200-9 (paper)

Printed on acid-free paper

Canadian Cataloguing in Publication Data

LaCapra, Dominick, 1939–
History and reading : Tocqueville, Foucault, French studies

(Green College lecture series)
Includes bibliographical references and index.
ISBN 0-8020-4394-1 (bound)   ISBN 0-8020-8200-9 (pbk.)

1. France – Study and teaching.   2. France – Historiography.
3. Literature and history.   4. History – Methodology.
5. Tocqueville, Alexis de, 1805–1859. Ancien régime et la révolution.
6. Foucault, Michel. Folie et déraison.   I. Title.   II. Series.

DC36.9.L32 1999   944′.007′2   C99-932802-6

A version of Chapter 1 was published in *The American Historical Review*
100 (1995), 799–828.

The University of Toronto Press acknowledges the financial assistance
to its publishing program of the Canada Council for the Arts and
the Ontario Arts Council.

University of Toronto Press acknowledges the financial support for its
publishing activities of the Government of Canada through the
Book Publishing Industry Development Program (BPIDP).

Canadä

For Véronique

Contents

Introduction
3

1 History, Reading, and Critical Theory
21

2 Rereading Tocqueville's *Old Régime*
73

3 Rereading Foucault's 'History of Madness'
123

4 Reconfiguring French Studies
169

Index
227

HISTORY AND READING

Introduction

My goals in this book are both broad and restricted – my subject is the relationship between history and reading, particularly with respect to the area of French studies, but I attempt to exemplify this relationship in two limited case studies. In the chapters focusing on Alexis de Tocqueville's *The Old Régime and the French Revolution*[1] and Michel Foucault's 'History of Madness' (*Folie et déraison: Histoire de la folie à l'âge classique*)[2] I hope to realize at least some of the ambitions of the initial and concluding theoretical or programmatic chapters, but they do not answer all of the challenges raised.[3] The purpose of the first and final chapters is to explore certain possibilities

---

1 Alexis de Tocqueville, *The Old Régime and the French Revolution*, trans. Stuart Gilbert (1858; New York, 1955). The French edition is *L'Ancien Régime et la révolution*, intro. Georges Lefebvre (Paris, 1952–3).
2 Michel Foucault, *Folie et déraison; Histoire de la folie à l'âge classique* (Paris, 1961). Partial translation (based on Foucault's abridged edition) by Richard Howard as *Madness and Civilization* (New York, 1965).
3 The reader might also be interested in consulting my *History and Memory after Auschwitz* (Ithaca and London, 1998), especially chaps. 3 ('Rereading Camus's *The Fall* after Auschwitz and with Algeria') and 4 ('Lanzmann's *Shoah*: "Here There Is No Why"').

and difficulties in the largest of senses, and I hope the reader will find them thought-provoking without seeking a perfect 'fit' between their arguments and the case studies. Indeed, especially in the final chapter, my explicit intention is to have my reach extend beyond my grasp in order to indicate my sense of French studies as a crucial area in which the problem of history and reading is at issue, especially with respect to the interaction between the fields of history and literary studies. The first and last chapters may also provide a basis for both framing and constructively criticizing the two case studies by indicating the ways in which the reading of texts I undertake must be expanded and transformed if reading is to become a crucial component of newer forms of historical and cultural inquiry.

In the first chapter I delineate five modes of reading that may be variously combined in the works of different figures. My two case studies focus on texts of authors who interweave various reading practices in ways that may achieve a significant degree of distinctiveness on the general level of modes of interpretation and analysis. To some significant extent, moreover, they may be seen as engaging in the kind of reconstruction of and dialogic exchange with the phenomena of the past that I delineate and defend in the first chapter – what Foucault theorized as genealogical analysis stimulated by, or at least having a bearing on, problems of the present with an eye to future possibilities. My own approach to Tocqueville and Foucault attempts to identify the virtues and limitations of two specific texts within the larger context of their authors' thought as a whole.

Both Tocqueville's and Foucault's work contains much of value. Through largely sympathetic, although at times rigorous, criticism, a dialogic exchange between the perspectives they elaborated may be generated – an exchange that will not result in a simple affirmation of one of the two perspectives and that may even reveal essential tensions. A principal incentive for discussing Tocqueville and Foucault between the covers of the same book is my belief that scholars working in the traditions of one of these important figures rarely read either the works of or commentary on the other. Such an exchange would be mutually beneficial and one of my goals is to initiate it, in good part because it might well lead to a re-examination of certain assumptions. To put it bluntly, those interested in Tocqueville often share his liberal assumptions, which are not subjected to critical scrutiny. They also tend to focus on the mainstream institutions, social formations, and cultural tendencies that Tocqueville addressed: the state, the family, education, the workplace, classes, and bureaucracy, as well as representative or prevalent ideas, mores, and mentalities. Those working on Foucault may similarly share his assumptions (although perhaps to a lesser extent than those working in Tocqueville's liberal tradition), and they may equally fail to approach his assumptions and important concepts with a sufficiently critical eye. Moreover, scholars working on or with Foucault tend to focus on more diffuse, cross-disciplinary, and marginal (or marginalized) groups or phenomena: the mad, sexuality, disciplinarity, the body, and homosexuality. They tend not to have Tocqueville as a reference point.[4] Those relating to

---

4 See, for example, the important work of Judith Butler, notably *Gender Trouble: Feminism and the Subversion of Identity* (New York and London, 1990); *Bodies That Matter: On the Discursive Limits of 'Sex'* (New York and London, 1993), and *The Psychic Life of Power: Theories in Subjection* (Stanford, Ca., 1997). Two other important figures working in a post-structural frame of reference, for which Foucault is at least pertinent, are Ernesto Laclau and Chantal Mouffe. They develop their concept of radical democracy with little reference to Tocqueville, even though he might be significant for revealing the limits of populism and the importance of a liberal admixture even in radical democracy, notably

Tocqueville or, more generally, to the liberal tradition to which he contributed, rarely devote sustained attention to the difficult and experimental thought of someone like Foucault; to the extent that they do, it may well be only (or at least primarily) to warn of its dangers, bemoan its consequences, or question its acuity.[5] This contrast may be somewhat overdrawn, but it serves heuristically to under-

---

in terms of constitutionalism and minority rights. See esp. Laclau and Mouffe's *Hegemony and Socialist Strategy* (London, 1985).

5 See, for example, Luc Ferry and Alain Renaut, *French Philosophy of the Sixties: An Essay on Antihumanism*, trans. Mary H.S. Cattani (1985; Amherst, Mass., 1990), which may well be the most important critique of Foucault and other post-structural figures that is both philosophical in the fundamental nature of its arguments and situated within a broadly Tocquevillian tradition. The French title is more telling than its English translation: *La Pensée 68*. '68 thinking' implies that, with respect to the political events of 1968 in France, '68 philosophy is part of a meaningful whole whose importance it illuminates while being illuminated by it' (62) – a circular, hermeneutic (or perhaps symptomatic [xix]) relation between context and thought or text whose very circularity Ferry and Renaut criticize when Foucault applies it in his analysis of Descartes (86). In their understanding, 1968 is the latest incarnation of the revolutionary tradition in all its sterile, misguided agitation that so preoccupied – and engendered anxiety in – Tocqueville. Foucault (along with Derrida) is a prime instigator and vehicle of '68 thinking, and 'The History of Madness' is seen as 'the inaugural work of '68 philosophy' (81). Ferry and Renaut find Foucault's thought incoherently divided between 'a Nietzschean / Heideggerain critique of reason in the name of "unreason," if not in fact irrationality, and a [Marxist] critique of bourgeois rationality in the name of another rationality, if only a potential one' (79) – despite Foucault's explicit attempts to distance himself from Marx. Ferry and Renaut attempt to demonstrate the dubiousness of extreme antihumanism and an all-or-nothing logic, which they usefully counter with a postmetaphysical humanism and a modified conception of autonomy. But their own humanism remains exclusively anthropocentric and is founded on invidious distinctions *vis-à-vis* other beings, and they are able to see antihumanism's presumed critique of the 'catastrophic effects' of humanism only in terms of serving 'man's' interests ('for whom if not for man?' they ask rhetorically [xxv]). Moreover, despite their pre-emptive efforts to avoid being called 'simplistic' (229), their argument does at times oversimplify issues and is close to a dismissive or debunking polemic. For example, it is hyperbolic and open to question to claim that

Introduction 7

score the interest of discussing Tocqueville and Foucault together and to initiate both comparisons and modes of possible interaction between the forms of inquiry that they undertook and for which they have become icons. Both Tocqueville and Foucault have been particularly important, in France and elsewhere, as what Foucault terms 'initiators of discursive practices.' We refer to 'Foucauldian' analyses of problems, and the conversion of a proper name into an adjective signals the fact that someone has initiated a discursive practice or provided a way of analysing and conceptualizing issues. 'Tocquevillian' analysis is less common, although this denomination does occur. But Tocqueville's texts have given rise to various,

---

'The History of Madness' is 'the inaugural work of '68 philosophy.' Moreover, it is not clear why a Marxist critique, which appears at best as a subtheme in 'The History of Madness' and, if anything, is not sufficiently sustained throughout Foucault's works, may not reinforce a Heideggerian / Nietzschean critique insofar as the latter cannot be reduced to a simple opposition between reason and '"unreason," if not in fact irrationality.' The model for Ferry and Renaut's approach to the role of intellectuals in France was perhaps set by Tocqueville in *The Old Régime* (which I discuss later); its more recent avatar is Raymond Aron's spirited *Opium of the Intellectuals*, trans. Terence Kilmartin (Garden City, N.Y., 1957). For an approach that may be instructively contrasted with that of Ferry and Renaut, see Mark Poster, *Existential Marxism in Postwar France* (Princeton, N.J., 1975) and *Cultural History and Postmodernity* (New York, 1997). The latter book includes a discussion of both Foucault and François Furet's use of Tocqueville in interpreting the French Revolution. For political and social theorists who have primarily negative or very mixed responses to Foucault but who raise issues worthy of consideration, I would make special mention of Nancy Fraser, Michael Walzer, Charles Taylor, and Jürgen Habermas. See Fraser, *Unruly Practices: Power, Discourse and Gender in Contemporary Social Theory* (Minneapolis, Minn., 1989), Walzer, 'The Politics of Michel Foucault,' and Taylor, 'Foucault on Freedom and Truth,' in David Couzens Hoy, ed., *Foucault: A Critical Reader* (New York, 1986), 51–68, and 69–102. Habermas also has an essay in this collection ('Taking Aim at the Heart of the Present,' 103–8). But see esp. his *Philosophical Discourse of Modernity* (Cambridge, Mass., 1987), chaps. 9 and 10.

more or less distinctive forms of political, social, and cultural analysis, for example, in the work of such important scholars as Louis Hartz, Raymond Aron, and François Furet.[6] A close analysis of key texts of Foucault and Tocqueville that is sensitive to the broader dimensions of their work and its impact or later reinscriptions should prove rewarding. Tocqueville has recently become a reference point for neoliberals or liberal-neoconservatives (such as Mark Lilla in the United States or Luc Ferry and Alain Renaut in France) who – in a kind of generational Oedipal revolt involving an intellectual return to the perspectives of less fashionable fathers (such as Aron) or even great-grandfathers (such as Tocqueville) – would like to counteract if not eliminate the recent and pervasive influence of Foucault and other figures labelled 'poststructuralist.' Despite the valuable attempt to question

---

6 See Louis Hartz, *The Liberal Tradition in America: An Interpretation of American Political Thought* (1955; New York, 1983); Raymond Aron, *Main Currents of Sociological Thought*, 2 vols. (1967; Garden City, N.Y., 1968–70); and François Furet, *Interpreting the French Revolution*, trans. Elborg Forster (1978; Cambridge, 1981). See also Marcel Gauchet and Gladys Swain, *La Pratique de l'esprit humain: L'Institution asilaire et la révolution démocratique* (Paris, 1980), for an attempt to criticize Foucault's history of madness on Tocquevillian grounds. Gauchet and Swain argue that the modern treatment of the mad is an effect not of exclusion but of inclusion relating to democratization and the *de jure* equality of conditions (in contrast to medieval hierarchy, which allowed familiarity because of the assumption of the radical otherness of the mad with whom one could not communicate). One may question some of their readings of Foucault (for example, they appear to believe that Foucault simply dichotomizes between exclusion and inclusion or integration), and their argument consists largely of counter-claims made in a manner that seems to render adjudication between them and Foucault's ideas impossible. In *French Philosophy of the Sixties*, Ferry and Renault take their argument as quite flatly refuting Foucault (90–7), but Gauchat and Swain make use of Foucault's later views in 'refuting' his history of madness. For example, they see the asylum as a panoptic utopia that employed a regimen of discipline and internalization in attempting to bring the mad to reason.

extreme antihumanism and to rethink the liberal tradition, this recourse to Tocqueville at times tends to obscure his more radical analytic endeavours and either to resist theory or to flatten it in order to make it accord with liberal-conservative or neoconservative inclinations. One goal of my discussion of Tocqueville is to reveal the tensions in his own thought that make evident the limitations of this recent turn.[7]

The idea of a Foucauldian analysis or 'reading' applies, I think, primarily to approaches derived from Foucault's later studies, notably *Surveiller et punir: Naissance de la prison*.[8] In the work of so-called new historicists, particularly those for a time gathered around the journal *Representations*, this approach has involved postulating a prevalent if not dominant sociocultural or political discourse or discursive practice (for example, panoptic discourse) and tracing the more or less complex, primarily 'symptomatic' ways in which artifacts, particularly those of 'high' culture,

---

7 Ferry and Renaut's *French Philosophy of the Sixties* is intentionally more limited than Tocqueville's analysis of the old régime in that, except for a chapter in which they discuss on a theoretical level the interpretations of May '68 offered by others (indicating a preference for Raymond Aron's *La Révolution introuvable* (*The Elusive Revolution: Anatomy of a Student Revolt* [1968; New York, 1969])), they focus predominantly on thought and intellectuals. Their understanding of larger cultural forces is for the most part restricted to the role of individualism in Tocqueville's sense of withdrawal from the political sphere, a turn to private life, apathy, hedonism, and even narcissism – which they both see as linking '68 to the eighties and contrast with the conception of the autonomous subject they defend. In Tocqueville, as we shall see, there is at least some basis within the argument of *The Old Régime* for criticizing the tendency to scapegoat intellectuals, for, despite the economic limitations of his analysis, Tocqueville goes far in revealing the social, political, and cultural problems that helped create instability and revolutionary agitation in France.

8 Michel Foucault, *Surveiller et punir: Naissance de la prison* (Paris, 1975); trans. by Alan Sheridan as *Discipline and Punish: The Birth of the Prison* (New York, 1978).

have recycled, reinforced, or 'policed' it.[9] The results have been impressive, but the risk incurred is a levelling or homogenizing understanding both of discourse and of the relations of artifacts (notably literary texts) to it.[10] What tends to be eliminated in this approach are the more critical and transformative dimensions of the interactions both within discourse and in the relation of artifacts to prevalent or dominant sociocultural or political discourses and practices.[11] Foucault's understanding of discursive practice and of the relations of artifacts to it tends, however allusively, to be somewhat more intricate and open to various possibilities in his history of madness, and this is one reason for a rereading of it. Indeed, his study of mad-

---

9 See, for example, D.A. Miller, *The Novel and the Police* (Berkeley, 1988). In its very inclusions and exclusions, the reader edited by Paul Rabinow is a good indication of the aspects of Foucault's work that were most important for new historicists, especially the *Representations* group at Berkeley. See *The Foucault Reader* (New York, 1984).

10 In an interview (first published in 1986) Foucault was asked the question: 'What place, what status, have literary works in your research?' He answered: 'In *Histoire de la folie* and *Les Mots et les choses*, I merely indicated them, pointed them out in passing. I was the kind of stroller who says: "Well, when you see that, you cannot but talk about *Le Neveu de Rameau*." But I accorded them no role in the actual economy of the process.' Referring to the next phase of his work, he adds: 'I moved from the expectative (pointing literature out when I happened to encounter it, without indicating its relations with the rest) to a frankly negative position, trying to bring out positively all the nonliterary or parallel discourses that were actually produced at a given period, excluding literature itself. In *Surveiller et punir* I refer only to bad literature ...' 'The Functions of Literature,' in Michel Foucault, *Politics, Philosophy, Culture: Interviews and Other Writings 1977–1984*, ed. with an intro. by Lawrence D. Kritzman (New York and London, 1988), 307–8.

11 For an elaboration and defence of this view, see my *History, Politics, and the Novel* (Ithaca and London, 1987) and 'Ideology and Critique in Dickens's *Bleak House*,' *Representations* 6 (1984), 116–23 (reprinted in Jeremy Tambling, ed., *Bleak House: Contemporary Critical Essays* (New York, 1998), 128–38).

ness radically tests and contests the assumptions of both Tocquevillian liberalism and conventional historiography. Even if we disagree with certain dimensions of its argument or style, *L'Histoire de la folie* enables us to recognize and question those assumptions.

I would, in an introductory fashion, like to make explicit certain comparisons between Tocqueville and Foucault that are at times left implicit in the body of the text. I shall begin with general similarities which, although worth noting, should not be the only level of inquiry, as they would then obscure specific problems in the critical analysis and reading of their work. Still, both are concerned in different ways with the relations among customs, institutions, practices, affect, and thought. Tocqueville employs an older vocabulary, invoking such terms as 'mores,' 'feelings,' and 'ideas.' Yet he also engages in what Foucault discusses in terms of the genealogy of practices and discourse analysis. Tocqueville even comments that 'a study of the connection between the history of language and history proper would certainly be revealing.' One of his most famous instances is his tracing of the history of the term '*gentilhomme*' in France in contrast to that of 'gentleman' in the English language. In England, the connotation of the term 'steadily widened ... as the classes draw nearer to each other and intermingle. In each successive century we find it being applied to men a little lower in the social scale. Next, with the English, it crosses to America. And now in America it is applicable to all male citizens, indiscriminately. Thus its history is the history of democracy itself.' In France, by contrast, 'there has been no question of enlarging the application of the word *gentilhomme*, which as a matter of fact has, since the Revolution, dropped out of common use. This is because it has always been employed to designate the members of a caste – a caste that has never ceased to exist in France and is still as exclusive as it was when the term was coined many centuries ago.'[12]

Genealogical history in both Tocqueville and Foucault begins with an important if not burning issue in the present and traces it back to its often concealed or repressed roots in the past. The purpose of such inquiry is not purely antiquarian. History for both men involves an at times intense involvement or implication of the historian in the object studied and an active exchange between the present and the past in ways that may be useful in shaping the future. In both Toqueville and Foucault, moreover, there is at least an implicit understanding of historical time in terms of displacement rather than simple continuity or discontinuity. Tocqueville is known for the thesis concerning the continuity of centralization through the French Revolution, in contrast to the belief that the Revolution constituted a break with the past and that it created a new relation between state, bureaucracy, and society. Although Foucault does not take the French Revolution as a crucial reference point, when he does refer to it, it is clear that in many basic ways it was not a turning point for him; indeed, the processes with which Foucault is concerned (such as the treatment of the mad) seem to continue or are even exacerbated through the Revolution. For both Tocqueville and Foucault, the Revolution seems to have worsened conditions rather than improved them, whether in terms of political turbulence that achieved little structural change or in terms of the treatment of marginalized groups whose 'liberation' is at best deceptive. Underlying continuity in both Tocqueville and Foucault is the role of a more crucial

---

12 *The Old Régime and the Revolution*, 83–4.

process of displacement – or repetition with more or less significant and disruptive (or traumatic) change. Practices, institutions, and processes do not simply continue through inertia or become discontinued through a pure separation from the past; they are reproduced or regenerated in varying ways. And their reproduction or (more or less compulsive) repetition may be masked or occluded by a consciousness or experience of change.

One key area of social and cultural life in which displacement is crucial involves secularization, or the movement from the religious to the secular. Tocqueville will indicate that, while the Revolution was manifestly antireligious in delimited ways, notably in its attack on the church as a social and political power, it also displaced religion in its secular ideology and practices – its cult of reason, its redoing of the calendar, its collective effervescence and at times fanatical élan, and its cycle of holidays and feasts. Despite his explicit emphasis on epistemological breaks, we shall also find important instances of displacement in Foucault's history of madness. While Foucault stood at a critical distance from psychoanalysis (as he understood it or perhaps especially as it had been institutionalized) and despite his famous critique of the so-called repressive hypothesis in the *History of Sexuality*[13] he also worked with a notion of repression and the return of the repressed. Indeed, it is most fruitful to see him as criticizing a delimited, overgeneralized concept of repression based on a narrowly negative notion of power – and especially the utopian idea that the end of sexual repression would bring, or at least be accompanied by, full bodily and political liberation. But repression and the

---

13 *The History of Sexuality, Volume I: An Introduction* (1976; New York, 1978).

return of the repressed in disguised and often distorted form are crucial to Foucault's own analyses. For example, the forces of unreason in the modern period do not simply disappear; they are for him driven underground and tend to return in often disguised, uncontrolled, and radically disconcerting ways.

The importance of religion was recognized by both Tocqueville and Foucault. Religion had manifest personal and political importance for Tocqueville, and one of the things he feared most was its secular displacement in a revolutionary political ideology that promised redemption or salvation, typically through quasi-sacrificial, regenerative violence. The 'death of God' is an often-neglected aspect of Foucault's indebtedness to Nietzsche, and the role of religion and its displacements are extremely significant factors in his history of madness. One of the dynamics of his thought in general may be his Nietzschean attempt to think through the death of God and to arrive at an atheism that sees divinity not in terms of loss or death but in terms of absence and the affirmative need to come to terms with that absence in personal and social life.[14]

---

[14] Here one may also note that the notion of the death (or absence) of man is related to the death of God insofar as man or humanity is defined as a function of divinity, either as the creation of God in a religious context or as the heir to God's powers in a secularized one. One crucial form of the displacement of divine powers onto humans is radical constructivism, a mode of secular creationism in which humans are believed to confer all meaning and value on the world. A related form is that which justifies anything done to others if it somehow furthers human interests, for example, experimentation on other animals or the destruction of natural habitats. Despite the extreme and apocalyptic tones in which it appears in Foucault's work – for example, in *Les Mots et les choses* (1966; *The Order of Things: An Archaelogy of the Human Sciences* [New York, 1971]) – the notion of the death of man need not entail the end of all humanism or a carte-blanche denial of human rights but rather the critique of the type of anthropocentrism that depends on secularized, displaced religious motifs and centres everything on

The limited but significant similarities between Tocqueville and Foucault should not obscure their differences, many of which will be touched on in this study. One significant difference has already been identified: Tocqueville's stress in his principal texts was on mainstream institutions, movements, and practices while Foucault focused on the marginal or marginalized. Increased interaction between their principal concerns is of obvious value. Moreover, Tocqueville was a political liberal whereas Foucault was radical in ways often difficult to classify in standard political terms. Tocqueville presents us with the problem of how to rethink liberalism in more differentiated terms – we might want to retain certain aspects of the liberal tradition (notably in terms of constitutionalism, minority rights, and human rights in relation to the demands of solidarity, social justice, and the claims of other beings) but we may equally wish to scrutinize other aspects more critically than Tocqueville or his followers are prone to do (notably economic liberalism in terms of a capitalistic, market economy). The difficulty in classifying Foucault's radicalism bears in part on stylistic and rhetorical issues that I shall take up in Chapter 3 – ways in which his thought is radically transgressive or disruptive. But it is also related to Foucault's generalization of the political in terms of an at times indiscriminate conception of 'positive'

---

humans. In this respect, human rights, while not denied, would be limited in different contexts by the need to recognize and account for the claims of other species or beings, and humans would be situated in a larger frame of reference allowing for ecological considerations. In Foucault and others, a concern for transforming the very location and self-understanding of humans in the world owes much to Heidegger, but it need not simply replicate all of Heidegger's views (or stylistic manoeuvres), for example, an at times incantatory prose style or the questionable idea that animals do not have a world.

or 'productive' power. This conception involved a provocative breakdown of the distinction between the political, the social, and the bodily. For example, it cast critical light on the politics – particularly the micropractices – of everyday life and the more or less subtle and imperceptible ways in which modes of oppression and subjection operated. Its drawback was the tendency to downplay the importance of the state (or other determinate centres of power) and to obscure the difference as well as the relation between power and authority or hegemony. Foucault's discourse either bracketed assumptions and distinctions prominent in the liberal tradition (including that between power and authority, including issues of legitimacy) or was insistently delegitimating in ignoring them, and it was forceful in bringing into prominence the ways in which marginalization, subjection, and abjection could take place even in the seemingly most liberal or enlightened policies and practices. This basic dimension of Foucault's work should not be forgotten But it tended to obscure both the actual and the desirable relations between power and normative legitimation that are necessary for *de facto* and *de jure* relations involving authority and hegemony (however democratic). Foucault and those following his lead are often prone to confuse normalization – that is, misleadingly taking the statistical average or the mainstream (for example, heterosexuality) as normative – and normativity in general. Hence the defensible critique of normalization may eventuate in a tendency to obscure or foreclose the problem of alternative normativities as they relate to desirable structural change in society, the polity, and culture – normativities that would not abjectify the 'mad' or alternative sexualities but give them a different status and raise normative questions in a different key. Tocqueville and other figures who do not have a prominent place in Foucault and Foucauldianism (including Emile Durkheim) might play at least a limited role in compensating for deficiencies in Foucault and indicating lines of analysis, critique, and social reconstruction.

The striking stylistic and rhetorical differences between Tocqueville and Foucault in responding to somewhat similar situations also merit comment. Both Tocqueville and Foucault wrote in what they perceived as post-traumatic or crisis-ridden times. For Tocqueville the French Revolution was still a potent and destabilizing force, especially in its after-effects for a paradoxical revolutionary tradition that disrupted political and social life and did not give rise to a stable, liberal democracy. One might almost say that in Tocqueville's view the reality of the Revolution lay in death and devastation during its occurrence and in its belated effects in post-Revolutionary France and Europe. It thus had the classical characteristics of a collective trauma, in which later generations confront the problems of their transferential implication and the need to come to terms with it through compulsive repetition (or acting out), working over, and, in the best of circumstances, working through. In part due to the massive extent of the Revolution's impact, Tocqueville's response, I shall argue, did not fully overcome acting out. He tended to project his anxieties onto the intellectuals of the Enlightenment, who, to some extent, become the scapegoats of his account, and he was able to provide only a relatively cosmetic rhetorical resolution to the tension between his proposed liberal-conservative responses and the severe problems his analysis disclosed both in the old regime and in its post-revolutionary aftermath. I shall also argue that Tocqueville's style is in a sense internally dialogized in terms of 'scientific,' interpretive (especially narrative), and ideological levels of discourse, yet his voice remains relatively unchanged throughout these levels, attaining only at times a lyrical enthusiasm with respect to his supreme value of liberty. In other words, his voice and style do not register the unworked-through trauma and the attendant socio-political and cultural problems he objectively observes in post-revolutionary France, and he may rhetorically make a premature return to a pleasurable mode of address and a sense of balance in discourse that he has not fully earned with respect to the problems he himself has described and analysed.

It is unclear whether, by the time Foucault writes, the French Revolution has been worked through in French society or whether it has been forgotten or left aside. François Furet, among others, tries to retire it, using at times a conceptualization reminiscent of the end-of-ideology approach common in the 1950s, for example in Daniel Bell and, to some extent, Raymond Aron. In any case, the French Revolution is not highly 'cathected' or charged with affect and value in Foucault. Perhaps it has simply been submerged by a series of catastrophes, genocides, and crises in the twentieth century that link the post-traumatic and the postmodern or post-structural.[15] Although the Holocaust receives almost no explicit attention from Foucault, there is a sense in which his thought and writing register its effects as well as those of other modern phenomena that have had extremely destabilizing effects in post-war France (notably the Vichy regime and the Algerian war).[16] Indeed, there is a sense in which

---

15 On this theme, see Eric Santner, *Stranded Objects: Mourning, Melancholia, and Film in Postwar Germany* (Ithaca and London, 1990), as well as my *Representing the Holocaust* (Ithaca and London, 1994).
16 For the post-war effects of Vichy, see Henry Rousso, *The Vichy Syndrome: History and Memory in France since 1944* (Cambridge, Mass., 1991).

the 'History of Madness' may be read as a displacement of more immediate problems and a commentary on a series of hidden texts. Foucault's style, unlike Tocqueville's, has itself post-traumatic characteristics and the ability to involve the reader in its disorienting sweeps and swerves. I shall discuss Foucault's style and voice in terms of three tendencies or dimensions: 'scientific' (or even positivistic), lyrical, and a more undecidable or marginal voice in closest proximity to the voices of unreason. The first two dimensions (as well as the role of narrative) have at least rough analogues in Tocqueville, but the third is radically different from Tocqueville's balanced and anti-extremist approach, especially from his generally poised, unflappable prose style. Here Foucault speaks or writes not so much about or even for the 'mad' (or the voices of unreason) but with them, not only participating in the threat and temptation they pose but internalizing them and allowing his own voice to be split apart by alien or different voices. The question, however, is whether the result is at times a new, riven or 'schizoid' monologism that does not recognize others as distinct others whose voices should be respected, at least in the form of extensive quotation and commentary. The further question bears on the political implication of this paradoxical mode of internal dialogization, bordering at times on monological fragmentation and abyssal or 'sublime' nonsense.

It might be hyperbolic, even within sight of the year 2000, to contend that Tocqueville furnished an exemplary exploration of the possibilities of historical and cultural analysis in the nineteenth century, while Foucault provided a comparable challenge in the twentieth century. But it is undoubtedly the case that Tocqueville and Foucault inquired into and enacted certain crucial dimensions of historical and cultural understanding in ways that contested neat disciplinary boundaries and, in the process, brought historical understanding into sustained contact with problems often housed in other disciplines, notably political science, literary studies, and philosophy. In these senses, it is not far-fetched to discuss in one book both key texts of these two figures and issues of a broad theoretical or programmatic nature.

I thank Tracie Matysik for her help in preparing the index.

1

History, Reading, and Critical Theory

Prominent in Peter Novick's *That Noble Dream: The 'Objectivity Question' and the American Historical Profession*[1] is a conception of the recent period in historiography as characterized not simply by an heightened intensity of questioning but as involving a more specific focus on the problems of language and signification. This emphasis on language also typifies the influential review essay of John Toews on the 'linguistic turn,' which I shall discuss later in this chapter.[2] The linguistic turn, which has many and at times incompatible variants, is most fruitfully understood as involving a recognition of the problematic nature of language or any signifying practice (ritual, music, or dance, for example).

---

1 Peter Novick, *The Noble Dream: The 'Objectivity Question' and the American Historical Profession* (Cambridge, 1988).
2 John Toews, 'Intellectual History after the Linguistic Turn: The Autonomy of Meaning and the Irreducibility of Experience,' *The American Historical Review* 92 (1987), 879–907. See also John H. Zammito, 'Are We Being Theoretical Yet? The New Historicism, the New Philosophy of History, and "Practicing" Historians,' *Journal of Modern History* 65 (1993), 783–814. Zammito's basic argument draws much from Toews's article.

Language in this sense is not a purely transparent medium that may simply be looked through (or bracketed) in the interest of (re)presenting the object or findings of research. It poses problems for the historian (or other analyst) and signals the manner in which the observer is constitutively implicated in the object of research. With reference to psychoanalysis, Freud framed this problem in terms of transference, and transference involves both the tendency of the analyst-analysand relation to repeat typically inappropriate parent-child relations and the more general tendency of an analytic discourse to repeat the problems at issue in its object of analysis.[3] The goal for Freud was to pass from a perhaps inevitable and necessary tendency to 'act out' (or compulsively relive) these problems – a tendency particularly insistent with respect to traumatic events – to the attempt to recall them in memory and critically work through them.[4]

Needless to say, the linguistic turn brings with it an openness to literary and critical theory, including aspects of (continental) philosophy, in the effort to rethink the nature and acceptable boundaries of historiography. It also mitigates the stark dichotomy between history and metahistory, if by the latter one means critical and self-critical theory bearing on the practice of history itself. Insofar as the professionalization of the discipline was experienced as requiring boundary setting, and litera-

---

3 See Dominick LaCapra, 'History and Psychoanalysis,' in *Soundings in Critical Theory* (Ithaca and London, 1989), 30–66, as well as *Representing the Holocaust: History, Theory, Trauma* (Ithaca and London, 1994).
4 See esp. 'Remembering, Repeating and Working Through' (1914), in *The Standard Edition of the Complete Works of Sigmund Freud* 12, trans. James Strachey (London, 1958), 145–56, and 'Mourning and Melancholia' (1917), in *The Standard Edition* 14 [1957], 237–60.

ture, literary theory, and philosophy were either positioned as largely negative identities or harmonized with science in a deceptively ideal unity, the recent turn to theory and the controversies it stimulates may be interpreted as a return of the repressed. Moreover, the varying fortunes of narrative in historiography indicate the role of a variable proximity to a certain dimension of literature and literary theory, but this proximity – both in those who cultivate and in those who excoriate it – has until recently typically been enacted or acted out rather than lucidly theorized. And the recent emphasis on narrativity has not brought consensus among historians either about the role of narrative in historiography or about the precise nature and status of narrative procedures in history and literature.[5] The possibility that the turn to narrative theory (and to the 'literary' more generally) may be a sign of a returning repressed also helps to explain the excesses in the gesture, including the tendency at times to cannibalize literary theory and to apply it to historiography in an unmediated and uncritical fashion. Moreover, it induces

---

5 See, for example, Philippe Carrard, *Poetics of the New History: French Historical Discourse from Braudel to Chartier* (Baltimore and London, 1992); Lionel Gossman, *Between History and Literature* (Cambridge, Mass., 1990); Hans Kellner, *Language and Historical Representation: Getting the Story Crooked* (Madison, Wisc., 1989); Louis Mink, *Historical Understanding*, ed. Brian Fay, Eugene O. Golob, and Richard T. Vann (Ithaca, N.Y., 1987); and Hayden White, *Metahistory: The Historical Imagination in Nineteenth-Century Europe* (Baltimore, Md., 1973), *Tropics of Discourse: Essays in Cultural Criticism* (Baltimore, Md., 1978), *The Content of the Form: Narrative Discourse and Historical Representation* (Baltimore, Md., 1987). Narrative may be understood in an excessively homogeneous or inflated manner and identified with (or at least seen as essential to) all language use or discourse. Such views obscure the diversity of narrative, including the role of experimental narratives that are self-questioning and resist closure; they also simplify the problem of the relation of narrative to such forms as theory, hypothesis formation and testing, the essay, or the lyric.

opponents of the turn to castigate indiscriminately those who have shown an interest in it as herdlike creatures in a night in which all cows are grey.[6]

There is a sense in which placing language or, more generally, signification, in the foreground of attention and having it apply self-reflexively to the practice of the historian creates a crisis or at least a minor trauma in historiography. For the linguistic turn means that the historian cannot remain fixated on the object of research, construe this object in a purely objectified manner, and provide unproblematic, 'sun-clear' reports about its nature. Moreover, language or signification cannot be situated in a merely instrumental and subordinate position, nor can it be confined to the status of simply one more object of investigation. Indeed, with the turn to language (or, more generally, signifying practices), an entire research paradigm may in certain ways be placed in question.

A relatively self-sufficient research paradigm was to a significant extent important for the professionalization of history as a discipline, and attacks on tendencies that question it may be taken as one indication of the degree to which it is still understood (perhaps misleadingly) as essential to the discipline even today. This paradigm enjoins gathering and analysing (preferably archival) information about an object of study in contrast to reading and interpreting texts or textualized phenomena. (In this exclusionary sense reading a text, especially a published text, is *not* doing research.) In its self-sufficient form, which may be common to conceptions of history as science and as narrative art, the research paradigm is at

---

6 Indiscriminate polemic based on excessively homogenizing reading is pronounced in Bryan D. Palmer, *Descent into Discourse* (Philadelphia, 1990), and Gertrude Himmelfarb, 'Post-modernist History and the Flight from Fact,' *Times Literary Supplement*, 16 October 1992, 12–15.

least loosely modelled on a certain objectifying idea of science (or, for that matter, narrative) in which there is a definitive separation and relation of cognitive mastery between the observer and the observed. The observer makes assertions or puts forth hypotheses about the observed that are subject to confirmation or disconfirmation through empirical investigation.

Obviously, important elements of this paradigm, such as the gathering and analysis of information or the testing of propositions, may be defended and distinguished from their role in what I am terming a relatively self-sufficient research paradigm, and the very concept of what counts as research may change (initiatives I deem desirable). Moreover, this paradigm or model should be seen as objectivist or one-sidedly objectifying rather than as simply objective, for it is possible to have a conception of objectivity that does not depend on it, and criticisms of it should not be seen as entailing an indiscriminate scepticism or a theory of history (or historiography) as based (or foundering) on radical constructivism in which all structures of narration or explanation are ultimately fictive projections of the historian.

An alternative conception of objectivity would stress the importance of thorough research and accuracy, the referential dimension of both individual assertions and more comprehensive structures, and the role of discussion and debate among historians as well as other significant interlocutors.[7] It would nonetheless recognize that language

---

[7] The question of who constitutes a relevant interlocutor is crucial in the definition of a field or discipline. Both the constitution of a discipline and the attempt to question it – at times in the interest of a more inter- or cross-disciplinary perspective – depend on the recognition of pertinent interlocutors, and this changing recognition is a key factor in the history of disciplines. A criterion of restricted professionalism is the exclusion of all non-professionals – whether practitioners of other disciplines or 'lay people' – from the sphere of those taken seriously as interlocutors or critics.

plays a performative part in constituting its object, historical statements depend on inferences from textualized traces, and the position of the historian cannot be taken for granted. There would be an active awareness that such issues as the subject-position(s) and voice(s) of the historian are an integral component of historiography complicating research and that the elucidation of the historian's implication in a contemporary network of research and methodological-theoretical-ideological controversy is not a dispensable matter of 'metahistory' or a specialized activity to be relegated to the 'think-piece.' Moreover, we could no longer rely on the idea that objectivity is a normal given of historiography that is assured by established procedures or that bias is a deviation from normality for which we can simply 'correct.' Rather, our perspective would be transformed: the constitutive place of the historian in the research project would be recognized and objectivity seen not as the simple opposite of subjectivity but as a tenuous yet valuable goal of a process of elaborating a range of subject-positions (for example, those of researcher, reader, and theorist or intellectual) by negotiating 'transferential' relations in a critical and self-critical manner. Research would be combined with reading and interpretation in a larger, more problematic conception of historiography in which the work of different historians would justifiably show different weightings and articulations and the decisive opposition between texts and documents would be questioned. Documents would be read textually, and the manner in which they construct their object in an institutional and ideological field would be a subject of critical scrutiny, while the documentary dimensions of texts would be posed as an explicit problem and elucidated.[8]

---

8 For a recent attempt to address these problems, see my *Representing the Holocaust: History, Theory, Trauma*, chap. 1. The notion of subject-position points

Reading in both its literal and metaphoric senses is a crucial constituent of the problem of language, and it is reciprocally related to writing. A mode of reading implies a mode of writing (and vice versa). In this sense, a different mode of reading would imply that the writing of history would also undergo significant variations and that historical works might take different forms. I do not think there is any simple choice between research and practices of reading and writing, although there is a tense and at times agonistic relation between them. But the problem in historiography is to conjoin them and to attempt to determine what range of practices combines in an acceptable manner a revised understanding of research and modes of reading and writing (or, more generally, practices of signification). I am here assuming that historiography as a professional discipline need not be – and in fact has not been – predicated upon one monological disciplinary practice but that it requires a certain coherence that can be satisfied by a range of practices evincing dif-

---

to the intersection of subject and society – the manner in which the subject is positioned and positions him- or herself in society. It also indicates the need to relate psychological or psychoanalytic concerns to social, historical, and political issues. Any individual occupies a number of more or less compatible subject-positions that provide the starting point for a response to problems. 'Identity' is a problematic articulation of subject-positions, and it cannot be reduced to either subjectivity or social roles and group affiliations alone. Moreover, subject-positions and 'identity' can to some extent be transformed through social practice, including the manner in which we respond to problems. In any event, the purpose of critical thought is not simply to legitimate subject-positions but to acknowlege their role and at least to enable testing and possible transformation. One significant question is whether the professionalization of history has tended to confine the historian to one dominant subject-position – that of a relatively restricted conception of professional historian, notably in the context of a research paradigm – in a manner that obscures or excludes the role of other subject-positions, for example, critical reader and public intellectual.

ferent emphases (for example, between research and reading or interpretation, including the role of metahistory and critical theory raising questions about research orientations, procedures, or findings). What this range of practices is, however, should be seen as contestable and not subject to decision in an *a priori* manner. It should be a matter of informed argument and debate. In this sense we should not be able to rule someone out of the profession in an apodictic or unargued manner because we disagree with his or her practice.[9]

We should also be open to the possibility that, in the event a certain practice is not 'properly' historical, a given individual may combine it with historical practices in hybridized roles or subject-positions. The question of what modes of hybridization are acceptable would raise debates about historiography to another level and reinforce the argument that the definition of historiography is contestable, perhaps essentially contestable. Such hybridized or cross-disciplinary positions could be seen as blurred only from within secure, decisive disciplinary enclosures, and such a view of them might well obscure newer articulations that are being formulated in and through them – articulations that may be most suitable for addressing problems that themselves cut across disciplines (such as the relation between text and context or between the present and the past). In practice of course decisions have to – and would be – made, and such material matters as whether new departments or programs should be instituted or who

---

[9] One may argue that there has been in professional historiography a marked imbalance between theory and research – the predominance of the latter at times associated with an invidious distinction between 'practising' or 'working' historians and all others who do not give unquestioned priority to (preferably archival) research. Attempting to redress this imbalance in no sense implies a denigration of the importance of research.

should be hired for a given position would provide a pragmatic court of appeal, but one whose determinations might well change over time, with changing conceptions of the acceptable range of disciplinary practices. For example, the combination of research, self-critical theoretical reflection, and close reading – or the hybridization of historian with critical theorist or public intellectual – might be deemed acceptable, indeed desirable if the latter role did not involve direct propagandizing in the classroom or the use of professional arenas, such as conventions or the pages of the *American Historical Review*, for narrow partisan-political activities.

I would propose that there are at present at least five important approaches to reading relevant to the practice of history. It should be evident that I am presenting a typology of important reading practices, no one of which may inclusively and exhaustively define the activity of any given historian or group of historians (such as social, cultural, or intellectual historians). Any given historian may employ or even combine two or more approaches, although it is often the case that one approach is most prominent in a historian's work; it shapes the character of inquiry and is used to determine what aspects of the other four are particularly useful or open to appropriation. In any event, there are more or less pronounced tensions involved in the combination of at least certain types with one another in discursive practice. The goal of the typology is to locate important protocols of reading that cut across both thematic emphases on issues such as class, gender, race, and sexual orientation (prominent in Marxism, feminism, ethnic studies, and gay and lesbian studies) and disciplines (notably history, philosophy, social theory, and literary criticism), although certain protocols may be much more prominent in certain emphases or disciplines than in others. Problems of race, gender, class, and sexual orientation are of crucial importance, and they should be addressed. The question for further inquiry is whether they are best addressed through one or more of the protocols of reading I shall discuss – or whether another approach I do not envision would be better still.

The Denial or Repression of Reading

Here the dominance of a seemingly self-sufficient research paradigm leads to an inability to recognize reading as a problem. All texts and documents are assimilated to a homogeneous status as source or evidence that enables the determination of certain findings. Research findings are often 'written up' rather than written in a stronger sense, and an unadorned plain style is favoured. Typically, literary or philosophical texts are reduced to the status of unreliable sources because they do not yield solid evidence or clear-cut facts about empirical states of affairs. They tend to be excluded from the record or at most referred to in brief, allusive ways as possibly suggestive for research. In any event, whatever they yield must be checked against more reliable documents, thus rendering their status redundant.[10]

---

10 In Louis Chevalier, *Classes laborieuses et classes dangereuses* (Paris, 1958), documents such as police reports are used to check the 'findings' derived from novels, as if both police reports and novels did not require more complex protocols of reading. Of Eugène Sue's *Mystères de Paris*, Chevalier writes: 'The social importance of this novel, like that of other great novels of the time, comes from the fact that their authors describe a society and an epoch to which they belong ... The extraordinary authenticity of *Les Mystères de Paris*, like that of *Les Misérables*, comes from the fact that these works passively register the demographic and economic evolutions that we have evoked. They are of their time and can do nothing other than attribute to the society they describe the characteristics that their authors know in the same manner in which they were known at the same moment by the most uncultivated [*incultes*] inhabitants of the city' (514–15; my translation).

In this approach, a priority has often been placed on archival sources and extensive archival research in which the critique of sources is limited to validating the authenticity of documents.[11] But this priority is in no sense necessary, and texts of both high and popular culture may be treated in accordance with a research paradigm for which reading is not a problem. Motives and ideological 'bias' in the historical figures investigated may of course be suspected, but such bias refers primarily to conscious intentions or well-defined strategies that may be established with the same certainty as the meaning of a text through straightforward reading of its content. Ideally, other texts (such as letters) give grounds for the ascription of ideological intentions that may be compared with the manifest content of documents. The goal is to elaborate either a particularistic or a more panoptic, panoramic account of a context in relation to which texts are strictly subordinate if not merely symptomatic documents. Instruction at the graduate level tends to take the form of devising research projects that emulate valued exemplars of successful research, thus avoiding the lures of approaches to history that do not conform to a self-sufficient research paradigm. Research itself is successful if it revises a hypothesis or retells a story in a manner that adds to, revises, or, in rare cases, overturns earlier respected examples of successful research on the basis of

---

11 The problem of reading in the archives has increasingly become a concern of those doing archival research, thus leading historians who do extensive archival work to become interested in problems raised later in this chapter. See, for example, Robert Darnton, *The Great Cat Massacre and Other Episodes in French Cultural History* (New York, 1984); Natalie Zemon Davis, *Fiction in the Archives: Pardon Tales and Their Tellers in Sixteenth-Century France* (Stanford, Cal., 1987); Steven L. Kaplan, *Adieu 89* (Paris, 1993); and Emmanuel Leroy-Ladurie, *La Sorcière de Jasmin* (Paris, 1983).

extensive (ideally, exhaustive), solidly grounded empirical inquiry.

At present, the above description may seem like a caricature, but the question is the extent to which the caricature still captures crucial aspects of actual practice and graduate training. To refer briefly to a 'then' of which I still have a vivid memory, my own graduate training in the 1960s by and large conformed to this model. It was rare, even in a seminar in intellectual history, to discuss in common a text that all members of the class had read. Research seminars met for a few initial sessions in which possible research topics were brought up and perhaps a few models of research read but they were not discussed in any critical form that addressed their assumptions or manner of conceiving history. Then members of the class went off for six weeks or so to conduct independent research, following which they reassembled to report their findings and to benefit from the reactions of others in the class. Shortly after my period of graduate study, a methodology seminar was introduced in which there was discussion of common readings. But priority in selecting texts was frequently given to very recent historiography, which might be directly emulated or 'trashed' by aspiring professionals. In preparation for general examinations, the prevalent ideal was to read a book a day in accordance with a kind of academic Fordism that helped the student to accumulate an impressive array of bibliographical references and a synoptic knowledge of the contents or theses of various studies.

Whenever I am inclined to believe that at present the preceding caricature no longer applies, I encounter a historian who arises to enact or act it out even while he or she may want to dismiss it as inapplicable. To the extent my experience is representative, it bears witness to inner division and anxiety in the profession provoked by recent critical-theoretical initiatives. Still, certain procedures have been modified and in certain places (such as my own university) drastically overhauled, at least in some areas of history. These procedures embodied virtues that many (myself included) would like to retain in a different conception of research, reading, and graduate education – virtues such as the insistence on extensive (ideally exhaustive) research; a thorough knowledge of the literature relevant to one's object of inquiry; an ability to conduct independent research; meticulous care in making assertions and in validating their more empirical or constative aspects; critical discrimination in assessing and selectively assimilating various critical theories (rather than learning one or another of them as a primary language and projectively reprocessing everything in its terms); and the judgment necessary to make significant distinctions and to frame explicitly (but not simply to exclude) as speculative or hyperbolic certain dimensions of an account or argument. But the limitations of a narrowly construed, exclusionary research paradigm need not be belaboured, notably confinement of historical understanding to a restricted, constative, empirical-analytic model and unconcern (if not disdain) for critical and self-critical theory.[12] It is no doubt true that a lack of concern for theo-

---

12 Even so important and sophisticated a historian as J.G.A. Pocock resorts to the invidious binary opposition between the 'working' historian and his or her 'other,' the metahistorian, thereby reducing an interest in critical theory to what might facetiously be called an 'attitude problem.' Hence Pocock writes: 'It is possible to define "intellectual history" as the pursuit by the "intellectual" of an attitude towards "history," and to write it as a series of dialogues between the historian himself, as intellectual, and his probably French or German predecessors, in the attempt to arrive at a "philosophy of history" or something to take the place of one. Such "intellectual history" will be metahistory, meaning that it will be reflection about "history" itself.

retical problems, including the complexities of reading texts and documents, facilitates both a mellifluous, accessible writing style and the acquisition of large amounts of empirical information, while problematizing certain procedures can have an inhibiting effect or at least subject certain procedures to time-consuming and possibly doubt-creating critical processes. But the issue is not simply whether the gains of problematization outweigh the losses but whether certain procedures of exclusion are acceptable or even cognitively responsible once compelling questions about them arise.

Synoptic Reading

The synoptic approach to reading, typically with a focus on content or theme, in a sense makes explicit the practice of reading that is operative when reading is not taken as problematic in a research paradigm. It thus may help open certain practices to inspection and debate, enabling a more precise idea of their virtues and limitations. Furthermore, literary or philosophical texts may now be objects of extended study or even focal points of research. But the synoptic or paraphrastic approach remains geared to reporting the 'findings' of reading or summarizing the meaning of large runs of texts or documents in a concise, lucid manner. Moreover, it downplays nuances and is geared to the reconstruction of the object, often to

---

But it is also possible to imagine a "working historian" who desires to be a historian but not (in this sense) an intellectual, who desires to practise the writing of history but not to arrive at an attitude towards it, and who does not look beyond the construction of those narrative histories of various kinds of intellectual activity which she or he knows how to write ... It is such a working historian of this kind whom I have presupposed in this article.' 'A New Bark Up an Old Tree,' *Intellectual History Newsletter* (1986), 8.

the exclusion (or occlusion) of a more dialogic, critical exchange with the past and its artifacts. Synopsis may of course be the primary method of reading in intellectual and cultural history as well as in other subdisciplines. Typically the goal of such reading is to derive reliable information, to state the manifest meaning of a text or document, and to develop some overarching thesis about a period, phenomenon, or development to which specific texts contribute primarily as symptom, illustration, or evidence.[13] One may at times grant priority to

---

[13] A recent, extremely successful, and genuinely valuable instance of the synoptic approach is Steven E. Aschheim, *The Nietzsche Legacy in Germany 1890–1990* (Berkeley, 1992). Aschheim writes: 'We have had to sacrifice some of the complexity and creative intensity characteristic of so many of these individual encounters in order to retain a synoptic perspective ... The philosopher is not only free to judge and evaluate – he is obliged to do so. Cultural historians, however, must be exceedingly wary of such exercises. It is the dynamic nature of Nietzsche's influence, the complex diffusion and uses of his ideas, not their inherent truth, falsity, or even plausibility that must lie at the center of historical analysis ... For the historian interested in the role, dynamics, and effects of ideas within a political culture, the question of valid or invalid interpretation and applications must be set aside' (3–5, 316). Yet, in contradictory or at least insufficiently examined fashion, Aschheim also wants to argue that something inherent in Nietzsche's thought allowed or even invited the diverse and at times divergent interpretations and uses he so skilfully traces. 'Nietzsche's congeniality to so many contrary tendencies and interests and capacity to elicit open-ended responses reflected a central property of his post-Hegelian thought and method' (7–8). One danger in Aschheim's approach to reception is that it surreptitiously assumes an interpretation of Nietzsche as completely open-ended or even threatens to turn Nietzsche's texts into mere Rorschach tests and to eventuate in the uncritical belief that *esse est percipi*. Aschheim, however, goes on to allude briefly to such factors as Nietzsche's rejection of systems, his aphoristic style, his shifting narrative perspective or voice, and his sustained celebration of creativity (8). Here Aschheim in a minimal way does explicitly read, interpret, and enter into an exchange with Nietzsche's texts. But one might argue that, in light of the 'centrality' he himself gives to them as well as the contextual reconstruction of their reception, Aschheim might at least have raised certain questions about the factors to which he alludes. For example, does the rejection of system imply a disavowal of all systematicity or coherence? Are

texts and documents from which facts can be extracted to reinforce or supplement a particular reconstruction of a phenomenon or period. Texts (such as those of James Joyce, Virginia Woolf, Samuel Beckett, or even Jacques Derrida) that render precious little for this method may be declared to be unreadable, unintelligible, or obscurantist, and their authors deemed hermetic or nihilistic. The difficulty in some periods, including the modern one, is that so many texts and writers tend to fall into this category that the historian is inclined to develop reductive theses about their disastrous effects or their status as mere symptoms of the worst modernity has to offer. They by and large bear witness to a destruction of reason, a misguided departure from cherished Enlightenment ideals, a death-dance of principles, a past imperfect, or an 'after-everything' phantasmagoria.[14]

---

certain appropriations and uses of Nietzsche more defensible than others? Is an aphoristic style or a shifting narrative voice necessarily open to misinterpretation or can it guard against certain abuses? It might be argued that Aschheim has done enough in the book he has written and that the exploration of such questions was not required of him. But one might nonetheless insist that inquiry into such questions, even when they cannot be answered in a fully adequate or satisfactory manner, is permissible and even desirable for the historian and that such inquiry is demanded to complement and supplement the truly informative kind of contextual history of reception that Aschheim provides. Moreover, such an insistence would entail a closer and more interactive relation between the historian and the philosopher than Aschheim envisions.

14 For a range of perspectives on these problems, see Georg Lukács, *Die Zerstörung der Vernunft* (Berlin, 1954); Jürgen Habermas, *The Philosophical Discourse of Modernity*, trans. Frederick Lawrence (Cambridge, Mass., 1987); Carl Schorske, *Fin-de-Siècle Vienna: Politics and Culture* (New York, 1980); Tony Judt, *Past Imperfect: French Intellectuals, 1944–1956* (Berkeley, 1992); John Lukács, *The Passing of the Modern Age* (New York, 1970); and Roland N. Stromberg, *After Everything: Western Intellectual History after 1945* (New York, 1975). A.J.P. Taylor writes: 'Literature tells us little when we deal, as we must in the twentieth century, with the people of England. The novels of Virginia Woolf, for example, were greatly esteemed by a small intellectual group, and

The synoptic approach shares with the denial of reading a focus on the signified (or meaning) and the referents of texts to the virtual exclusion of a concern for the work and play of the signifier or, more generally, for the way a text does what it does. It is in good part for this reason that reading (and writing) remain relatively unproblematic in this approach. But one should recognize that synopsis and its attendant procedures remain a basic and important level of all reading concerned with meaning, reference, and the reconstruction of the object of study.[15] Moreover, certain procedures that typically attend it are desirable, for example, the insistence on thorough research, the importance of substantiating empirical statements, and the careful distinction between empirical and more speculative assertions – procedures that are ingrained as common sense in professional historiography. This insistence may at times be misplaced insofar as it inhibits or invalidates more insistently interpretive or speculative ventures, even when they are clearly framed as such. But it is nonetheless valuable as a characteristic of research and a check upon more extravagant tendencies in reading and interpretation.

---

their destruction of the tight narrative frame has influenced later writers. They are irrelevant for the historian.' *English History, 1914–1945* (New York and Oxford, 1965), 311. (I thank Jonathan Sadowsky for calling my attention to this reference.) 'A small intellectual group' is apparently not part of 'the people' for Taylor, and the irrelevance of Woolf's novels is so obvious that an apodictic *non sequitur* is sufficient to establish it.

15 For a cogent defence of synopsis that is also sensitive to certain of its limitations, see Martin Jay, 'Two Cheers for Paraphrase: The Confessions of a Synoptic Intellectual Historian,' in *Fin-De-Siècle Socialism and Other Essays* (New York and London, 1988), 52–63. For an erudite, magisterial synoptic history of the problem of vision in recent French thought, which includes elements of critical, dialogic exchange, see Jay's *Downcast Eyes: The Denigration of Vision in Twentieth-Century French Thought* (Berkeley, 1994).

It is arguable that the synoptic approach and procedures related to it have become hegemonic or conventional in the historical discipline. But what is taken for conventional changes over time and with different disciplines or discursive-institutional areas of society, and the attempt to determine what is or is not hegemonic in a complex field, especially at a time of intense controversy and change, is tentative at best. For example, New Criticism – which did pay attention to the signifier, if only in a restricted, formalistic manner geared to the discovery of formal principles and the integrating role of irony and paradox – may now be conventional, even old-fashioned in literary criticism. In historiography, however, New-Critical formalism is not conventional, and certain theorists who, from a literary-critical point of view, might be seen as in good measure New-Critical (such as Hayden White in *Metahistory*) may be taken as radical or revolutionary within the historiographical field. Indeed, the goal of a counter-hegemonic practice (in contrast to an endlessly transgressive or anarchistic one) is to establish new conventions and norms in a discursive practice, although the norms deemed more desirable may be more open and self-questioning, notably with respect to the role of hybridization and the need for contestation or periodic transgression.

Deconstructive Reading

Deconstruction is a complex, heterogeneous movement that has been more prominent in literary criticism and certain branches of Continental philosophy than in history. But historians have shown interest in it if only to learn enough to criticize it and its 'lures,' often, if not typically, understanding it in reductive or truncated terms.[16] Given the complexity of deconstruction and the variety of ways in which it is construed or employed, it is difficult not to be reductive in making generalizations about it or its more prominent practitioners, and I cannot claim to have escaped this difficulty in my own discussion.

In deconstructive reading, there is a pronounced suspicion of synoptic or contextual reductionism, and virtually everything is to be found in nuance and the close reader's response to it. This approach to reading often brings extremely dismissive reactions to synoptic, content-oriented, and constative (or representational) reading practices – reactions especially evident in radical forms of deconstruction. Paul de Man and those modelling themselves on him tend to be radically deconstructive in the sense I am invoking. The writings of Derrida are more divided and at times involve countervailing forces, although they have a strong pull in a radically deconstructive direction that has perhaps been exacerbated with de Man's death and Derrida's inclination at times to identify with his theoretical views and reading practices.[17] In any

---

16 See, for example, James Kloppenberg, 'Objectivity and Historicism: A Century of American Historical Writing,' *American Historical Review* 94 (1989), 1011–30. Contrast the more positive and constructive approach to deconstruction in Joan Wallach Scott, *Gender and the Politics of History* (New York, 1988), or Dominick LaCapra, *A Preface to Sartre* (Ithaca and London, 1978), *Rethinking Intellectual History: Texts, Contexts, Language* (Ithaca and London, 1983), and *Soundings in Critical Theory* (Ithaca and London, 1989). See also Keith Jenkins, ed., *The Postmodern History Reader* (London and New York, 1997), esp. Part IV. Rather than repeat some of the things I have written about deconstruction, I shall try to take the discussion in somewhat different directions related to my understanding of some recent developments in deconstruction itself.

17 See Jacques Derrida's *Mémoires for Paul de Man*, trans. Cecile Linsdsay, Jonathan Culler, and Eduardo Cadava (New York, 1986), and 'Like the

case the problem of the relationship between de Man and Derrida over time has received inadequate analysis because of the prevalent tendency of American deconstructionists to amalgate the writings of de Man and Derrida into an insufficiently differentiated deconstructive reading practice or mode of criticism.[18]

By radical deconstruction I mean the tendency to take the important resistances to meaning and the internal contestations or tensions in texts and to become fixated on them by reading all texts in terms of an almost compulsively repeated process of locating an aporia, *mise en abîme*, uncanny nodal point, or process of internal undoing. The resistance to meaning thus threatens to become an externally predictable but internally compelling evacuation of meaning, and all roads in reading seem to lead to the aporia. Meaning (or the signified) tends to be eliminated, or at least bracketed, and attention is riveted on the enigmatic play of the signifier, which becomes arbitrary, mechanical, inhuman, 'free' play. Moreover, the valuable emphasis on the conditions of possibility of a phenomenon or an historical process may be absolutized such that they displace rather than inform history and lead to an abstract, meta-metaphysical mode of analysis in which specificity is lost or obscured.[19]

Sound of the Sea Deep within a Shell: Paul de Man's War,' trans. Peggy Kamuf in *Critical Inquiry* 14 (1988), 590–652 (reprinted in a slightly revised form in Werner Hamacher, Neil Hertz, and Thomas Keenan, eds., *Responses: On Paul de Man's Wartime Journalism* [Lincoln, Neb., 1989]). See also my critique of the latter essay in *Representing the Holocaust*, 125–33.

18 For a lucid discussion of this problem, see Jeffrey T. Nealon, 'The Discipline of Deconstruction,' *PMLA* 107 (1992), 1266–79.

19 Derrida at times struggles against this tendency while de Man tends, in a displacement of the New Criticism, to legitimate the notion of the literary as an unstable but autonomous 'domain' whose aporetic conditions of possibility are tracked and replicated in literary theory. See esp. de Man's *Resistance to*

In de Man, there is a marked contrast or unstable binary opposition between hermeneutics and poetics. Hermeneutics is interpretation that seeks the meaning of texts, while poetics focuses on the play of the material signifier that is both the condition of meaning and the force that prevents meaning from being satisfying or even at times from constituting itself in any readable manner.[20] De Man sees an inevitable 'fall' into hermeneutics even in the most 'rigorous' critical practice, but this movement to meaning is evidently a 'fall' in the strong sense, bringing with it displaced religious connotations. The ideal is an ascetic practice of criticism in which rigour entails resistance to meaning – particularly unearned meaning – and its seemingly all-consuming ideological lures. (De Man himself repeats this oppositional structure leading to an aporia in various guises, for example, in terms of the relation between metaphor and metonymy or semiotics and rhetoric.)[21] A crucial question in reading de Man is whether the aporia marks a terminal impasse or immobilizing disorientation – inducing the endless acting out of a repetition compulsion, including a compulsive mode of analysis – or whether (as Derrida generously believes) it also helps to generate new questions and possibilities, thus opening at least provisional paths to working through problems.[22]

In Derrida, one may distinguish between two related

Theory, ed. Wlad Godzich (Minneapolis, Minn. 1986), 7, 12, and 19. On the aporia, see Jacques Derrida, *Aporias*, trans. Thomas Dutoit (Stanford, Cal., 1993).
20 See *The Resistance to Theory*, esp. 55–6.
21 See *Allegories of Reading: Figural Language in Rousseau, Nietzsche, Rilke, and Proust* (New Haven and London, 1979), esp. chaps. 1 and 3.
22 For Derrida's view of de Man on the aporia, see *Mémoires for Paul de Man*, 132.

processes that have different weights in his various writings: deconstruction and dissemination. Deconstruction involves the analysis of the tensely related, internally 'dialogized' forces in a text that place its author's explicit goals or intentions in more or less extreme jeopardy. Most prominently, an author's reliance on traditional binary oppositions (inside/outside, identity/difference, male/female) and an attendant desire for totalization may be upset, undercut, or disoriented by less readily classifiable, more disconcerting movements in a text that leave undecidable residues, remainders, or hybridized (in-between) elements. Since binaries are typically arranged in a 'violent' hierarchy, deconstruction involves interrelated movements or phases: reversal (wherein the subordinate term is given priority) and generalized displacement. The latter movement requires an attempt to counteract the simple inversion of hierarchy that remains within a given frame of reference and establishes a new form of dominance, but where it leads is less clear. It often involves generalizing the residue or remainder and refiguring the subordinate term until one has a less stable field of meaning that may suggest (while never quite seeming to work out) newer articulations. It may also lead in the direction of dissemination where wordplay is pronounced and articulations are at best elusive and extremely labile. At the limit, undoing a text or phenomenon may make any attempt at reconstruction or rearticulation seem hopelessly naive, and the utopian may remain insistently vacuous or be figured as that which never comes (or is always *à-venir* – to come in a future that is never a present). In any case, deconstruction does not simply exclude or bracket meaning and reference; it places them within a general text or interplay of textualized traces that they do not simply transcend or master. The notorious statement that 'there is no outside-the-text [*il n'y a pas de hors-texte*]'[23] certainly questions any idea of full, unmediated presence (for example, of an experience, meaning, or divinity), but it does not eliminate all meaning or reference. Rather, it situates meaning and reference within a network of instituted traces or a generalized trace-structure, and it makes their situation a matter of a function within, or an inference from, such a 'structure.'

For Derrida, moreover, a text never simply conforms to its author's intentions, and its language is never fully transparent. More specifically, a text puts into play longstanding assumptions of the metaphysical tradition – assumptions that are not themselves fully homogeneous and that receive more or less critical and explicit formulation in the texts of significant philosophers. In his early 'Structure, Sign, and Play in the Discourse of the Human Sciences,' Derrida provided this principle for distinguishing between the relative critical and self-critical strengths of texts: 'But if nobody can escape this necessity [of being within traditions and, in the West, within the tradition of inherited metaphysical concepts], and if no one is therefore responsible for giving in to it, however little, this does not mean that all the ways of giving in to it are of equal pertinence. The quality and fecundity of a discourse are perhaps measured by the critical rigor with which this relationship to the history of metaphysics and to inherited concepts is thought.'[24] In his discussion of Paul de Man's Second World War journalism ('Like the Sound of the

---

23 *Of Grammatology*, trans. Gayatri Chakravorty Spivak (Baltimore and London, 1974), 158.
24 Richard Macksey and Eugenio Donato, eds., *The Structuralist Controversy: The Languages of Criticism and the Sciences of Man* (Baltimore and London, 1970), 252.

Sea Deep within a Shell: Paul de Man's War'), Derrida himself seemed to forget this important principle, for there he tried unconvincingly to argue that a propagandistic, ideologically saturated text that remained rather blindly within anti-Semitic stereotypes could be read to reveal inner tensions if not strong forms of self-deconstruction or self-questioning implying self-reflexive rigour. The result was not only apologetic with reference to de Man; it threatened to reprocess the object of study in terms of a rashly generalized reading technology and unconsciously to validate the most hostile and extreme claims of critics that deconstruction could be used tendentiously to rewrite the past and prove virtually anything.

Another way of seeing Derrida's unfortunate article on de Man is to read it as a misapplication of disseminatory writing that in other areas may be justifiably experimental or thought-provoking. Disseminatory writing may be related to, but not conflated with, another practice in recent criticism that stems from the work of Harold Bloom: strong misreading. Bloom sees strong misreading as a typical way in which major poets relate to dominant, fatherlike predecessors, but it may characterize criticism that emulates poetry or 'creative' writing. Indeed, Derrida's article is an exceptionally 'strong' and 'creative' misreading in that it takes what is often weakest in de Man's early writing and makes something powerful and even subversive out of it. This procedure may be praiseworthy as an act of 'creative' writing when it is a question of Beckett rewriting Flaubert, or Derrida rewriting Genet, but it is altogether misplaced as historical reading and critique.

Dissemination in general supplements deconstruction through an active intervention in which a text is indeed rewritten in terms of possibilities that were underexploited or even unexplored by its author and perhaps remain submerged in the text. At its most extreme this rewriting is a ludic improvisation that follows associative processes of a waking dream, making more or less regulated and lucid use of the processes Freud disclosed in dream-work (condensation, displacement, secondary revision, and suitability for staging or *mise en scène* [*Darstellbarkeit*]). Disseminatory writing thus enacts or acts out 'free' association and dream-work, especially in response to a trauma that disrupts a text (in the broad sense that may include a life).

In Freud, of course, 'free' association is not simply arbitrary in that it brings out significant relations that may be repressed or denied by consciousness. The most effective associations are 'free' in this disclosive sense. Reading that follows associative processes is thus a procedure that emulates psychoanalytic mechanisms. Its performative quality indicates that it does not simply copy or imitate the manifest content of the text being read but actually makes something happen (or makes history in its own way) through its associations and improvisations. Oneiric improvisation accounts for the 'through-the-looking-glass' quality of certain deconstructive readings where what is made of a text departs drastically from anything a more conventional reading might reveal. Moreover, disseminatory writing and strong misreading may put into play a practice of radical decontextualization or diremption whereby textual segments are severed from their own time or place and made to take on new, unheard-of significations in their rewritten form.[25]

In literary criticism that emulates creative writing, a reading may be praised to the extent that it is a strong mis-

---

25 See Jacques Derrida, 'Signature, Event, Context,' in *Margins of Philosophy*, trans. Alan Bass (1967; Chicago, 1982), 307–30.

reading and engages its object in an unpredictable, even strangely disconcerting or uncanny, performative manner. Indeed the stronger the misreading the better, insofar as the strength of a misreading is indicative of the extent to which it appears performative, creative, or even original and brings out what is not evident in the text that becomes its pretext. The process is most remarkable when the resultant reading is as ingeniously creative as the text being read, for example, in many of Derrida's texts (notably *Glas*) or in Roland Barthes's *S/Z*, where Honoré de Balzac's *Sarrasine* is decomposed and put together again in a fashion that would have astounded Humpty-Dumpty. Disseminatory writing and strong misreading are somewhat comparable to the 'riff' in jazz, wherein one musician improvises on a tune or on the style of an earlier musician. As in jazz, the more traumatic or disjunctive variations (or changes within repetition) may from a certain point of view be the most impressive. In this respect, Derrida may perhaps be seen as the John Coltrane of philosophy or of some hybridized genre that remains difficult to name.

It is, of course, difficult to determine whether a style emulating dream-work generates associations that are genuinely disclosive about both the text being read and a contemporary relation to it. Moreover, the improvisational procedure may border on the questionable, even in literary criticism or philosophy, when it becomes overwhelmingly projective reprocessing in which the 'voice' or perspective of the other is not attended to but is assimilated into a participatory discourse or generalized 'free indirect style' that amounts to a monologic approach, however internally dialogized or self-contestatory it may be. This is, for example, the style in which Foucault's *Folie et déraison: Histoire de la folie à l'âge classique*[26] is at times written, and it is one reason why the book is 'exciting' as a mode of writing but questionable as history. In it, the 'voices' of those classified as 'mad' or radically 'other' are not directly quoted or even commented on but are made to agitate Foucault's own tortured, flamboyant prose and his internally divided, self-questioning style – a style that is internally dialogized but may still in an important sense be monologic (or narcissistic) insofar as it assimilates or incorporates the voices of others without respecting their resistances to assimilation. An internally dialogized, indeed radically fragmented style that projectively reprocesses the voices of others may be theorized and defended as 'schizophrenic' writing that attempts to break up the 'paranoid' rigidities of classical or conventional writing. But the dangers are obvious in the view that a desirable alternative to paranoia is a strategic, willed release of 'schizo' flows of energy and desire.[27]

The preceding discussion may enable a delimitation of the point at which deconstruction and its disseminatory supplement – and, more generally, certain post-structural tendencies – have the most dubious relation to historical reading and interpretation. It might be argued that historical reading should pay close attention to the 'voices' of the other and try to reconstruct these 'voices' or perspectives as closely and carefully as possible, however problematic

---

26 Michel Foucault, *Folie et déraison: Histoire de la folie à l'âge classique* (Paris, 1961).
27 See, for example, Gilles Deleuze and Félix Guattari, *Anti-Oedipus: Capitalism and Schizophrenia*, trans. Robert Hurley, Mark Seem, and Helen R. Lane (New York, 1977), and *A Thousand Plateaus*, trans. Brian Massumi (Minneapolis, Minn. 1987). These books seem to take as their premise a naive, utopian conception of desire opposed to all forms of limiting norms that are indiscriminately identified with repression and paranoia or even with fascism.

the undertaking may be. This is one reason why contextualization is important even in approaches stressing the significance of reading and interpretation, although the precise form and limits of contextualization in historiography may certainly be debated.[28] It could also be argued that the historian should elicit the possibilities and the repressed or denied dimensions of texts or documents. But the attempt to specify these dimensions of a text or phenomenon is always tentative, problematic, and even speculative. At the minimum one would demand in historical reading and interpretation a specification of a configuration (or an articulation of the repeated and the changed) that would help to delimit better what may be ascribed to the past and what is being added in the present. Moreover, in history, the principle cannot be that the stronger the misreading the better, for here history does not emulate creative writing and is constrained by different norms of inquiry. At the very least, there is in history a basic distinction between the attempt to reconstruct the object of inquiry, including its meaning or possibilities at its own time or over time, and the entry into a dialogic exchange with it that tries to bring out its potential in the present and for the future. The question is whether deconstruction, disseminatory writing, and related post-structural tendencies tend to conflate or collapse the distinction between reconstruction and dialogic exchange through a kind of generalized free indirect style or middle voice that may neutralize or collapse not only binary oppositions but all distinctions.

    The historian may, however, take up another role and

---

28 On this problem, see my *Rethinking Intellectual History: Texts, Contexts, Language* (Ithaca and London, 1983), esp. chap 1; *History & Criticism* (Ithaca and London, 1985); and *Representing the Holocaust: History, Theory, Trauma*, esp. chap. 1.

engage in freer variations or speculations insofar as they are explicitly framed as such and not placed on the same level or indiscriminately intertwined with other readings and interpretations that are more explicitly controlled and subject to ordinary processes of validation. Here, one would have a hybridized role or genre of writing that is more or less close to that of Derrida. But how justifiable the specific instances of this genre might be requires further investigation and argument. As I noted, its use in the case of Derrida's rewriting of de Man's propagandistic journalism is objectionably indiscriminate and converges, even if unintentionally, with revisionism in the limited sense of a normalizing view of the Nazi period and the Shoah. A hybridized genre involving clearly framed speculations would seem most acceptable to the extent that it is indeed difficult to determine what belongs to the past and what to the present, notably with respect to deep-seated philosophical assumptions and the repressed dimensions of a culture or tradition – for example, those related to a quest for origins, full presence, and purity that may be conjoined with displaced sacrificial and scapegoating mechanisms. But even here it should not lead to the loss or elimination of all historical specificity in treating phenomena.

I would make further mention of one important tendency in contemporary criticism that is evident in many writers sympathetic to deconstruction and at times in Derrida himself.[29] This is an ethos of renunciation combined

---

[29] See esp. Leo Bersani, *The Culture of Redemption* (Cambridge, Mass., 1990). In opposing both conventionality and totalizing tyranny, Bersani elaborates a theory of presumably nonviolent masochistic desire in which the explosively narcissistic self seeks 'the ecstatic suffering of a pure ébranlement' (38) or self-shattering, thus averting frustration that, for Bersani, causes violence

with a propensity for a generalized aesthetic of the sublime.[30] Renunciation appears in methodological humility or modesty that avoids direct, 'aggressive' criticism of the other as well as in the quest for an undecidable 'position' that neutralizes or disempowers opposites such as activity and passivity. It also arises in the tendency to abandon not only mastery but seemingly all control in the more disseminatory extreme where language in its most hyperbolic forms takes over and, in a self-sacrificial or immolating gesture, distributes the decentred self in the flow of discourse. (This stance may be most appealing to men who are striving for sensitivity, especially in the face of feminist critiques of 'phallocentrism' and patriarchy. In the case of women or minorities, it may have the tendency to reinforce unfortunate stereotypes of abjection.) The *mise en abîme* of the text may even coincide with the much-heralded (and greatly exaggerated) death of the author: language is presumably left to write itself in unpredictable, aleatory movements reminiscent of automatic writing in surrealism and open to the possibility (or necessity) of misreading. Yet the movement towards the abyss, in which all meaning and reference threaten to be lost, brings with it the possibility of reaching infinite heights – or at least infinite deferral of meaning – as the self confronts symbolic excess (or dire lack) that simulates death and transfiguration. Trauma (including the induced

---

and aggression against others. Here one may ask whether Bersani's intricate, probing, and demanding analyses, which provide arresting insight into the problematic nature of modern writing, seem at times to be based on a utopian anarchism close to the viewpoint of Deleuze and Guattari.

30 See the independently developed but convergent analyses in my *Representing the Holocaust: History, Theory, Trauma* and Steven Connor, *Postmodernist Culture: An Introduction to Theories of the Contemporary* (Oxford and Cambridge, Mass., 1990), esp. chap. 8.

trauma of the *mise en abîme* of the text) is transvalued in an aesthetic of the sublime into an occasion for ecstasy and exhilaration.[31] And the very ability to confront death, however symbolically, empowers the self and brings an intimation of the sublime as one steps away from the near annihilation threatened by the 'abyss' of a radical excess or lack of meaning. The fascination with excess that gestures towards death and a secular sacred – indeed, towards a secularized, symbolic sacrificial process that may paradoxically undo itself by playing itself out – is a powerful force in post-structural thought in general, and it harks back to the work of Georges Bataille, Maurice Blanchot, and Martin Heidegger. The problem is that its fascination is often so great that it induces a quasi-transcendental mode of thinking in which the deconstruction of metaphysics – including the very important deconstruction of the binary logic that subtends scapegoating and victimization – continues to gravitate in a meta-metaphysical orbit. To the extent that the inverted or parodic tracking of metaphysics prevails, the role of history and politics loses its specificity and becomes at best allusive and utopian (as well as impossibly mournful or endlessly melancholic), and any sense of limits or guard rails (whose importance Derrida at times invokes) easily becomes only a faint memory. The actual victims of history may be lost in an indiscriminate general-

---

31 For this transvaluation, the works of Jean-François Lyotard and Slavoj Zizek are especially significant. See esp. Lyotard, *The Postmodern Condition: A Report on Knowledge*, trans. Geoff Bennington and Brian Massumi (Minneapolis, Minn. 1984), *The Differend: Phrases in Dispute*, trans. George Van Den Abbeele (Minneapolis, Minn., 1988), and *Heidegger and 'the jews,'* trans. Andreas Michel and Mark S. Roberts (Minneapolis, Minn., 1990); Zizek, *The Sublime Object of Ideology* (London, 1990), *Looking Awry* (Cambridge, Mass., 1991), and *Enjoy Your Symptom!* (New York, 1992).

ization of victimage (or abjection), a levelling identification of all history with trauma, and an abstract, tortuous conception of witnessing, all of which tend to have apologetic functions and to incapacitate knowledge, judgment, and practice.[32] The attendant difficulty is a near fixation on trauma, as well as its transvaluation in the sublime, that induces a compulsively repetitive acting out of traumatic crisis and disorientation.

Deconstruction to some extent relies on a homeopathic process in creating discursive antidotes – antidotes that employ a proper dosage of a prevalent cultural malaise (such as unlimited excess) in the attempt to facilitate a cure.[33] But when excess, or that which is beyond determination and representation, is fixated on, there is a marked inclination to overdose on the antidote. Moreover, that which can be represented even in extreme experience or limit cases is passed over in silence or treated in overly indirect, vague, and at times confusing terms. At this unrestrained, hyperbolic point any more comprehensive working through of problems tends to be foreclosed, and the sublime itself may become somewhat routinized and threadbare insofar as it is repeatedly alluded to, in increasingly tedious, predictable terms, and has no strong resistances against which to assert itself. One may even have what Flaubert in *The Sentimental Education* (1869) termed 'the sublime at bargain-basement prices' [*le sublime à bon marché*].

---

32 These tendencies are especially marked in the discussion of de Man in Shoshana Felman's 'Paul de Man's Silence,' *Critical Inquiry* 15 (1989), 704–44 (reprinted as 'After the Apocalypse: Paul de Man and the Fall to Silence,' in Shoshana Felman and Dori Laub, M.D., *Testimony: Crisis of Witnessing in Literature, Psychoanalysis, and History* (New York, 1992), 120–64
33 One of Derrida's best discussions of the antidote is his 'Plato's Pharmacy,' in *Dissemination*, trans. Barbara Johnson (Chicago, 1981).

Redemptive Reading

The more extreme form of deconstruction or its disseminatory supplement may, as in de Man, lead one repeatedly to the abyss with any redemptive gesture adamantly refused. Alternatively it may hint, however obliquely or paradoxically, at redemption through a self-effacing, secularized sacrifical process, an aesthetic of the sublime, or a utopia that is always to come. Another variant of reading, often in opposition or reaction to deconstruction, is more prevalent in historiography; it takes a rather sober if not placid approach to the redemption of meaning in and through interpretation. Close reading or attention to nuance is not the forte of this tendency. Reading instead becomes integrated into harmonizing interpretation, especially when a neo-Hegelian frame of reference explicitly encourages a model of speculative, dialectical transcendence that is often combined with a phenomenological notion of experience as the foundation of meaning. And interpretation is easily reconciled with the most conventional use of contextualization as the full meaning of a text or experience is presumed to be available to the interpreter through an attempt to capture the meaning-in-context of a past text or phenomenon – even of an entire series of events or sweep of a tradition. But redemptive reading often leads to a projective reprocessing of the past that is more secure and self-satisfying in its results than that operative in deconstruction, for the meaning that is redeemed is typically that which is desired in the present, and figures in the past tend to become vehicles or mouthpieces for contemporary values. This possibility is perhaps most available in its extreme form for historians and theorists who employ a neo-Hegelian frame of reference that applies to history the model of the speculative dialectic, in which a past phenomenon is 'transcended' or 'sublated' (*aufgehoben*) in time with only minor and essentially recuperable losses. Thus, where radical forms of deconstruction tend to evacuate or endlessly defer meaning even where it seems to be significant, hermeneutic approaches may find ultimately satisfying or full meaning by filling in or covering over traumas and gaps that would seem to mark its limit.

The more moderate advocates of this approach to history as the story of 'symbolic' meaning may look to Clifford Geertz and a delimited 'anthropological' understanding of the nature of historical inquiry. Geertz's work is especially appealing because of its remarkable insights and relative accessibility, as well as its stylistic charms, which often are quite distant from the more difficult or even 'rebarbative' nature of deconstructive and, more generally, post-structural approaches. Moreover, it provides a stimulating alternative to cut-and-dried approaches, especially those relying on 'number-crunching.' It also allows for a measure of fictionalization not as pronounced or blatant as that evoked by strong misreadings – one that supports a turn to forms of narrative in historical writing. The beautifully orchestrated, finely crafted, arrestingly dramatized narrative of the Balinese cockfight may here be seen as a *locus classicus* for a certain kind of history, and Geertz often seems to be the *genius loci* in the work of a signficant number of historians.[34]

---

34 See, for example, John Higham and Paul K. Conkin, eds., *New Directions in American Intellectual History* (Baltimore, 1979). Among European historians, Robert Darnton acknowledges the influence of Geertz. See *The Great Cat Massacre and Other Episodes in French Cultural History* (New York, 1984) and 'The Symbolic Element in History,' *Journal of Modern History* 58 (1986), 218–34. For Geertz's treatment of the Balinese cockfight, see 'Deep Play: Notes on a Balinese Cockfight,' in *The Interpretation of Cultures* (New York, 1972).

More recently, the influence of Charles Taylor has brought into renewed prominence a neo-Hegelian model that is insistent and comprehensive in its construction of history as the story of meaning. This hermeneutic approach may be combined with a phenomenological notion of experience, as it was in the work of earlier theorists and historians such as Wilhelm Dilthey. But the redemptive model of reading is quite prevalent, often on a nontheoretical, conventional level in which there is a determined striving to seek out the meaning of past experience, frequently in terms that put into play or even help to validate contemporary desires and values.[35] In a recent publication,[36] I have discussed in terms of redemptive reading two important, extremely readable, yet exceptionally sophisticated books on a theoretical level: Caroline Walker Bynum's *Holy Feast and Holy Fast: The Religious Significance of Food to Medieval Women*[37] and Charles Taylor's *Sources of the Self: The Making of the Modern Identity*.[38] A par-

---

For a critique of it, see Vincent Crapanzano, 'Hermes' Dilemma: The Masking of Subversion in Ethnographic Description,' in James Clifford and George E. Marcus, eds., *Writing Culture: The Poetics and Politics of Ethnography* (Berkeley, 1986), esp. 68–76. Crapanzano argues that Geertz's treatment is characterized by the absence of the native's point of view, the excessive, decontextualized stylization of performance, the transcendental perspective of the narrator, and the avoidance of a dialogic relation to the other.

35 For a truly masterful instance of the redemptive model, see M.H. Abrams, *Natural Supernaturalism: Tradition and Revolution in Romantic Literature* (1971; New York, 1973). For a different approach to history as the story of meaning, one less concerned with contemporary values and more attuned to ideological conflict in the past, see Keith Michael Baker, 'On the Problem of the Ideological Origins of the French Revolution,' in Dominick LaCapra and Steven L. Kaplan, eds., *Modern European Intellectual History: Reappraisals and New Perspectives* (Ithaca and London, 1982), 197–219.

36 LaCapra, *Representing the Holocaust: History, Theory, Trauma*, 178–87.

37 Caroline Walker Bynum, *Holy Feast and Holy Fast: The Religious Significance of Food to Medieval Women* (Berkeley, 1987).

38 Charles Taylor, *Sources of the Self: The Making of the Modern Identity* (Cambridge, Mass., 1989).

ticularly dubious example of the ideological work of the speculative dialectic in redeeming meaning, repressing or marginalizing trauma, and recuperating loss in history is Taylor's ameliorative (perhaps unintentionally revisionist) characterization of the Nazis as marking an unsuccessful interruption of a victorious ethic of reducing suffering – an ethic Taylor sees as coming to its fullest historical fruition in a triumphant modern identity.[39]

In the present context, I would like to turn briefly to John Toews's substantial, justly influential review essay, 'Intellectual History after the Linguistic Turn: The Autonomy of Meaning and the Irreducibility of Experience' – an essay that concludes with a favourable appreciation of an essay by Taylor that predated *Sources of the Self.* Toews's contribution appeared at a crucial juncture in the recent history of the profession. Variants of the 'linguistic turn' had captured the interest of historians,[40] and some histo-

---

39 Ibid., 575. Here Eric Santner's notion of narrative fetishism is pertinent: 'By narrative fetishism I mean the construction and deployment of narrative consciously or unconsciously designed to expunge the traces of the trauma or loss that called that narrative into being in the first place ... [It] is the way an inability or refusal to mourn employs traumatic events; it is a strategy of undoing, in fantasy, the need for mourning by simulating a condition of intactness, typically by situating the site and origin of loss elsewhere.' 'History beyond the Pleasure Principle: Some Thoughts on the Representation of Trauma,' in Saul Friedlander, ed., *Probing the Limits of Representation: Nazism and the 'Final Solution'* (Cambridge, Mass., 1992), 144.
40 See Martin Jay, 'Should Intellectual History Take a Linguistic Turn? Reflections on the Habermas-Gadamer Debate,' in Dominick LaCapra and Steven L. Kaplan, eds., *Modern European Intellectual History: Reappraisals and New Perspectives* (Ithaca and London, 1982), 86–110. See also the essays in Lynn Hunt, ed., *The New Cultural History* (Berkeley, 1989). The role of a linguistic turn has also preoccupied practitioners of, and commentators on, the new historicism in literary studies. See Brooke Thomas, *The New Historicism and Other Old Fashioned Topics* (Princeton, N.J., 1991); H. Aram Veeser, ed., *The New Historicism* (New York and London, 1989); and Joseph Gibaldi, ed., *Introduction to Scholarship in Modern Languages and Literatures* (New York,

rians even seemed to be appropriating aspects of contemporary critical theory in their own work, while others were looking for a way to understand and respond to these newer or 'new-fangled' initiatives. Toews's essay quickly became the avenue through which many historians came to understand – and react to – the so-called linguistic turn in historiography and especially the use in the profession of deconstructive and more generally post-structural thought. It also helped to inaugurate a significant turn in the *American Historical Review* in the direction of questions of theory and method as at least a necessary and valuable supplement to monographic research. The level of Toews's discussion is consistently high, and, whether or not one agrees with all of his arguments, the strenuous thought – what Hegel in the preface to *The Phenomenology of Mind* called the *Ernst des Begriffs* (the seriousness of the concept) – that lies behind them and the critical inquiry they are able to prompt must be appreciated.

Toews's basic argument is summarized in his subtitle: the autonomy of meaning and the irreducibility of experience. In accordance with his neo-Hegelian view, culture is a medium (or mediation) to make experience meaningful, and language is its primary means of accomplishing this (redemptive) feat. The engaging movement of the review essay, similar to Hegel's *Phenomenology of Mind*, involves bringing each work under discussion to the cliff-hanging juncture of some internal difficulty, which then motivates the move to the next work, until one arrives at a penultimate point of dialectical reversal and at least a hint of the ultimate hope of speculative synthesis. The dialectical reversal indicates that not only must meaning be

---

1992), esp. Robert Scholes, 'Canonicity and Textuality,' 138–58, and Annabel Patterson, 'Historical Scholarship,' 183–200.

redeemed from experience but experience itself must be saved from meaning in a two-way repudiation of reductionism that is not completely terminal insofar as there is the abiding hope of some form of reconciliation or integration. Meaning, experience, and language triangulate Toews's argument as its threefold conceptual foundation, but their definition, relations, and history may be more problematic than Toews allows. It is, for example, significant that contemporary linguistic theories of meaning stem in good part from Ferdinand de Saussure. Saussure's narrowly linguistic orientation is explicitly criticized by Mikhail Bakhtin and his school, who argue against its abstract, ahistorical formalism and by contrast defend a theory of language in historical use involving the problem of contextualization.[41] Foucault takes the latter understanding of language-in-use in the direction of power and institutions, while Derrida elaborates a notion of a generalized text or a network of institutionalized traces that does not exclude reference, reality, or 'experience' but attempts (however debatably at times) to situate them in a critical manner and to explore their limits. Moreover, meaning is contested internally and limited by forces that relate language to other phenomena in complex ways (for example, phonemes, drives, and bodily processes – including psychosomatic ones – that have complex relations to signification but cannot be reduced to it).[42]

---

41 See in particular V.N. Volosinov, *Marxism and the Philosophy of Language*, trans. Ladislav Matejka and I.R. Titunik (New York and London, 1973), esp. 52–63.

42 The very play of material signifiers affects the body on a level undercutting signification – the level of imagination and even sensation that Julia Kristeva relates to the pre-Oedipal condition of the infant (or the *chora* in Plato). See her *Révolution du langage poétique* (Paris, 1974) (partial translation as *Revolu-*

History, Reading, and Critical Theory 59

The most problematic term in Toews's discussion may well be 'experience,' for in other quarters it has become something of a scare word that intimidates opponents (those who do not share or at least empathetically understand the 'experience' in question — those who really have not been through it).[43] It is also a means of authenticating one's own position or argument. Experience often func-

---

tion in *Poetic Language*, trans. Margaret Waller [New York, 1984], and *Black Sun: Depression and Melancholia* (New York, 1989).

43 My point here is not to incriminate Toews's argument through a specious appeal to guilt by association but to bring out ways in which he does not sufficiently guard against certain abuses of the concept of experience. At the very least 'experience' in Toews's essay is insufficiently differentiated for use as a critical in contrast to a relatively uncritical or foundational concept. For example, Toews does not elaborate a distinction among subject-positions with respect to experience — both subject-positions of historians and subject-positions of their objects of study. In brief, he does not consistently relate the concept of experience to that of subject-position, which I deem necessary for a critical use of 'experience.' Hence a series of questions is not addressed. Should the historian make explicit his or her own subject-positions to the extent that they are pertinent to research and argument? Should the historian treat in the same way perpetrators, victims, bystanders, collaborators, rescuers, and so forth, especially with respect to extreme or limit events that involve trauma? What, precisely, in the work of the historian is to be related to his or her personal experience? Is it necessary to be autobiographical? How does the historian relate his or her own experience to the experience of those studied? How is experience in historiography related to non-experiential factors (as well as evidence for them), notably objectified or structural movements as well as aspects of language or signification in general? A crucial question here is the role of empathy, which Toews surprisingly does not mention although it would seem vitally important for any attempt to stress the role of experience in history. Empathy has tended to drop off the historical agenda, in part because of its earlier 'romantic' or even somewhat 'mystical' uses and the professionalization of the discipline under the banner of objectivity, often conflated with objectivism. Especially dubious in earlier uses of empathy was the tendency to conflate it with projective identification rather than to relate it to the problem of recognizing the alterity (or otherness) of the other. Yet transference and notions of observer participation bring into question extreme objectification that denies a voice to the other, and they should also lead in historiography to a critical re-examination of empathy and the role of affect in

tions as the blackest of black boxes in general usage and perhaps to some extent in Toews's own sophisticated, well-developed argument.[44] If one means by experience the common-sense notion of having lived through something, for example, the experience of the Holocaust or of rape victims, it retains an important role. But the nature of this role should be specified and its implications assessed. For example, it might be argued that experience provides a basis for a subject-position that, especially in certain cases (such as that of victims), should be respected and attended to, and it may even give a *prima facie* claim to knowledge. But experience in and of itself neither authenticates nor invalidates an argument or point of view, and it cannot be invoked to silence others – either

---

understanding (which make the latter more than cognition in the narrow sense of processing information). Empathy poses special challenges with respect to traumatic events and the relation of perpetrators and victims in them. In my judgment it leads not to projective identification and vicarious experience (inducing surrogate victimage on the part of the historian who identifies with the victim) but to virtual experience respectful of the other as other and related to critical (and self-preservative) distance (including the role of certain objectifying devices, such as constative statements and footnoting). Virtual experience generates what might be called empathic unsettlement in the historian's account that resists any denial of the traumatic events calling it into existence. At the very least the empathic unsettlement registering in the account of the historian (or other secondary witness) signals the dubiousness of a quest for full narrative closure or dialectical synthesis.

44 Joan Scott observes: 'Experience for Toews is a foundational concept ... [It] thus provides an object for historians that can be known apart from their own role as meaning makers and it then guarantees not only the objectivity of their knowledge, but their ability to persuade others of its importance. Whatever diversity and conflict may exist among them, Toews's community of historians is rendered homogeneous by its shared object (experience). But as Ellen Rooney has so effectively pointed out, this kind of homogeneity can exist only because of the exclusion of the possibility that "historically irreducible interests divide and define ... communities".' '"Experience,"' in

those having or those not having it.[45] Moreover, there are many types of experience, including that of reading or writing texts, and the latter may in certain cases be quite significant. They may even be crucial components in working through other experiences or even traumas.[46]

One should not peremptorily dismiss the concept of experience or the need to come to terms with it, and Toews's article is extremely helpful in prompting significant questions about it. One of the merits of his complicated account is to introduce unexpected intricacies into the very conception of 'experience' and to indicate how a contemporary development of Hegel's thought – or even a fair appreciation of it – would resist a facile tendency to reject all constructive, substantively rational activity as redemptive or totalizing. But three further points may be made concerning the way this concept may function to exclude crucial possibilities. One concerns the role of trauma, which escapes experience in the ordinary sense and upsets the movement of a harmonizing or synthesizing speculative dialectic. The 'significance' of trauma is

---

Judith Butler and Joan Scott, eds., *Feminists Theorize the Political* (New York and London, 1992), 32.

45 Those with extreme experience, such as rape victims, may be placed in the double bind of being authenticated as witnesses but invalidated as knowledgeable commentators concerning that experience. Thus, on talk shows, the victim typically appears as witness but the expert (for example, the psychiatrist) is the one who knows the meaning of the experience. (I thank Linda Alcoff for this insight.) This double bind is more generally at play with respect to those in subordinate or 'abject-ified' and objectified positions, for example, 'native informants.'

46 Aside from its ordinary senses, 'experience' was of course a crucial concept for Hegel. Jean-François Lyotard observes: 'The word *experience* is *the* word of the *Phenomenology of Mind*, the "science of the experience of consciousness." Experience is the "dialectical process which consciousness executes on itself" ... In the sphere that belongs to it, experience supposes the speculative element, the "life of the mind" as a life which "endures death and in death maintains its being" ... This abode liberates the *Zauberkraft* [magical

that it disrupts experience and cannot be integrated into it. For Freud trauma cannot be located punctually but takes place belatedly (*nachträglich*) as a later, seemingly insignificant 'experience' somehow recalls an earlier one, charged but unassimilated. The trauma in the technical, psychoanalytic sense is marked by an interval between experiences, and it involves a period of latency between the initial and triggering 'experiences.' More generally, trauma does not conform to either a phenomenological or a common-sense model of experience, and it is typically repressed or denied in a manner that induces its compulsive re-enactment and the need to work through it. Rather than repressing or excessively mitigating its role (as in Taylor's *Sources of the Self*), a critical historiography would allow trauma to register in the (perhaps never fully successful) attempt to work it through. Moreover, it may, paradoxically, be the case that the only 'full,' prepossessing experience is phantasmatic, and its relation to meaning is problematic: the experience of compulsively acting out a (real and/or imagined) traumatic past that is relived as if it were entirely present (rather than remembered with the risk of gaps and other difficulties that memory brings). One may also insist that working through trauma does not deliver full meaning or speculative synthesis but instead permits a significant measure of critical control that may never entirely – at least in cases of severe trauma – dispense with at least the possibility (and in all probability the reality) of acting out.[47]

---

force] of the mind, the power to convert the negative into Being, the "*göttliche Natur des Sprechens*'" [divine nature of speech]. *The Differend: Phrases in Dispute*, 88–9.

47 For a discussion of the way in which the concept of experience has been used in post-war Germany to deny, repress, or mitigate trauma, see Eric L. Santner, *Stranded Objects: Mourning, Memory, and Film in Postwar Germany*

History, Reading, and Critical Theory 63

A second point is that one of the main purposes of history is to inquire into the significance of what we have *not* experienced and what we are able reconstruct on the basis of multiple remains, including at best the traces of others' experiences and traumas. In this sense we cannot simply ground history in experience, and the problem is not to guard against the reduction of experience to meaning but to enable ourselves and others to understand and remember what may be distant from our personal experience or that of our community (or what we take that experience to be). How understanding and memory should work is debatable, for example, in terms of the role and relative importance of empathy, the interpretation of meaning, and the active recognition of the limits of both empathy and meaning. But that history extends beyond (or falls short of) experience, without simply providing either full meaning or deceptively vicarious experience, should be evident.

(Ithaca and London, 1990), esp. the analysis on 89–97. On trauma, see also my *Representing the Holocaust: History, Theory, Trauma* and 'European Intellectual History and the Post-traumatic State,' an interview in *iichiko intercultural* 1994, no. 6, 108–26. In his sensitive, informative book, *The Texture of Memory: Holocaust Memorials and Meaning* (New Haven and London, 1993), James E. Young writes of concentration camps as memorials and specifically of Majdanek: 'The ruins here are material evidence not only of these crimes [against Jews and other victims of the Shoah] but also of a state's reasons for remembering them. Indeed, there is little reason for preserving the ruins outside of the meaning preservation imputes to them' (121). Young's assertions may be qualified by noting that memorial ruins may also mark trauma and delimit meaning. Besides being *lieux de mémoire* (in Pierre Nora's term), they are also *lieux de trauma*, that is, sites for acting out problems that resist being imbued with satisfactory meaning and that may not be adequately remembered or worked through. It might also be noted that despite the ideological individualism and adamant rejection of psychoanalysis as applied to collective phenomena in his preface (xi), Young, in his substantive discussions of the role of memorials in various social contexts, makes frequent appeals to psychoanalytic concepts such as repression.

A third consideration is that a prevalent characteristic of 'postmodern' culture is the commodification of experience, and the invasiveness of this process may raise doubts about the uncritical invocation of the term. We now buy and sell experiences and not simply goods and services – the experience of visiting an Indian reservation, of getting to know Santa Fe, of living for a while in a monastery, of attending a university such as Harvard or Yale, or even of spending an afternoon in a Holocaust museum participating in certain 'experiences' of victims. With the advent of virtual reality, we now can market simulated experiences detached from their 'real' referents. We try to escape from commodification through a phenomenon that is readily fed back into the commodity loop through soap operas and popular literature: the meaningful experience itself. The meaningful experience does not reduce experience to meaning (the move Toews fears); it joins the two in a blissful *Aufhebung*, which shows how Hegel, too, can be conventionalized, provide one facile way to shoot the gap between high and mass culture, and be made to render good service for contemporary life. ('His pain, our gain,' as one postmodern, Christological T-shirt has it.)

Dialogic Reading

Since I have attempted in my own work to develop and apply a dialogic approach to reading and interpretation, I shall tend in this section to speak more fully in my own voice. Yet a strong caveat is in order. 'Dialogue' is itself a contemporary 'buzz word' that is like 'experience' in that it too has been thoroughly commodified if not banalized. And it is difficult in discussing an approach one has advocated to avoid an upbeat Hollywood ending that strikes a redemptive note. For these reasons, dialogism must be distinguished from dialogue in the ordinary, banalized sense. Dialogism refers in a dual fashion both to the mutually challenging or contestatory interplay of forces in language and to the comparable interaction between social agents in various specific historical contexts. (Especially in the former sense, its concerns parallel those of a certain mode of deconstruction.) Basic to it is a power of provocation or an exchange that has the effect of testing assumptions, legitimating those that stand its critical test and preparing others for change. (This is, I think, the crucial sense of dialogism in Bakhtin that involves the role of the carnivalesque.) Moreover, in my understanding of it, a dialogic approach is based on a distinction that may be problematic in certain cases but is nonetheless important to formulate and explore. This is the distinction between accurate reconstruction of an object of study and exchange with that object as well as with other inquirers into it. This distinction itself indicates that there are limits to dialogism that prevent it from achieving the status of a redemptive or totalizing perspective. It is both necessarily supplemented by other perspectives, such as reconstruction, and questioned by forces it does not entirely master (such as differences in power, the effects of trauma, or the workings of the unconscious).

History in accordance with a self-sufficient research paradigm gives priority if not exclusive status to accurate reconstruction, restricts exchange with other inquirers to a subordinate, instrumental status (signalled textually by a relegation to footnotes or a bibliography), and is forced to disguise dialogic exchange as reconstruction, often in a manner that infiltrates values into a seemingly objective or value-neutral account. It is less deceptive to argue that one may make a problematic yet significant distinction between reconstruction and exchange and that exchange is permissible – indeed, both unavoidable and desirable – for the historian, with respect both to the object of inquiry and to other inquirers. The distinction between reconstruction and exchange does not imply the feasibility of a binary opposition or separation of the two into autonomous activities or spheres. Exchange with other inquirers is constitutive of research, for it helps to shape the very questions posed to the past and establishes a contemporary context (typically involving ideological issues) that should be critically elucidated rather than occluded, repressed, or relegated to a secondary position. In this sense, there is a mutually reciprocal relation between research and dialogic exchange, for the object of research is constructed in and through exchange with past and present inquirers. In addition, exchange with the object of inquiry (which is always mediated by exchange with other inquirers) is necessary, notably with respect to intensely 'cathected' or traumatizing objects, such as the Holocaust, or texts that themselves raise problems of continuing concern and demand a response from the reader not restricted to purely empirical-analytic inquiry or contextualization.

A dialogic approach involves the recognition that projection is to some extent unavoidable insofar as objects of inquiry are of intense concern to us because they pose questions that address significant values or assumptions. At times they may pose such questions precisely because they differ drastically from what we hold, or would like to believe we hold, our basic values or assumptions to be. This point applies both to the beliefs and practices of very different cultures or time periods and to more recent phenomena that upset cherished convictions about the nature of our civilization. The difficulty in coming to terms with the Nazi period and the desire to normalize it in one way or another, if only by showing the prevalence of genocide or, on the contrary, the manner in which it was presumably anomalous or marginal in German or Western history, attest to the manner in which we tend to refuse to see that it was indeed a real possibility for an important part of 'our' civilization and thus for 'us' under certain conditions. An obvious but basic point is that something would not shock us if it were not already in us, in however potential, subdominant, or repressed a form. If it were not already in us, it would not provoke anxiety but simply leave us indifferent as an object of idle curiosity. The incredulity evinced by the fact that the Shoah could have happened in the land of Goethe and Kant is remarkable both because of its naiveté and because of the manner in which it signals the occurrence of a shock or trauma we find difficult to assimilate.

A combination of accurate reconstruction and dialogic exchange is necessary in that it accords an important place to the 'voices' and specific situations of others at the same time as it creates a place for our 'voices' in an attempt to come to terms with the past in a manner that has implications for the present and future. It is in this sense that it remains important to provide quotations from a text being interpreted or from agents in the period being discussed. The principle here is that such quotations should be extensive enough to provide the reader with a basis for a possible counterreading or interpretation in the event that the latter is indeed called for. In reading the past, one may formulate the combination of reconstruction and dialogic exchange most simply in terms of two related questions: What is the other saying or doing? How do I – or we – respond to it?

This formulation is simplistic in that it does not address

the complexity of understanding others in history or explicate the divergent possibilities of response. To arrive at a measure of understanding requires some determination of literal and figurative meaning, the role of irony, parody, and 'voice' or positionality in general, the possible intervention of unconscious forces such as repression and denial, and the articulation of inherent assumptions of the text or activity. It also requires sensitivity to the projective dimensions of our attempts at reconstruction that become more insistent to the extent that the object of inquiry is still highly charged for us. Here there is the possibility of a post-deconstructive notion of objectivity that supplements rather than obviates the role of dialogic exchange: a notion of objectivity in which we attempt to check projection and prevent it from becoming a unilateral if not narcissistic reprocessing or monologic rewriting of the phenomenon or text. Instead we employ contextualizing techniques, requiring meticulous research and the attempt to substantiate statements, precisely as checks on projection. Deconstruction may signal points at which the attempt at dialogic exchange is blocked because the traumatic aspect of the text or phenomenon is so great that it makes exchange and perhaps language in general break down in a more or less telling way – a possibility that entails not the futility of all dialogue but the recognition of its limits. Moreover, radical deconstruction tends to stay within trauma and to act it out or perform it, and this procedure, while to some extent necessary in the face of traumatic crises or limit cases, is especially misleading when it is autonomized and does not broach the question of how to work through problems. Still, deconstruction can be of value in bringing out the internal tensions, contradictions, and aporias of texts or phenomena, and such inner contestations may well indicate problems that were not – and may still not be – acceptably thought and worked through. In certain of its forms (notably in Derrida's writings), it may also bring out the significance of play and laughter as well as their possible role in working through problems. But a dialogic approach does not postulate an antinomy between reading and interpretation, hermeneutics and poetics, work and play. Rather, it takes those relations to be problematic as it investigates the possibility and limits of meaning in the past in its bearing on the present and future. Here the attempt at reconstruction itself broaches the question of how to engage in dialogic exchange.

Dialogic exchange indicates how the basic problems in reading and interpretation may ultimately be normative and require a direct engagement with normative issues that are often concealed or allusively embedded in a seemingly 'objective' account. It also brings out the problem of the relations among historiography, ethics, and politics. For the dialogic dimension of inquiry complicates the research paradigm and raises the problem of the voice and subject-position(s) in which we respond to the past in a manner that always has implications for the present and future. The use of the 'I' is relatively uncommon in historiography and is often restricted to a preface or coda. It is becoming more common, perhaps too common, in literary criticism and anthropology. Its use is, in any case, ambivalent or even equivocal. It disrupts a value-neutral façade and raises questions about the possibilities and limits of objectivity. It foregrounds the problem of subjectivity. But the use of 'I' easily reinforces an individualistic ideology, obscures the problem of subject-positions, and may foreclose other possible responses, such as collective and more politically germane ones. The notion of subject-position signals the intimate relation of subject and subjectivity to social positionality and the manner in which 'voice' is not a purely individual or subjective issue. It also brings 'voice' in contact with ethical and political issues that are not confined to the individual psyche or biography, thus forcing the issue of the nature of a desirable dialogic response to the past. The dialogic dimension of research in which a response is required of the investigator has been acknowledged in a restricted manner in the notion of observer participation. This dimension heightens awareness of, even anxieties about, the historian's interactions with the object of inquiry. It is thus worth returning to the proposal that we consider these transactions in psychoanalytic terms – as involving a transferential relation to the object of study (as well as to other inquirers). Transference in Freud rested upon the tendency to repeat, either in a compulsive form of acting out (in which the individual relived a typically traumatic past as if it were fully present) or in a more critically controlled 'working through' that allowed for significant change and a reinvestment in life. The transferential repetition in the clinical context of the relationship between parent and child was seen by Freud as occurring in less controlled or safe environments such as the adult romantic or even the work relationship. Even in its restricted, orthodox Freudian sense, transference may have a bearing on the relation among scholars (notably the teacher–graduate student relationship) that has yet to be sufficiently acknowledged and accounted for.[48] But the

---

48 On this issue see Peter Loewenberg, *Decoding the Past: The Psychological Approach* (New York, 1983), 45–80. I should note that my conception of transference does not imply that a process or structure exists in the past as an 'objective' ready made to be replicated in the present. The process of repetition involves elements of projection and, more generally, of interaction with the past. But, in acting out, this process is undergone blindly, and it is as if what is repeated is fully there in the past and comes to exert com-

more general and basic sense of transference as a tendency to repeat applies as well to the way in which processes active in the object of study tend to be replicated in our accounts of them. This transferential relation in the broad sense requires that we come to terms with it in one way or another – through denial (as in positivism or notions of pure objectivity), repression (in research that brackets or marginalizes values only to see them return in encrypted or covert form), acting out (as in certain views of performativity or active rewriting), or working through (the goal of a critically controlled dialogic exchange with the past). Insofar as the fundamental concepts of psychoanalysis (such as transference, repression, denial, resistance, acting out, and working through) are not restricted to the individual psyche or the one-on-one clinical situation but recognized as undercutting the opposition between the individual and society and linked with the notion of subject-position, they provide a way of rethinking the problem of reading and interpretation in history. They may even furnish the basis for developing an ethics of reading that is not insensitive to the role of play, laughter, and carnivalesque forces in general.[49]

In concluding, I would reiterate the basic point that different historians may justifiably embody in their work a different combination of reconstruction of the object, involving contextualization in terms of the past, and dialogic exchange with it which itself calls for self-contextual-

---

pulsive force in the present. Moreover, when the repetition is disclosed, we may be shocked by the way the past returns and haunts or possesses us in the present. The active recognition of the difference between past and present helps initiate the process of working through problems.

49 In this request the work of Bakhtin is of obvious importance. See my discussion of Bakhtin in *Rethinking Intellectual History: Texts, Contexts, Language*, chap. 9.

ization in a present network of discussion and debate. Indeed, different works or portions of a work by the same historian may show differing stresses and strains. This view considerably broadens the field of history without depriving it of all coherence. Rather it introduces into historiography the need for informed argument about boundaries and the recognition of how certain forms of testing – or even periodic transgressing – of those boundaries may be fruitful for the self-understanding of historians and the reconsideration of disciplinary definitions. Finally, it also raises the question of what combinations of subject-positions should be deemed allowable or desirable even when they involve the passage beyond a delimited disciplinary conception of the historical profession.

2

Rereading Tocqueville's Old Régime

An excellent introduction to recent scholarship on Tocqueville is provided by Matthew Mancini's *Alexis de Tocqueville*.[1] Lucid, sober, and judicious, it is a worthy companion to Tocqueville's own writings. Mancini, however, like many recent commentators, tends by and large to share Tocqueville's basic assumptions and liberal orientation and those assumptions consequently tend to remain implicit and thus not subject to critical analysis, even when Mancini demurs from certain of Tocqueville's tendencies (notably with respect to imperialism and colonialism). The primary purpose of my own analysis shall be to elicit the assumptions on which Tocqueville relied and which typically are shared by his commentators. On the level of his basic assumptions Tocqueville is as much a figure of the present as of the past; as I indicated in the Introduction, these assumptions are embedded in the work of an influential group of political theorists (notably, Louis Hartz in the United States and Raymond Aron in

---

1 Matthew Mancini, *Alexis de Tocqueville* (New York, 1994).

France) who were pivotal commentators on Tocqueville and the essentials of whose approach have not been sufficiently questioned or transcended. In this discussion I shall focus on Tocqueville's *Old Régime and the French Revolution*, which is probably his most important work for historians, while *Democracy in America* receives more attention from political scientists and the general public. I shall attempt, however, to place *The Old Régime* in the larger context of Tocqueville's thought.[2]

With Tocqueville's interpretation of the Revolution, we move from the religious perspective of Joseph de Maistre to a more secular and familiar form of thought. The late-twentieth-century reader experiences relatively little culture shock from Tocqueville's attempts to explain why the Revolution happened in France. For the historian, in fact, the critical problem may be to defamiliarize Tocqueville – just as the contrasting problem may be to demonstrate that the thought of someone like Maistre has some relevance to contemporary problems. Maistre interpreted the French Revolution as a collective ritual process centrally involving sacrifice and collective regeneration in and through violence. The Terror was the instrument of God's will: shedding the blood of innocents would serve as punishment and compensate for the sins of wayward élites (including the aristocracy and clergy) in the old régime. Thus for Maistre the Revolution could not be turned back and the attempts of counter-revolutionaries to reverse its course were misguided. The Revolution had to play itself out in order ultimately to achieve a renewed

---

2 *The Old Régime and the French Revolution*, trans. Stuart Gilbert (1856; New York, 1955). *Democracy in America*, trans. George Lawrence, ed. J.P. Mayer (vol. 1, 1835; vol. 2, 1840; New York, 1969). All page references will be to these editions and will be included in the text.

and reinvigorated old régime, as people came to their senses and returned to ancient wisdom, legitimate monarchy, and old-time religion. In *The Old Régime* Tocqueville refers in passing to Maistre without closely analysing or lending credence to his views. Sacrifice and related 'excesses' are not prominent in Tocqueville's understanding of religion in general (although they may be with respect to its secular displacements), and by and large they remain a missing chapter in the work of later commentators. In Tocqueville, religion is seen generally as a positive force, except when its exogenous political role and uses provoke certain groups to unrest and even to revolution (as in the case of peasants subjected to tithes and other exactions by the church under the old régime). Unlike most commentators, Mancini stresses religion in Tocqueville. Indeed, the stress on the presence of religion supportive of democracy comes to supplement (without questioning) the emphasis of earlier commentators on the absence of a feudal past in the United States. This absence is presumably a key determinant of the stable democratic régime found on this side of the Atlantic, whereas political turmoil is part of the destabilizing heritage of a democratic revolution in the context of European feudalism and aristocratic privilege. For Tocqueville religion serves to underwrite and solidify democracy in America, uniting the head of mankind with its heart. Religion becomes a necessity in democratic societies, serving to limit desire and check political turbulence.[3] Thus religion is a crucial component of the 'habits of the heart' – the mores or what Pierre Bourdieu would term the *habitus* – required to maintain stable, viable

---

3 Mancini, *Alexis de Tocqueville*, 51.

democracy. Needless to say, in this vision of religion and its relation to society and politics, only selected elements of the religious phenomenon are treated; the more disorienting aspects (including fanatical fundamentalism and blood-letting) that Maistre recognized and at times emphasized tend to be downplayed or eliminated.[4] Other aspects or possible kinds of religion tend to be downplayed as well. Tocqueville's understanding of Americans, in the second volume of *Democracy in America*, as 'natural' or 'unschooled' Cartesians tends to overlook the role of a certain kind of religion (radical sectarian Protestantism, especially Puritanism in the New England context) in fostering or even generating the traits he identifies from a French perspective as Cartesian – traits that go in a direction contrary to his moderate Catholic and generally positive understanding of religion. (Here

---

4 Mancini's treatment of religion is limited in other ways. In line with Max Weber and Jürgen Habermas, Mancini sees modernity in terms of disenchantment and the separation of spheres of activity – the religious, social, economic, political, and so forth. What this perspective obscures is the role of countervailing forces into which Tocqueville himself provided insight. Religion in Tocqueville tends not simply to disappear nor is the world simply disenchanted, although a crisis may be evident with traumatic consequences for those who find their faith shaken or out of touch with modern conditions. Despite crisis and trauma, Tocqueville recognized ways in which religion might be displaced in secular institutions, practices, movements, and ideologies that themselves promised re-enchantment and an analogue of salvation or redemption. Indeed, one of his fears was that politics might be understood as redemptive and inspire revolutionary movements that held out the hope of secular salvation. Commentators (including Mancini) notice that the French Revolution was seen by Tocqueville as giving rise to a secular or civil religion, with its elation and rituals, but they may not extend this observation to a more general account of secular displacements of religion in modernity. Moreover, Tocqueville recognized the renewed quest for wholeness that militated against the separation of existence into discrete spheres, and saw that displaced religion might itself be a primary vehicle for this quest. On Maistre see Owen Bradley, *A Modern Maistre: The Social and Political Thought of Joseph de Maistre* (Lincoln, Nebr., 1999.)

an important dimension of Max Weber's work, particularly his *Protestant Ethic and the Spirit of Capitalism*, serves as a supplement to Tocqueville's analysis.) These putatively Cartesian traits include the belief in an absolute break with the past, an ethos of self-reliance, and a scorn for forms and rituals.[5] Moreover, the role of a certain type of religion in fostering these traits in America would contradict or at least qualify Tocquevile's belief that religion would perforce act as a constraint on, or counterforce to, such traits and hence in this respect as an unambiguous support of a certain kind of liberal democratic polity. Finally, we might underscore the point that Tocqueville saw America almost exclusively from the perspective of Puritan New England, however restricted his understanding of that perspective and its implications may have been. He gave little autonomy, for instance, to the point of view of the plantation south or of Indian tribes that

---

5 Here is Weber on the doctrine of election: 'In its extreme inhumanity this doctrine must above all have had one consequence for the life of a generation which surrendered to its magnificent consistency. That was a feeling of unprecedented inner loneliness of the single individual. In what was for the man of the age of the Reformation the most important thing in life, his eternal salvation, he was forced to follow his path alone to meet a destiny which had been decreed for him from eternity. No one could help him. No priest, for the chosen one can understand the word of God only in his own heart. No sacraments, for though the sacraments had been ordained by God for the increase of His glory, and must hence be scrupulously observed, they are not a means to the attainment of grace, but only the subjective *externa subsidia* of faith. No Church ... Finally, even no God. For even Christ had died only for the elect ... This, the complete elimination of salvation through the Church and the sacraments (which was in Lutheranism by no means developed to its final conclusions), was what formed the absolutely decisive difference from Catholicism ... The genuine Puritan even rejected all signs of religious ceremony at the grave and buried his nearest and dearest without song or ritual in order that no superstition, no trust in the effects of magical and sacramental forces on salvation, should creep in.' *The Protestant Ethic and the Spirit of Capitalism* (1904–5; New York, 1958), 104–5.

were displaced and at times decimated by various 'errands into the wilderness.'[6] In Tocqueville's account, the plantation south and the heritage of slavery, as well as the life of American Indians, became at most objects of observation and delimited, objectified sources of difficulties for democracy, rather than the source of alternative visions of American history as a whole.

Thus, in some recent accounts, the role allotted to religion supplements, often without raising questions about, other aspects of Tocqueville's thought. This is especially true with respect to an earlier assumption that has by now reached canonical if not essentialized status: the idea that democracy in America – in marked contrast to the situation in France – is stable and viable because America, unencumbered by a feudal past, did not have to go through a turbulent revolution to achieve it. In *Democracy in America*, Tocqueville is often understood as providing 'us' in North America with a self-image – a way to read ourselves. In a sense, Tocqueville is credited with having discovered America, for *Democracy in America* is often read as the mirror on the wall; predictably enough, 'we' turn out to be the fairest of them all. In *The Old Régime*, Tocqueville presumably provided 'us' with an equally necessary, complementary image of the other 'over there' – what we were not and are not, and what the French were and perhaps still are. One crucial question is whether these readings are somewhat limited, or even dubious, and whether a partial reversal (but not a simple inversion) of perspectives is necessary whereby we can also, to

---

6 On religion in Tocqueville, see also Doris S. Goldstein, *Trial of Faith: Religion and Politics in Tocqueville's Thought* (New York, 1975). Like Mancini, Goldstein stresses the general importance of religion in Tocqueville's conception of democracy.

some significant extent, recognize ourselves in *The Old Régime*.[7] In saying this, I am not drawing a literal analogy between pre-1789 France and contemporary America (or modern societies in general) but rather pointing to an aspect of Tocqueville's approach that is all too tempting to repeat. In his manner of addressing difficult and at times intractable problems Tocqueville tended to displace his own anxieties onto others and to offer solutions that did not seem adequate to problems as he himself analysed them.[8]

While Edmund Burke is seen as a conservative and Joseph de Maistre as an ultra-conservative, Tocqueville is often presented as a liberal-conservative. This label is most appropriate for his practical politics and for certain of the explicit conclusions of his thought. But it does not do justice to the complexities of his thinking, which has at times radical dimensions (radical in the basic sense of going to the root of problems). While Tocqueville does not dwell on dimensions of the Revolution that preoccupied Maistre and although his prose does not attain the rhetorical force and emotional pathos of that of Burke, the thought-provoking complexity of his work, with its

---

7 François Furet's influential interpretation, which I shall discuss later, is a different form of reversal, indicating that Tocquevillian liberals in France believe that France has – or should – become more like 'us' at least ideologically.

8 It should be clear that I am not simply arguing that we should now see Tocqueville as 'regressive' or that his vision of liberal democracy is irrelevant in the contemporary American and global context. On the contrary, certain aspects of his thought, including some of his very omissions or exaggerations, may be instructive in that they parallel or corroborate recent tendencies that are open to criticism. I am also arguing for a distinction between the political and constitutional dimensions of liberalism, which I would join Tocqueville in defending, and certain of its economic, ideological, and imperial-colonial dimensions, which I would criticize.

sophisticated interweaving of dimensions, is still significant today. For purposes of analysis, I find it useful to distinguish among three dimensions of Tocqueville's thought: 1) the descriptive, analytic, and explanatory (or 'scientific') 2) the interpretive, particularly in terms of narrative and 3) the ideological, especially in relation to Tocqueville's basic values such as liberty (his primary value). These dimensions arguably form the basic conceptual underpinnings or assumptions of Tocqueville's approach to problems. They tend to remain invisible to commentators who share them without having sufficient critical perspective on them.[9]

The descriptive, analytic, and explanatory dimension is ostensibly the most important in *The Old Régime* and has been the most influential among historians. I shall say a little about the other two dimensions before turning to an extensive discussion of it. I would note in passing that one problem with François Furet's stimulating analysis in *Interpreting the French Revolution* is its somewhat truncated and overly scientific conception of Tocqueville as wavering between two 'hypotheses' about the causes of the French Revolution: administrative centralization and the role of mentalities and the intellectuals. Furet does not inquire into the nature of this seeming indecision and its relation

---

9 The aesthetic or literary dimension of Tocqueville, as well as certain ideological implications, is the focus of analysis in Hayden White's *Metahistory: The Historical Imagination in Nineteenth-Century Europe* (Baltimore and London, 1973), chap. 5. White's analysis is penetrating, especially with respect to certain tensions in Tocqueville, but it is limited by the fact that it does not systematically relate aesthetic and ideological dimensions to the more scientific impetus that has been of greatest influence among historians and that is an insistent dimension of Tocqueville's thought. White also exaggerates the role of a putative 'fall' into the impasses of irony, a reliance on mechanistic explanation, and what he sees as an almost nihilistic sense of degeneration in Tocqueville.

to other tensions and ideological forces in Tocqueville. The Revolution is clearly overdetermined for Tocqueville, and the problem is, I think, less his indecision between the two factors Furet stresses than the manner in which his emphasis on them is conjoined with a diminished or inadequate concern for other problems.[10] As we shall see,

---

10 See François Furet's *Interpreting the French Revolution*, trans. Elborg Forster (1978; Cambridge, 1981). I try to provide a frame of analysis grounded in an intertextual reading of *The Old Régime* and *Democracy in America*, while Furet makes primarily local and circumscribed references to the latter text. (Furet also seems to accept the prevalent if not canonical idea that democracy in America was 'not only a state of society, but a founding principle, brought over and built up *ex nihilo* by democratically-minded men who never had to struggle against an opposing principle, an opposing history and opposing traditions' (156). It is unclear where this view leaves slavery, plantation society, and the Civil War, as well as the treatment of American Indians.) As I note above, Furet's encompassing interpretive gesture is to see Tocqueville as suffering 'from a kind of conceptual block' because of his tendency to 'waver' between 'two basic hypotheses about French history': the 'hypothesis of administrative centralisation' and a 'hypothesis' about the role of revolutionary ideology and its relation to violence (161–2). Furet is correct in pointing out the limitations of Tocqueville's analysis of ideology and the dynamic of revolution (as well as his exaggerated idea of the degree of administrative centralization in the old régime). His observation that 'Tocqueville has given us not so much the history of "The Ancien Régime and the Revolution" he had meant to write as an interpretative description of the Ancien Régime and some fragments of a projected history of the Revolution' (162) also has merit. But Furet does not discuss Tocqueville's animus against the intellectuals; he treats only the manner in which prior developments (such as administrative centralization) prepared for the importance and dissemination of ideology and for the role of intellectuals as leaders. Furthermore, Furet exaggerates the issue of the two hypotheses and relies too heavily on them to provide coherence in his own analysis, for I fail to see why these so-called hypotheses would cause a 'conceptual block' rather than at most a degree of tension in matters of emphasis. After all, in the logic of Tocqueville's argument administrative (as well as political) centralization might further the appeal and effectiveness of ideology even among the privileged insofar as centralization could be seen as breaking down practices and habits of self-rule, particularly those of the intermediary bodies, whose importance Furet fails adequately to address or situate in Tocqueville's explanatory structure. In general, Furet is very close to Tocqueville in terms

these problems include the role of socio-economic forces, the very understanding of the process of centralization, and the skewed treatment of the role of intellectuals. Moreover, Furet's animus against Marxism and Marxist-inspired accounts of the Revolution (which parallels Tocqueville's animus against socialism) is useful in bringing out simplifications that Tocqueville's analysis helps to pinpoint and place in doubt, especially the misleading idea that the old régime was a solid feudal order upset by rising capitalism and its putative bearer – a class-conscious, modernizing bourgeoisie. Indeed, most historians today would probably join Furet in finding Marx's picture of the forces responsible for the Revolution much too simple, if not misleading, even when they might be more inclined than Furet to criticize other aspects of Tocqueville's account.[11] But certain aspects of Marx – especially his general understanding of critical theory and his specific critique of a commodity system – may both corroborate general critical-theoretical tendencies in Tocqueville (including a desire to relate theory and practice) and raise questions about his defence of a market system, as well as his relatively unproblematic conjunction of capitalism with liberal democracy (another feature of his thought that has found its analogues in certain perspectives on recent history, especially with the fall of communist regimes).

What I have referred to as the second dimension of

---

of both methods of analysis and ideological commitments. For an extended analysis and critique of Furet in the context of the Bicentennial in France, see Steven L. Kaplan, *Adieu 89* (Paris, 1993).

11 See the analysis in Seymour Drescher, 'Why Great Revolutions Will Become Rare: Tocqueville's Most Neglected Prognosis,' *Journal of Modern History* 64 (1992), 429–54. See also Drescher's *Dilemmas of Democracy: Tocqueville and Modernization* (Pittsburgh, 1968).

Tocqueville's thought is interpretive. Tocqueville not only tries to describe and explain things, he attempts to provide some idea of the meaning or significance of the events and processes he discusses. Noteworthy in this respect is the manner in which he tells a story and depends on a narrative construction of events. Among the standard elements of narrative on which he relies are plot, characterization, voice, and point of view. In some ways the story he tells is similar to that in Stendhal's *The Red and the Black*, for example, with respect to the status of narrative voice, problems in characterization, and the role of a tragic plot. And the general reading of French society has significant parallels in Tocqueville and Stendhal. For both, post-Revolutionary society is marked by an atomization of individuals and a factionalization of groups, which produce a situation marked by stalemate and a lack of cooperation, even when the interests of social agents tend to coincide.[12]

What is the plot of *The Old Régime*? In one respect the story seems tragic, especially viewed from an aristocratic perspective. In *The Old Régime* we have an account of the decline and fall of the old order and the nobility and the corresponding rise of a despotic, centralizing monarchy and egalitarian movements. Here we may note one of Tocqueville's central themes – the link between extreme egalitarianism or democracy and despotism. For Tocque-

---

12 The similarities between Tocqueville and Stendhal do not necessarily imply that both relied projectively on ultimately fictive structures of interpretation, as Hayden White tends to assert in other contexts. On the contrary, one can argue that novels may involve truth claims, for example, in the manner in which they read the times or provide insight into phenomena or developments. In any case, the relation between fact (or more generally truth claims) and fiction is too intricate to allow for a simple reduction that postulates the priority of one or the other.

ville as for Aristotle or Montesquieu, extreme equality invites despotism because it eliminates intermediary safeguards, especially the existence of an aristocracy. The process of decline and fall of the old régime culminates in what is – or seems to be – revolutionary upheaval. For Tocqueville, however, the very idea of a French Revolution is in important respects a misleading fiction, for the Revolution did relatively little of a positive nature in changing basic structures and institutions, and the factors that caused instability in the old régime continued through the Revolution to create instability in post-revolutionary France. Modern France inherited some of the worst features of the old régime, notably a highly centralized bureaucratic and administrative structure. (Here Tocqueville's emphasis brings him close to Max Weber or to the Marx of *The Eighteenth Brumaire.*) One real effect of the Revolution for Tocqueville was ideological: the Revolution gave birth to a revolutionary tradition, which exacerbated later instability. It is precisely this revolutionary tradition that concerns, indeed generates anxiety in, Tocqueville at his own time, and one crucial impetus of his account is to counter it by showing how the Revolution produced more harm than good. It was largely a wasted or a needlessly destructive and destabilizing effort: 'Even if it had not taken place, the old social structure would nonetheless have been shattered everywhere sooner or later. The only difference would have been that instead of collapsing with such brutal suddenness it would have crumbled bit by bit' (20).

There are, however, dissonances in the process that Tocqueville seems to view as tragic. One problem common to Tocqueville and certain dramatists and novelists is whether the processes of modern history are too fragmented, messy, and declassé to support a classical tragic structure.[13] Can key agents in the modern period be cast in the role of tragic heroes? Marx tried at times to see the old régime as a solid feudal order overthrown by an heroic bourgeoisie in its pursuit of limited political democracy and a capitalistic economy. Thus the bourgeoisie in pre-Revolutionary France was cast in the role of tragic hero, while the proletariat in post-Revolutionary society could be seen as a hero promising a possibly successful 'comic' resolution of events through revolution. In his classic account of the emergence of working-class consciousness, Marxist historian E.P. Thompson seemed to see an heroic, albeit now more tragic, role for the workers in early nineteenth-century England.[14] But for Tocqueville the role of hero remained without convincing players in France. The old régime as Tocqueville describes it was not a solid, legitimate order. By the eighteenth century, it was a shambles rather than a firm feudal structure or cosmos. The most important vestiges of an earlier time were onerous feudal dues detached from their supports in the distant past (these vestigial dues were indeed eliminated in the course of the Revolution).

Tocqueville seems at times to cast the aristocracy as a collective tragic hero. Its fall was clearly for him a catastrophe and the failure of the aristocracy to retain its legitimate functions in society was lamentable. The nobility, in Tocqueville's rather legendary if not at times fabulous account of it, was a bulwark of liberty in the distant past of a genuinely feudal monarchy (see pages 110–11). Indeed, the feudal monarchy of the fourteenth and fifteenth centuries is idealized by Tocqueville. (Furet observes that

---

13 Eric Auerbach discusses this problem in *Mimesis*, trans. Willard Trask (1946; Princeton, N.J., 1968).
14 E.P. Thompson, *The Making of the English Working Class* (New York, 1963).

Tocqueville knew little about French history before the eighteenth century and tended to exaggerate the degree of centralization even in the period before the Revolution.) For Tocqueville, in the older régime of the feudal monarchy (the good old days), the nobility helped to constrain a centralizing monarchy and provided the basis of a socio-political order combining aristocracy and liberty. But by the eighteenth century, the nobility for Tocqueville was a problematic hero at best. He presents it as more foolish than flawed, at times even treating the aristocracy ironically as a group blind to what he, from his superior vantage point, sees as its true interest and mission. Under the quasi-legendary feudal monarchy – an older old régime – the nobility was a proud elite. Back then the nobility lived on its lands and provided certain useful functions for its people, such as protection and judicial services, and it limited the powers of the king and his bureaucracy. By the eighteenth century, however, the nobility had sold its right to rule for a mess of pottage – material advantages such as tax benefits and life at court. The nobility in this sense was not what Burke thought it was. On the contrary, it was in good part the agent of its own undoing: it sold out to the king.[15]

In many ways the nobility in the eighteenth century was scarcely distinguishable from the bourgeoisie, but it nonetheless antagonized bourgeois groups by insisting on very clear and at times insulting status differences, even when

---

15 Given Burke's belief that the old régime was a basically solid, legitimate order based on the aristocracy, clergy, and monarchy, he has some difficulty in explaining why a revolution occurred at all. He resorts to conspiracy theory and tends to blame the Revolution on two classes of speculators: speculators in money, who invested in the government debt, and speculators in ideas – the intellectuals whom Tocqueville also tends to scapegoat in a manner that is more dissonant with his account than with Burke's.

status lines could be crossed, for example, by bourgeois buying offices. The bourgeoisie, rather than being a class-conscious carrier of capitalism and democracy, was highly diversified internally and often concerned with emulating the values (and the bickering) of its social superiors. Its most prominent segments wanted nothing better than to buy offices in the judiciary and the administration and to acquire landed estates – that is, to make its way in the old régime. Both the aristocracy and the bourgeoisie were for Tocqueville narrowly self-interested. But the villain of the piece is clearly the monarchy, and the intellectuals, as we shall see, attract their share of caricature and vilification.

Thus Tocqueville offers a varied set of collective characters who inhabit a highly fragmented, conflict-ridden social space. Worlds apart from a classic tragic structure characterized by protagonists who, however flawed, could be seen as heroic, pre-Revolutionary France – with its array of mediocre and self-interested figures – was more akin to a sorry 'sitcom,' which the Revolution did little to remedy.

What is the nature of the voice and viewpoint of Tocqueville as narrator? Sometimes he is closest to the aristocracy, but his retrospective understanding of the way in which they ignobly undid themselves gives him a disappointedly ironic and satirical perspective on their activities. At times his perspective is somewhat akin to that of Stendhal in relation to his characters in *The Red and the Black*,[16] but Tocqueville's irony occasionally goes beyond

---

16 One may note that the narrator's irony is undercut at the end of the novel when Julien Sorel's insight comes to match Stendhal's and the relation between narrator and character is destabilized. On this question, see my analysis in *History, Politics, and the Novel* (Ithaca and London, 1987), chap. 1. In *The Old Régime* there is no analogue of Julien Sorel, for no actor in the French Revolution apparently ever attains Tocqueville's degree of retrospective insight.

Stendhal's relatively gentle tones to approximate the bitterness and disillusionment of Flaubert.[17]

Tocqueville certainly wants to be meticulous in his research and accurate in his facts. He makes pointed reference to all the archives he has visited and is manifestly concerned about establishing his narrative and analytic authority. But he is also preoccupied with the problem of proximity and distance in his relation to his subject matter. And he does at times question himself, change voices, and make explicit but modulated use of irony, parody, and other rhetorical devices. Tocqueville thus enacts one form of dialogic exchange with the past, a form in some instances so pronounced that it may disconcert more conventional historians who might otherwise find congenial his methodology, his balanced and often mellifluous style, and his basic conception of historical discourse. He also manifests a tension between a desire for objectivity and an involvement or implication in the events he treats. At certain times his voice is explicitly normative and performative, particularly with reference to his desire to give his defence of liberty implications for the present and future. Thus he writes:

> I hope and believe that I have written the present book

---

[17] *Madame Bovary* was published in 1856, the same year as *The Old Régime*. On irony in Flaubert, see Jonathan Culler, *Flaubert: The Uses of Uncertainty* (Ithaca and London, 1974), and Dominick LaCapra, *'Madame Bovary' on Trial* (Ithaca and London, 1982). Tocqueville, however, retains both a pathos-charged sense of nostalgia for a legitimate aristocracy and an activist idealism or perhaps an 'optimism of the will' (which Gramsci linked with 'pessimism of the spirit') based on Tocqueville's supreme value of liberty. These characteristics are not in evidence in Flaubert's antidemocratic liberalism and more insistently critical, deflationary, and at times near-nihilistically ironic representation of social life. (One might note that Hayden White in *Metahistory* projectively tends to see Tocqueville almost as if he were Flaubert.)

without any *parti pris*, though it would be futile to deny that my own feelings were engaged. What Frenchman can write about his country and think about the age in which he lives in a spirit of complete detachment? Thus I confess that when studying our old social system under its infinitely various aspects I have never quite lost sight of present-day France. Moreover, I have tried not merely to diagnose the malady of which the sick man died but also to discover how he might have been saved. In fact, my method has been that of the anatomist who dissects each defunct organ with a view to eliciting the laws of life, and my aim has been to supply a picture that while scientifically accurate, may also be instructive. (xi–xii)

Despite his reliance on medical metaphors in the above passage, Tocqueville in general employs explicitly evaluative or normative language and does not rely on the type of crypto-normativism that deceptively conceals norms in a seemingly neutral, 'scientific' conception of normality, pathology, or other misleadingly medicalized analogies. His perspective as narrator is most closely bound up with the value of liberty. The narrator is almost a discursive statue of liberty holding a torch aloft. (Here we move to the dimension of ideology and value.)

Tocqueville directly and passionately affirms the value of liberty, and his writing is moved by the pathos of liberty besieged and beleaguered. He is in a sense inquiring into the past in order to provide a critical history of the present, and he clearly wants to initiate a dialogic exchange between past and present that might have implications for the future. Liberty for Tocqueville is essential for the well-being of the body politic, and it alone provides a sure defence against despotism. Tocqueville is close to a certain tradition of civic humanism and republicanism as recent historians (such as J.G.A. Pocock) have reconstructed it. He is never ironic about the value of liberty, and it has a very special status for him as a serious sanctuary of basic commitment, indeed a secular sacred – an end in itself. Historical forces in the modern period are militating against the value of liberty, notably a centralizing state and egalitarian movements – tendencies that converged in the Jacobin phase of the French Revolution. Moreover, the more general twin threats to liberty are posed by the complementary extremes of revolutionary agitation and apathy – forces that he comes increasingly to see as clear and present dangers in the modern world. And Tocqueville is hard-pressed to provide convincing responses to these threatening forces. Moreover, while Tocqueville is justifiably concerned with the modern tendency to make a displaced religion of political ideology, he himself participates in this tendency through his elevated, auratic idea of liberty – an idea that is at times invoked without being sufficiently defined.

One may signal the tensions between Tocqueville's effort at 'objective' reconstruction of the past and his dialogic exchange with it that was significantly shaped by his investment in the value of liberty (notably in the form of an insufficiently differentiated liberal ideology). Tocqueville was probably not sensitive enough to these tensions (both enabling and disabling), notably with respect to the way in which a necessary and at times beneficial projective inclination, related to his implication in actors and events, might have to be countered in the interest of 'objectivity' and the attempt to do justice to problems. I find this limitation especially evident in his discussion of intellectuals, who tend to become scapegoats onto whom are projected anxieties Tocqueville is loathe to recognize in himself, especially anxiety related to the tension between the seemingly radical implications of his own analysis and the explicitly liberal-conservative conclusions he would like to draw from it. For when Tocqueville transfers his value of liberty onto a practical level, he combines it with some rather moderate (if not tame) or even conservative views. And while he believes that the French Revolution may at a certain point have become historically inevitable, he clearly thinks it was undesirable and had pernicious consequences.

In terms of his own immediate context, it is well known that Tocqueville was active in politics for a significant portion of his career.[18] From 1839 to 1851 (during the July Monarchy and the Second Republic), he was elected by impressive majorities as deputy of the electoral district (the Vologne) where the château of the Tocqueville family was located. He apparently had a close, paternalistic relation to the people on his estate: in a sense, he tried to live out the features he idealized as operative under the older feudal system. During the revolution of 1848, some of the people from his estate even went to Paris to protect Tocqueville from the Parisian mob. They apparently identified more with him than with workers and artisans in Paris.

The year 1848 was crucial in Tocqueville's life and thought. His anxieties and concerns are evident in his *Recollections* as is the role of irony in expressing them.[19] Before 1848, during the July Monarchy, Tocqueville participated in upper-class, liberal, humanitarian causes such as criticism of slavery in the French colonies and prison

---

18 For Tocqueville's biography, see especially André Jardin, *Tocqueville: A Biography*, trans. Lydia Davis and Robert Hemenway (New York, 1988).
19 Alexis de Tocqueville, *Recollections of the French Revolution* (1893; Garden City, N.Y., 1970).

reform. (The latter was the reason for his trip to America.) But he did not oppose colonialism. Indeed, he strongly defended it. He did not, for example, invoke his liberal principles in defence of Arabs in North Africa; on the contrary, he defended military conquest and only criticized the military when they opposed the role of French civilian colonists. In the 1840s Tocqueville wrote: 'As for me, I believe that all means of desolating [or laying waste to – DLC] these tribes ought to be used. I make an exception only in case of what is interdicted by international law and that of humanity.'[20] As Melvin Richter observes, Tocqueville nonetheless 'remained silent in 1846 when it was revealed that hundreds of Arabs had been smoked to death in the course of the *razzias* he had approved for their humane quality.'[21] Liberalism and humanitarian morality apparently did not in any effective manner extend to Arabs when French interests were at stake.

Tocqueville defended imperialism not on narrowly racial grounds – which he opposed, for example, in his exchange with Gobineau – but on moral ones. He believed that imperialism and national sentiment were strong idealistic forces that might counteract selfishness, egoism, and dreaded apathy. Colonial ventures might serve as an antidote to decadence and mediocrity. In 1840, Tocqueville referred in a letter to the invasion of China by England, an event he applauded: 'Here is the European spirit of movement pitted against Chinese immobility. This is a great event especially when one remembers that it is only the ultimate consequence, the most recent in a whole series of events which gradually

---

20 Quoted in Melvin Richter, 'Tocqueville on Algeria,' *Review of Politics* 25 (1963), 380.
21 Ibid.

push the European race abroad to subjugate all other races ... Quite without anyone noticing it, our age is achieving something vaster and more extraordinary than anything since the establishment of the Roman Empire. I mean the subjugation of four-fifths of the world by the remaining fifth. Let us not scorn ourselves and our age, the men may be small, but the events are great.'[22]

Hegel and Marx did of course write similar things and the sense of European superiority was deeply rooted and widespread, at times cutting across other ideological differences. Still, one important current of liberalism could defend both liberal democracy in the West and imperialism and colonialism in non-Western areas of the world – with the far-distant hope that in good time other areas of the world would reach the stage of enlightenment and civilization that would render them worthy of liberal, democratic rule. This current should perhaps be seen neither as anomalous nor as unmasking the true face of liberalism; it was one important form liberalism could and did take. Tocqueville participated in it along with his friend and correspondent, John Stuart Mill. In Tocqueville, this orientation went against biologistic racism of the sort

---

[22] Letter to Henry Reeve of 12 April 1840, quoted in Richter, 385. In *The Old Régime* Tocqueville makes a disparaging remark about the use of China as a model by the physiocrats or economists: 'Being unable to find anything in contemporary Europe corresponding to this ideal State they dreamed of, our Economists turned their eyes to the Far East, and it is no exaggeration to say that not one of them fails, in some part of his writings, to voice an immense enthusiasm for China and all things Chinese. As a matter of fact, China was an almost unknown country in those days, and what they wrote about it was absurd to a degree. That unenlightened, barbarian government which lets itself be manipulated at will by a handful of Europeans was held up by them as a model to the world' (163). As in his discussion of American Indians in *Democracy in America* (to which I shall soon allude), Tocqueville's use of the passive construction in the last-quoted sentence serves to blame the victim.

found in Gobineau, but it was compatible with a cultural or 'moral' racism closely bound up with a theory of stages of civilization – a theory in which Tocqueville firmly believed. For him only the West had arrived at the highest stage of civilization; other peoples were mired in either barbarism or savagery, and a people at one stage might regress to a lower one. Hence the West was itself threatened by regression to barbarism, a threat posed by democratic despotism allied with apathy in the body politic. And a 'barbaric' people, such as emancipated blacks, might regress to 'savagery' (exemplified by American Indians). Here it is important to note the manner in which a seemingly 'scientific' theory of stages of civilization, so prevalent at Tocqueville's time, could be intimately bound up with racist presuppositions which, even if not biologistic, could take important cultural forms that might legitimate oppressive colonial and imperial policies.

I shall later note that one deficiency in *The Old Régime*, also apparent in *Democracy in America*, is the restricted role of economic analysis. It is significant that a noteworthy exception to this generalization relates to Tocqueville's analysis of emancipated slaves. Here Tocqueville relies on classical economics and argues that freed slaves should be prevented from owning small parcels of land and should instead become workers on the estates of their former masters. The creation of a class of proletarians who were former slaves was presumably a progressive stage on the way to civilization, whereas ownership of small holdings of land, which created an inclination for subsistence farming, would signal a regression from barbarism (the state of blacks) to savagery (aligned with hunting and gathering). (Tocqueville did not enter into the implications of this analysis for the prevalence of small landholdings in

France which – furthered but not caused by the French Revolution – was so prominent a feature of the French countryside both at his own time and until relatively recently.) Tocqueville apparently joined many 'liberal' abolitionists in believing that the responsibility for slaves stopped once they had been emancipated. With emancipation, the only problem for liberals was getting former slaves into the labour market as workers who would then be responsible for their own upward mobility towards civilization.[23]

A pronounced sense of Western superiority is blatant in Tocqueville's treatment of both American Indians and African-Americans in *Democracy in America*. He certainly recognizes and at times describes the brutal role and the brutalizing effects of oppression. As he phrases it with reference to American Indians: 'With my own eyes I have seen some of the miseries just described; I have witnessed afflictions beyond my powers to portray' (324). Tocqueville notes the way the federal and state governments alike broke their solemn pledges to tribes: 'There is less of cupidity and violence in the Union's policy toward the Indians than in that of the individual states, but in both cases the governments are equally lacking in good faith' (337). He even recognizes, at least in passing and with

---

23 See *Tocqueville and Beaumont on Social Reform*, ed. and trans. Seymour Drescher (New York, 1968), esp. 'On the Emancipation of Slaves,' 137–73. See also the discussion in Mancini, *Alexis de Tocqueville*, chap. 5. Mancini stresses Tocqueville's avoidance of moral argument and his reliance on economic analysis with reference to freed slaves and even allusively relates these tendencies to the discussion of American Indians in *Democracy in America*. But he somewhat apologetically provides no interpretation of this dimension of Tocqueville's thought, except to relate it without critical comment to Tocqueville's belief in stages of civilization – a belief that may have been shaped by Tocqueville's attendance at François Guizot's 1829–30 lectures at the University of Paris.

important qualifications, the appeal of other ways of life: 'There is something in the adventurous life of a hunting people which seizes the heart of man and carries him away in spite of reason and experience' (331n). But he also makes rather specious, ideologically freighted arguments that mitigate if not deny the role of oppression and assume the decisive superiority of European culture as representing a higher stage of civilization. Indeed, in Tocqueville's account as elsewhere, preconceptions about the barbarity and savagery of the stereotyped 'other' are crucial in establishing Europe's putative superiority, and evolutionary postulates underwrite the contrast between savagery or barbarism and civilized intellect and enlightenment. On these unexamined bases (or biases), Tocqueville argues that 'savages' who do not have civilization, enlightenment, and intellect refuse to accept them from those possessing superior power. As he states with reference to American Indians (whose various cultures he often assimilates through a deceptively homogeneous composite image of the savage 'other'): 'When the side that has the physical force has intellectual superiority too, it is rare for the conquered to become civilized; they either withdraw or are destroyed' (330–1). Tocqueville's passive construction ('are destroyed') obscures the role of European and American agency, as well as the nature and viability of diverse native cultures. Moreover, his concept of American Indian withdrawal from Western civilization and his stereotypical contrast between 'Indian' pride and 'Negro' servility serve to blame the victim.

Tocqueville even makes periodic use of ingratiating, exotic, and presumably tell-tale anecdotes that serve to reinforce prejudicial stereotyping. Worth quoting at length is a description of a strange, pathos-charged scene that brings the three 'races' into a seemingly illustrative *tableau vivant.* Tocqueville begins with a misleadingly lawlike statement or ideologically tinged general principle. In this way he gratuitously imputes psychological motivations to the 'other' and eschews any semblance of critical social and political analysis. 'The Negro would like to mingle with the European and cannot. The Indian might to some extent succeed in that, but he scorns to attempt it. The servility of the former delivers him over into slavery; the pride of the latter leads him to death.'

From this pseudo-generalization that culminates in an incredible metalepsis making slaves responsible for their enslavement and Indians for being killed, Tocqueville moves to the levels of narration and description:

> I remember that, passing through the forests that still cover the state of Alabama, I came one day to the log cabin of a pioneer. I did not wish to enter the American's dwelling, but went to rest a little beside a spring not far off in the forest. While I was there, an Indian woman came up (we were in the neighborhood of the Creek territory); she was holding by the hand a little girl of five or six who was of the white race and who, I supposed, must be the pioneer's daughter. A Negro woman followed her. There was a sort of barbarous luxury in the Indian woman's dress; metal rings hung from her nostrils and ears; there were little glass beads in the hair that fell freely over her shoulders, and I saw that she was not married, for she was still wearing the bead necklace which it is the custom of virgins to lay down on the nuptial couch; the Negro was dressed in European clothes almost in shreds.

Thus Tocqueville sets forth a scene in which a hierarchy is implicitly postulated (white over decadent black barbarian and savage Indian, the latter bearing dilapidated traces of 'barbarous luxury'), and the point is made that the white pioneer and the 'Indian' woman are not married. The 'Negro' seems to be a servant or nanny, but her status is unclear. The authority of Tocqueville's ethnographic voice is reinforced by his observation about the bead necklace, which attests to his knowledge of 'native' customs. Tocqueville resumes his narrative:

> All three came and sat down by the edge of the spring, and the young savage, taking the child in her arms, lavished upon her such fond caresses as mothers give; the Negro, too, sought, by a thousand innocent wiles, to attract the little Creole's attention. The latter showed by her slightest movements a sense of superiority which contrasted strangely with her weakness and her age, as if she received the attentions of her companions with a sort of condescension.
>
> Crouched down in front of her mistress, anticipating her every desire, the Negro woman seemed equally divided between almost maternal affection and servile fear, whereas even in the effusions of her tenderness, the savage woman looked free, proud, and almost fierce.
>
> I had come close and was contemplating the sight in silence; no doubt my curiosity annoyed the Indian woman, for she got up abruptly, pushed the child away from her, almost roughly, and giving me an angry look, plunged into the forest.

Tocqueville's curiosity apparently did not extend far enough to prompt him to inquire why his 'contemplation' might have annoyed the Indian woman who is one of his objects of observation and studied objectification. Here the status of the 'Negro' woman as servant is clear, and her relation to her child 'mistress' becomes seductive and marked by an equivocal mixture of 'almost maternal affection' and 'servile fear.' The 'savage woman,' by contrast, takes on decisively Amazonian characteristics, while the child, who passes in this paragraph (where the father is absent) from white to Creole, is, with the transition to the intermediate status of Creole, described as spoiled and prematurely supercilious. In marked contrast to the demonstrable empirical situation, the maternity rather than paternity of the child is more in doubt, for the 'Indian' woman is a mother only analogically and the 'Negro' woman is almost maternal through divided affection. Here the three 'races' form a confusing *ménage à trois* with the child in the role of indeterminate and suspect offspring. Tocqueville as narrator occupies the position of an unself-conscious *voyeur*, whose own problematic status receives no commentary or self-reflection. For what this scene portrays is Tocqueville's imagination as well as his penchant in certain situations for projective accounts devoid of empirical substantiation or critical analysis. He concludes his unverifiable description in this way: 'I had often seen people of the three races inhabiting North America brought together in the same place; I had already noted very many different signs of white predominance, but there was something particularly touching in the scene I have just described; here a bond of affection united oppressors and oppressed, and nature bringing them close together made the immense gap formed by prejudices and by laws yet more striking' (320).

As in a fable, the general conclusion or *leçon de morale* resonates (at least weakly) with the lawlike beginning of the scene, but it does not seem to follow from the intervening account. It is rather vague as well as symptomatic of wishful thinking. Nor does the narrator pause to question the possible gap between the scene as it occurred and the role of his own preconceptions, desires, or prejudices in rendering it. It is also significant that, in the next section, devoted to the 'Black Race' rather than to the 'Indian Tribes,' Tocqueville one-sidedly and tendentiously postulates that 'the most formidable evil threatening the future of the United States is the presence of the blacks on their soil' (340). He asserts that 'an aristocracy founded on visible and indelible signs [cannot] vanish' and that 'those who hope that the Europeans will one day mingle with the Negroes seem to me to be harboring a delusion' (342). He also sees little hope in sending blacks back to Africa, which might nonetheless have the side benefit of enabling 'European enlightenment ... to penetrate there' (359). He ends his discussion with a double bind: 'If freedom is refused to the Negroes in the South, in the end they will seize it themselves; if it is granted to them, they will not be slow to abuse it' (363).

It is significant that the entire treatment of 'Indians' and 'Negroes,' which is pessimistic if not bleak in tenor and followed by various and sundry speculations about the chances the Union will last, is explicitly introduced as a concluding supplement (317); it is relatively isolated from the entire preceding argument, which took almost no notice of the problems it addresses. The reader is hard pressed to reconcile the earlier, seemingly optimistic discussion of democracy in America with the treatment of 'Indian Tribes' and the 'Black Race,' and many readers have indeed kept them in the separate compartments that Tocqueville's own analytic approach seems to generate. What should be stressed is that both Tocqueville and, even more so, those who turn to him to defend a conception of American 'exceptionalism,' tend to emphasize the absence of both a feudal past and a democratic revolution in creating special conditions for stable democracy in

America, in marked contrast with France. But the idea of the exceptional position of America fails to account for the fact that both slavery and the treatment of American Indians may be seen, if one reads Tocqueville against the grain, as creating severe long-term problems for legitimate democracy in America – problems in certain ways comparable to those created by a feudal past in Europe. Here the analysis of African-Americans and American Indians constitutes a rather dangerous supplement to the main argument of *Democracy in America* and can serve to decentre or counteract its explicit, often upbeat emphasis (at least in volume one) on the nature and preconditions of stable democracy in America.

In the European context Tocqueville before 1848 advocated gradualistic social reform, which he optimistically believed was adequate to quell revolutionary unrest. The revolution of 1848 horrified him. It was for him the first real social revolution; it posed the clear-cut choice between what he saw as egalitarianism with servitude, on the one hand, and order, property, and some liberty, on the other. Tocqueville sided with the forces of law, order, and qualified liberalism. Even before 1848 Tocqueville was a staunch opponent of the socialists. He saw socialism as a pathological symptom of a revolutionary epoch – one of the excesses of democracy. (Here he is close to Max Weber and fits well with recent forms of liberal conservatism or neoconservatism.) Tocqueville rejected the idea that socialism was the last stage of the democratic revolution that, like democracy itself, had to be accommodated rather than rejected. He did not discuss even the theoretical possibility of applying the liberal political principle of self-rule to all participants in the economy – one way of defining liberal democratic socialism. He did not see socialism as a possible site for self-governing groups as intermediary bodies between the state and the individual, despite his crucial general insistence on the desirability of such groups as checks upon despotism. He saw only the possibility of authoritarian state socialism as a manifestation of democratic despotism.

Yet in 1851 the coup of Louis Napoleon was adamantly opposed by Tocqueville. The Napoleonic régime did not offer the kind of law and order that he found legitimate. In the 1850s he retired from public life and became a critic of the Second Empire as representing a form of democratic despotism that eliminated liberty. Active implicitly – and at times explicitly – in *The Old Régime* with its defence of liberty is an attack upon the régime of Napoleon III. In this respect Tocqueville's account is informed by a strongly polemical voice and had rather direct and forthright implications for his own time. Napoleon III posed as great a threat from the right to Tocqueville's brand of liberalism as did socialism from the left.

At this juncture another point becomes apposite. Tocqueville's predominant stress on continuity from the old régime through the French Revolution may function to mitigate or even repress the latter's traumatic impact both at its own time and in its aftermath, notably its role in creating the revolutionary tradition that so preoccupied Tocqueville. It is also striking that Tocqueville, in *The Old Régime*, does not discuss 1848 as a particularly significant moment in that tradition, in spite of the fact that it had such manifestly unsettling consequences for him and sensitized him to the need to look into the historical origins of the revolutionary activity that agitated France throughout the nineteenth century. Paradoxically, the very theme of continuity may serve as a placebo or a means of 'tension management' that reinforces a liberal-conservative position averse to 'radical' or even basic structural responses, even when one's own analysis uncovers deep-seated and long-standing structural problems in society.

Let us now look more closely at the first – the descriptive, analytic, and explanatory – dimension of *The Old Régime* and relate it to some recurrent themes of Tocqueville's thought. In *The Old Régime* Tocqueville makes use of what might be called pluralistic factor analysis. He analyses and explains events in terms of the interaction of a plurality of factors whose bearing on given events – such as the Revolution – is overdetermined. The factors he analytically singles out are organized in terms of an implicit typology of social and political forms that were crucial for all of Tocqueville's thinking. This typology presents democracy and aristocracy as primarily designating types of society, and liberty and despotism as designating types of government. As we shall see, various combinations of social and political types are possible (liberal or despotic democracy, liberal or despotic aristocracy). Tocqueville also makes a limited attempt to relate his analytic factors and types to provide both specific hypotheses and, in the last chapter of his book, a composite picture (however flawed) of France as a whole.

In terms of its manifest structure, *The Old Régime* is divided into three parts, each of which is subdivided into chapters. Each chapter focuses on a significant factor or set of factors in French history leading up to the Revolution. There is no overarching, conventional, sequential narrative, and, while there are narrative elements in the book as well as a metanarrative framework for Tocqueville's typology of factors or forms of society and government, the insistent analytic procedure in *The Old Régime* nonetheless poses a challenge to the recent tendency to see narrative as *the* basic instance of the human mind or the true infrastructure of all historical discourse.[24] In *The Old Régime* narrative elements are embedded in lines of thought that relate in complex ways. To some extent Parts One and Two analytically single out long-term structural causes or processes – what historians more recently have referred to as elements of *la longue durée*. Part Three treats causes and conjunctures especially important in the eighteenth century. In the last chapter Tocqueville makes some attempt to put it all together.

Perhaps the most crucial general explanatory dimension in Tocqueville is to be found in the typology of factors he uses to analyse problems and explain developments. As I intimated, the terms 'democratic' and 'aristocratic' refer primarily to types of society, whereas 'liberal' and 'despotic' apply to governmental régimes. The categories are not air-tight. But Tocqueville's focus is a broadly conceived political sociology relating society, culture, and politics. What do the terms mean?

Aristocratic society is based on inherited status and function, at times defined by law. It is characterized by privilege and inequality. The old régime was an aristocratic society that became rigidified into a castelike structure, and the aristocracy by the eighteenth century was subordinate to a centralized monarchy and no longer had functions that compensated for its privileges. By democracy Tocqueville means the equalization of conditions in society – a process that was already under way in the old régime. For him liberty does not define democracy, equal-

---

24 For these tendencies, see Fredric Jameson, *The Political Unconscious: Narrative as Socially Symbolic Act* (Ithaca and London, 1984), and Paul Ricoeur, *Time and Narrative*, trans. Kathleen McLaughlin Blamey and David Pellauer, 3 vols. (Chicago, 1984–8).

ity does. Democracy is not necessarily free, and political subjects can be powerless but equal under a despotic government. When Tocqueville correlates liberty and democracy, he does so in terms of the ideal state of affairs in modernity – one he saw at least sketched out in America as analysed in the first volume of *Democracy in America*. At least three observations may be made about Tocqueville's conception of a democratic society – observations that Tocqueville can be seen to have addressed in *Democracy in America*. First, it is the opposite of an aristocratic society and often viewed from the perspective of an aristocratic society. In a democratic society, there is no extreme, inherited inequality or privilege. But given Tocqueville's perspective, conditions often appear more equal than they might from another point of view, such as an egalitarian one at the other end of the spectrum. Tocqueville sees his own highly stratified society as more egalitarian than others would. And a democratic society is sometimes perceived in 'mass' terms that may obscure certain of its internal differentiations, tensions, and inequalities.

Second, there are more positive senses of democratic society. Politically, it is characterized by equality before the law. There are, for example, no special courts for privileged social groups such as the aristocracy. Socially, everyone feels he or she is the moral equal of everyone else. People tend to think: 'I am as good as you are.' The style of authority tends to be relatively cooperative, with a demand for open communication and what we would today call 'feed-back.' There is also a standardization of lifestyle, whereby people dress and look more or less alike (at least for those who do not make finer discriminations, such as – if you will pardon the anachronism – the cost of designer jeans!). Tocqueville is much vaguer about economic equality. He argues that no extreme differences of wealth are found in a democratic society, which is also characterized by an increasing equality of opportunity. Some economic basis for equality before the law and citizenship rights must exit, but there is no socio-economic equality, and what there is, is not defined with great precision. Indeed, Tocqueville in general tends to be relatively vague about economic problems with respect to the preconditions of legitimate liberal democracy.

Third, equality is for Tocqueville a providential fact. Tocqueville only explicitly uses the language of religious conservatives like Maistre with respect to the rising tide of egalitarianism. The bottom has risen, and the threat is that society may become entirely bottom. But Tocqueville tells reactionaries in their own providential language that democratization is an irreversible tendency in modern society. It cannot be turned back; at best it may be controlled. Tocqueville views democratization with awe and fear, for he believes it places in jeopardy what is for him the supreme value of liberty. The seemingly intractable problem is to stop egalitarian forces from going too far and preventing a viable balance between equality and liberty.

Here we pass on to types of government and their relation to society and culture. Liberty for Tocqueville has a crucial political sense: self-government in truly representative institutions. This is one extremely important meaning of liberty in Tocqueville, and he tries to distinguish it from licence, its abuse. But liberty also takes on less definable values and more nebulous connotations as it becomes the object of elevated paeans and insistent apostrophes. Then Tocqueville seems to indulge in poetic licence and operatic effects: liberty is given a golden aura and constituted as the be-all-and-end-all of social life – the imaginary and fetishized repository of all that is of utmost value in existence. In this vein Tocqueville's rhetoric can reach lyrical heights, at which liberty becomes a sublime object of ideology and the icon of displaced religiosity: 'What has made so many men, since untold ages, stake their all on liberty is its intrinsic glamour, a fascination it has in itself, apart from all 'practical' considerations. For, only in countries where it reigns can a man speak, live, and breathe freely, owing obedience to no authority save god and the laws of the land. The man who asks of freedom anything other is born to be a slave' (168–9).

Tocqueville can also take his resonant analysis in the extremely dubious direction of a conception of national character having (at least in the passing reference to 'blood') racial overtones that he otherwise rejects. This conception is allied with a positioning of liberty in a sublime, supralogical, ineffable position that makes it the secular analogue of an object of fervid religious devotion. Indeed, liberty at a certain point seems almost to be the last, lingering gasp of a disappearing aristocracy.

> Some nations have freedom in the blood and are ready to face the greatest perils and hardships in its defense. It is not for what it offers on the material plane that they love it; they regard freedom itself as something so precious, so needful to their happiness that no other boon could compensate for its loss, and its enjoyment consoles them even in their darkest hours. Other nations, once they have grown prosperous, lose interest in freedom and let it be snatched from them without lifting a hand to defend it, lest they should endanger thus the comforts that, in fact, they owe to it alone. It is easy to see that what is lacking in such nations is a genuine love of freedom, that lofty aspiration which (I confess) defies analysis. For it is something

one must *feel* and logic has no part in it. It is a privilege of noble minds which God has fitted to receive it, and it inspires them with a generous fervor. But to meaner souls, untouched by the sacred flame, it may well seem incomprehensible. (169)

Despotism is the opposite of liberty – the absence of self-rule and the institutions, habits, and sentiments that accompany it. It is invited by licence and facilitated by public apathy. And it is related to a highly centralized political and administrative control of society by government. Tocqueville fears that in modern society people will surrender self-rule for material advantages and greater equality of conditions.

Tocqueville's typology is not simply a static analytic system. It is related to a theory of structural change over time in Western societies that also constitutes a metanarrative. For Tocqueville there has been a movement from aristocratic to democratic society. In aristocratic society intermediary groups were attached to their privileges, which they called liberties. Aristocratic society did have a measure of self-rule, at least for the privileged groups. In the older old régime, groups such as the aristocracy, the church, guilds, and municipal organizations provided a check on central state power. The feudal monarchy in this sense was aristocratic and liberal. And the aristocracy had social and political functions to compensate for its privileges. In France, as I noted, the aristocracy gave up its real social and political functions but acquired or retained privileges such as tax breaks and feudal dues. This was for Tocqueville the highly unstable and unjust situation that Edmund Burke, with his vision of France filtered through the glitter of the English aristocracy, failed to see. The problem in modern society was whether democratic society would be combined with liberty or with despotism.

The social order for Tocqueville did not determine the political structure in any simple way. But their relation was not purely contingent. It depended upon intervening variables articulating their interaction. The key intervening variable between a type of society and a type of government was the intermediary body or group – the group between the individual and the state. The role of the intermediary body or group in Tocqueville's thought is at times not sufficiently appreciated by commentators.[25] Yet it is absolutely essential for him and one of the key elements of his brand of liberalism – an element that may even be extended in directions (notably in terms of liberal democratic socialism) that he explicitly resisted. In aristocratic society the intermediary groups that fostered self-government and averted despotism were corporative groups. In modern society, the intermediary group that Tocqueville's trip to America revealed to him was the voluntary association. But in *Democracy in America* Tocqueville is somewhat equivocal about the voluntary association. To have the full functions he deems necessary for a liberal democracy, the voluntary association cannot be simply a mathematical combination of interests, that is, it cannot be a mere special interest group or lobby. It must have corporate status or solidarity, and it must play an actively civic role in the public arena. At the very least, the association must be the exponent of enlightened self-interest that is not restricted to narrow egoism, including group egotism. In the America of his day Tocqueville saw lawyers as constituting a group with a cohesiveness that extended beyond particular interest and

---

25 It has, for example, no role in the commentaries of Matthew Mancini or Hayden White.

included a political culture and a civic role, but he also saw tendencies that might lead to democratic despotism. One was the tyranny of the majority, when it denied minority rights and became oppressive. (This was of course a concern shared by John Stuart Mill.) A second tendency was depoliticization and privatization, when the majority was overly passive or apathetic and succumbed to a more or less benign state despotism that allowed people their material well-being and economic endeavours but made them political infants. A third danger was the rise of what Tocqueville called an aristocracy of manufacturers. As we noted, Tocqueville, however tendentiously, saw the heritage of slavery and the condition of the blacks in the United States as creating difficulties. But he did not accord to this problem a status similar to that of the feudal past in Europe – that is, the status of a basic structural flaw that warranted more than supplementary treatment with respect to a stable liberal democracy. To this limited extent he laid the basis for ideological versions of American 'exceptionalism' that, as we have seen, stressed – or even became fixated upon – the absence of a feudal and aristocratic past which (at times together with the presence of religion supportive of democracy) was interpreted one-sidedly as creating the basis for genuine liberal democracy in America. These 'exceptionalist' visions converted what were at best contingent and contestable conditions of legitimate liberal democracy into complacently asserted (if not triumphalist) necessary and sufficient ones.

Tocqueville's idea of a viable democracy in America also combined genuinely representative institutions and politically conscious voluntary associations with the role of roughly equal, self-reliant individuals motivated by enlightened self-interest rather than narrow egotism. Individuals presumably would come together to form civic-minded voluntary associations when the need arose, and there would be no impediments to their doing so, as in fact there often are. Tocqueville's notion of despotic democracy envisioned the elimination of intermediary groups and the domination of atomized, politically ineffective individuals by a central state – even a central state that allowed politically disempowered citizens to make as much money or own as much property as they could. This was for him the state of France after the Revolution – a state furthered by important tendencies of the Revolution itself, such as Jacobinism.

One general problem with Tocqueville's ideal model of liberal democracy is that over the course of the nineteenth century conditions in both Europe and America increasingly tended to depart from it – a state of affairs that is reflected both in the more pessimistic tone of volume two of *Democracy in America* and in *The Old Régime*. Tocqueville's model probably corresponded most closely to the Jacksonian period in early-nineteenth-century America – the period of his visit.[26] And a key difficulty in Tocqueville's model – which is equally present in *The Old Régime* – is the weakness of its socio-economic analysis. Tocqueville does not provide a detailed account of the configuration of occupations and activities in the economy. More specifically, in neither *Democracy in America* nor *The Old Régime* does he even attempt to elaborate a theoretically informed discussion of industrialization and the relation of capital and labour in a capitalistic, industrialized economy. Marx may have been substantially wrong about the causes of the French Revolution, but his analysis of the post-revolutionary economy and society did

---

26 The standard work on Tocqueville's American journey is still George Wilson Pierson, *Tocqueville and Beaumont in America* (New York, 1938).

highlight the importance of factors Tocqueville and, at times, those who rely on him, tend to downplay or ignore.[27] In France industrialization proceeded relatively slowly and a liberal market was limited. Yet by the second half of the nineteenth century, industrial and capitalistic processes had become quite noticeable, and Saint-Simon and Fourier observed their role even in the earlier part of the century. Tocqueville did not adequately confront the issue of how industrial capitalism and the social groups and conditions it created affected his model of liberal democracy. In *The Old Régime* as well, he devotes very little attention to socio-economic problems.

Tocqueville discusses society largely in terms of its relation to culture, government, and administration. And his understanding of society and culture is itself almost entirely framed in terms of social psychology, collective mentality, and sentiments. *Pace* Furet, the problem is less his indecision in assigning causal roles to administration and mentality than his tendency to restrict attention to these areas. For example, in Part Three, all the more specific questions raised about the eighteenth century concern the central government, administration, political culture, and social psychology. One can observe this from

---

27 In certain respects Tocqueville's approach is not altogether divorced from that of Marx. His analysis of problems was often radical in a basic sense, and it included an emphasis on class relations. But Tocqueville devoted little time in his principal works to an account and critique of capitalism and a market economy, which he tended to accept as valid and linked to liberal democracy in a 'high' stage of civilization. In terms of alternatives to existing society, Marx combined blank utopianism, Messianism, and an insistence on the relation of theory to practice – a rather dubious and dangerous combination. Tocqueville also linked theory and practice and, whether optimistically or pessimistically, remained within the parameters of liberal democracy and capitalism. But, as I shall later suggest, he did at least have the basis of a structurally different alternative in his conception of the importance of intermediate groups in a legitimate liberal democracy.

the chapter headings alone: intellectuals and their role; antireligious feeling; desire for reform; rising expectations; and how central authority undermined law-abiding sentiments. These are all very important questions to which many historians, notably those in the *Annales* school, have been returning. In treating these questions, Tocqueville advances many stimulating hypotheses. (For example, he maintains that revolution is related to rising expectations rather than to a state of misery and that the most dangerous time for an oppressive regime is when it tries to reform.) What Tocqueville does not do in any sustained fashion is to relate problems of government, administration, political culture, and social psychology to the socio-economic process and the interests and problems it generates. It could of course be argued that an in-depth analysis must be focused and that Tocqueville's approach is valid for cultural and political history. But such a response is inadequate if the project in question is to explain a phenomenon such as the French Revolution and its aftermath. (For example, can the failure of groups in the aristocracy and the bourgeoisie to cooperate be attributed to the fact that they were affected differently by inflation?) If socio-economic problems are abandoned on the grounds that no one can do everything, at the very least the range of analysis must be circumscribed and its problematic nature explicitly indicated in a fashion that Tocqueville does not undertake.[28]

---

[28] Richard Herr, in *Tocqueville and The Old Régime* (Princeton, N.J., 1962), argues plausibly that the theme of centralization cannot be seen as the central argument of *The Old Régime* because it is found only in the first half of Part Two of the book. But Herr's contention that the true centre of the book is the emphasis on the effect of beliefs and ideas on society and political institutions is insufficiently specific. Moreover, it underwrites and compounds the limitations of Tocqueville's own focus without providing a critical perspective on it.

A further difficulty is the manner in which centralization is treated. It too appears as an inevitable, providential process, although Tocqueville does not explicitly use this language with reference to it. The attempt of the revolutionary government to decentralize is dealt with in an extremely obscure way. And Tocqueville omits mentioning a crucial reason why the attempt failed – war, which furthered centralizing tendencies.[29] The entire problem of the relation between centralization and decentralization in the Revolution receives one obscure reference (208). From this reference, it is difficult to tell precisely what Tocqueville is talking about when he praises the promising and genuinely idealistic early phase of the Revolution (which included an attempt to decentralize).

As I have indicated, Tocqueville's treatment of the intellectuals (or 'men of letters') is one area in which his analysis becomes decidedly projective and imaginary. He threatens to revert to the scapegoating tendencies of thinkers such as Burke and Maistre. The reason, I think, is that the anxieties and difficulties of his own analysis tend to be condensed and displaced onto the intellectuals of the Revolution, in spite of the fact that this process involves him in self-contradiction, notably in his inclination to presuppose – as a basis for his castigation of the intellectuals as a corrupt force – a 'healthy,' integrated state of society whose existence he has already denied. By taking as causes what are at most symptoms and ignoring the constructive potential of contestation, he attributes to intellectuals a fantastic power to affect society in overwhelmingly negative ways.

For Tocqueville the intellectuals indulged in 'abstract,

---

[29] This point is made by Georges Lefebvre in his Introduction to the French edition of *L'Ancien Régime et la révolution* (Paris, 1952–3).

literary politics' (139). They produced negative, destructive criticism with no idea of more constructive responses; they had no contact with reality, the facts of political life, and the exercise of power. Yet the intellectuals were able to lead the French people astray, for they filled what might be called an ideology vacuum, as France lost its other and presumably more legitimate guides to public opinion and policy (such as an aristocracy of the right kind). The 'men of letters' believed that you could simply sweep away 'the complex of traditional customs governing the social order of the day' and replace them with 'simple, elementary rules deriving from the exercise of human reason and natural law' (139). The intellectuals were thus hopelessly abstract, literary-minded theorists out of touch with reality but nonetheless holding the power to change its course.

On one level Tocqueville's assertions about 'abstract, literary politics' seem plausible and may apply to certain aspects of the thought of certain figures in ways he never takes the trouble to specify in sufficient detail. But, as I have suggested, there are severe difficulties in this view, which is often repeated almost compulsively in the treatment of intellectuals in France and elsewhere even today.[30] Tocqueville himself recognizes that the intellectuals in the

---

30 For a recent example from a liberal-conservative perspective in certain ways close to Tocqueville's, see Mark Lilla, 'The Politics of Jacques Derrida,' *The New York Review of Books* (25 June 1998), 36–41. The significant difference between Tocqueville and Lilla is that the latter eliminates the instructive tensions between Tocqueville's at times radical analyses and his conclusions by flattening the analyses to fit liberal-conservative (or neoconservative) conclusions. In the Introduction I have already referred to the more substantial but still problematic argument of Luc Ferry and Alain Renaut, *French Philosophy of the Sixties: An Essay on Antihumanism* (1985; Amherst, Mass., 1990). See also Keith Windschuttle, *The Killing of History: How a Discipline Is Being Murdered by Literary Critics and Social Theorists* (Paddington NSW, Australia,

old régime were cut off from political processes by the central state. And if French society and politics were in such bad shape in the eighteenth century, where was that 'complex of traditional customs governing the social order of the day' to which Tocqueville appeals to be found? He can locate the desired traditional complex only in an older feudal monarchy, which he tends to idealize. But that was long ago, in the older old régime. On Tocqueville's own analysis, the social order by the time of the Revolution was a mess consisting of undeserved privilege and central state power – power that was both excessive and inept. Indeed,

---

1996). The title of this book alone, wherein intellectual challenges are converted into death-threats, gives some idea of its 'arguments.' Here is but one of Windschuttle's sweeping indictments of the current critical scene: 'One of the most striking things about the output of late twentieth [*sic*] literary and social theory is how closely it resembles – through its slavish devotion to seminal texts and its unrestrained flight across all subject matter – the theology of the medieval clergy. Today's theorists have substituted French theory for Christian texts but are seeking to break down the disciplines in exactly the same way' (222). In this quotation, disdain for the Middle Ages is matched only by a flair for dubious analogy misconstrued as exactitude. Windschuttle's reliance on rather loose montage or collage as an overall organizational device is itself an 'unrestrained flight across all subject matter.' He makes only a few passing references to Tocqueville and devotes almost as much attention to Francis Fukuyama as to Foucault. If anything, he employs a less dismissive and aggressive tone with Fukuyama than with Foucault and he allocates more space to the former (over fourteen pages) than to truly important and influential literary critics and social theorists (such as Pierre Bourdieu, Jürgen Habermas, Fredric Jameson, and Paul Ricoeur, among others, whom he treats summarily). Windschuttle also slights historians and cultural analysts who have tried constructively, and not uncritically, to come to terms with recent critical tendencies – many of whom he fails even to mention (for example, Robert Berkhofer, Jr, Judith Butler, Iain Chambers, Geoff Eley, Nancy Fraser, Jan Goldstein, Harry Harootunian, Geoffrey Hartman, Martin Jay, Gareth Stedman Jones, Bruno Latour, Meaghan Morris, Peter Novick, Michael Roth, Joan Scott, Gabrielle Spiegel, and others). One may disagree with Foucault in basic ways (as I do), but to treat him and Fukuyama in a comparable manner is a serious lapse of judgment.

one might suggest that Tocqueville's harsh condemnation of the intellectuals is related to his resistance to drawing the conclusions that his own analysis would often seem to imply – conclusions about the need for basic if not radical change that he projects onto the 'men of letters' whom he upbraids in self-contradictory terms. One sign of this resistance is the fact that Tocqueville replicates in his discussion the very charges he levels against the 'men of letters' in what may be seen as a telling repetition compulsion. His own discussion is highly rhetorical, stereotypical, and devoid of extended treatment of specific figures and texts. His indictment is itself close to 'abstract, literary politics,' and his conception of alternatives remains at best on the level of abstract principle.

Tocqueville makes only passing references to figures such as Fénélon (146), Helvétius (154), Diderot (153 and 154), Morelly (164), and Voltaire (166). His only relatively substantial discussion is of Turgot and the physiocrats. As he puts it: 'Though the Economists figure less prominently than our philosophers in histories of the period and perhaps did less than they towards bringing about the Revolution, I am inclined to think it is from their writings that we learn most of its true character' (158). Yet Tocqueville's decontextualized indictment does not give much sense of the concrete conditions and problems Turgot faced. Here we may note summarily that Turgot turned to enlightened despotism or reform from above to institute a freer market, but the fact that key privileged groups in society opposed his reforms deprived his measures of the social support necessary for success – a classical double bind.[31]

---

31 See the discussion of Turgot in Steven L. Kaplan, *Bread, Politics, and Political Economy in the Reign of Louis XV*, 2 vols. (The Hague, 1976).

I have tried to indicate that Tocqueville's most pressing problem was to find a viable basis for his supreme political value of liberty and that in seeking it he resisted acknowledgment of the radical consequences his analyses seemed to imply. The lessons he sought to impart to the reader remained on the level of abstract principle if not 'abstract, literary politics' – a spirited defence of liberty, the application of which to his own society or to the past he could treat predominantly in terms of ideals and of idealizations of a lost past. Tocqueville's pessimism about the possibility of defending liberty in more institutional, practical, or concrete terms helps to shape his account of the tidal movement of egalitarianism and the threat of political despotism. One difference that the Revolution did effect was ideological: it instigated a revolutionary tradition that Tocqueville opposed and that caused him great anxiety, especially in the wake of 1848. The tensions in Tocqueville's analysis of the old régime and his difficulty in bringing together the various factors, processes, and dimensions active in his account help, I think, to explain the remarkable rhetorical flourish with which he ends the book. After returning to the theme of the great conflict between liberty and equality, Tocqueville concludes with a high-flying evocation of French national character as the ultimate explanation for why the Revolution occurred in France.

> When I observe France from this angle I find the nation itself far more remarkable than any of the events in its long history. It hardly seems possible that there can ever have existed any other people so full of contrasts and so extreme in all their doings, so much guided by their emotions and so little by fixed principles, always behaving better, or worse, than one expected of them. At one time they

rank above, at another below, the norm of humanity; their basic characteristics are so constant that we can recognize the France we know in portraits made of it two or three thousand years ago, and yet so changeful are its moods, so variable its tastes that the nation itself is often quite as much startled as any foreigner at the things it did only a few years before. Ordinarily the French are the most routine-bound of men, but once they are forced out of the rut and leave their homes, they travel to the ends of the earth and engage in the most reckless ventures ... Thus the French are at once the most brilliant and the most dangerous of all European nations, and the best qualified to become, in the eyes of other peoples, an object of admiration, of hatred, of compassion, or alarm – never of indifference.

France alone could have given birth to revolution so sudden, so frantic, and so thoroughgoing, yet so full of unexpected changes of direction, of anomalies and inconsistencies. But for the antecedent circumstances described in this book, the French would never have embarked on it; yet we recognize that though their effect was cumulative and overwhelming, they would not have sufficed to lead to such a drastic revolution elsewhere than in France. (210–11)

In this remarkable passage, Tocqueville places the French in all sorts of contradictory positions and construes them as the true people of paradox. The result is a decidedly 'abstract' and 'literary' evocation that both repeats the defects he imputes to pre-revolutionary intellectuals and would seem to possess cosmetic functions in concealing the stress lines and fissures of his own analysis. What I would suggest in conclusion is that while a great deal can be learned from Tocqueville's hypotheses about society, culture, and government, there is also much to learn from his tensions and even from his evasions and equivocations. In many important ways these have not been overcome in theory or practice and one is hard-pressed to come up with better responses than those of Tocqueville. This is especially the case if one simply dismisses, as Tocqueville did, even the possibility of a liberal democratic polity with some viable admixture of socialist concerns. These concerns are not eliminated either by the pronounced failures of communist regimes or by the recent turn to a triumphalist neoconservatism that is liberal in very limited ways and insists even more staunchly than Tocqueville on the virtues of a market economy and its essential links with what is called liberal democracy.

Emile Durkheim shared with Tocqueville the conviction that intermediary groups were essential in relating the individual and the state, counteracting the possibility of despotism and public apathy, and providing a venue for the participation of all social groups in the major institutions of modern life, notably those of the economy and the state. Durkheim might even be seen as an heir to Tocqueville who retained a genuine commitment to liberal democracy but tried to reconcile it with a conception of intermediary groups that involved the active role of both labour and capital. Such groups might be seen as Durkheim's functional equivalent for socialism in that they would organize the economy and become units of political representation in ways sensitive to the demands of social justice.[32] Even if it were argued that Durkheim's specific vision were obsolete, we would still be faced with the

---

32 For an analysis that stresses the importance of this dimension of Durkheim, see my *Emile Durkheim: Sociologist and Philosopher* (Ithaca and London, 1972; reissued Chicago, 1985).

problem of a constructive alternative that combined political liberalism with a social and economic critique in the attempt to bring into existence a desirable polity based on social justice for all relevant groups. Unfortunately, the influential type of radicalism represented in the work of Michel Foucault (to which I shall now turn) maintains a distance from Marx without assimilating either Tocqueville's sustained devotion to liberal democracy and its institutional and ideological foundations or Durkheim's modification of a commitment to liberalism through a democratic corporatism sensitive to the role of intermediary groups in organizing the economy in the interest of solidarity and greater social justice. Foucault's emphasis on the importance of marginalized and often silenced groups (the mad, homosexuals, prisoners) has the virtue of shifting socio-political analysis and critique in the direction of an angle of vision that reveals problems that may easily be overlooked from a standard liberal or liberal-conservative viewpoint. But his latter-day emphasis on a relatively undifferentiated notion of power and disciplinary control of society tended to cut him off from traditions of political, social, and cultural analysis – such as those represented by Tocqueville, Marx, and Durkheim – that focused on important institutions – the family, education, the workplace, and the state – and that raised the issue of possible alternative structures for modern societies.

3

Rereading Foucault's *'History of Madness'*

Michel Foucault's *Folie et déraison: Histoire de la folie à l'âge classique*[1] is entitled a history and would thus seem comparable to Tocqueville's explicitly historical *The Old Régime and the French Revolution*. In the Introduction, I pointed out certain similarities, as well as a few differences, between Tocqueville's and Foucault's projects. Yet in many basic ways the world of thought seems to change as one moves from Tocqueville to Foucault – a change measured less in centuries than in conceptual light years. Indeed it is paradoxical that both books may in some sense be termed histories, for they seem at extreme ends of a shattered spectrum. One way to characterize this divergence is to note that all professional historians would almost certainly recognize Tocqueville's book as a history

---

1 Michel Foucault: *Folie et déraison: Histoire de la folie à l'âge classique* (Paris, 1961). The appendix, 'La folie, l'absence d'œuvre,' may be found in the Gallimard edition of 1972. Page references are included in the text. Unless otherwise indicated, translations are my own. The English translation of Foucault's own abridged version is entitled *Madness and Civilization*, trans. Richard Howard (New York, 1965).

while many would question that designation for Foucault's.

A typical way of domesticating *L'Histoire de la folie* within historiography has been to read the book on a restricted thematic level and to subject its themes, theses, and specific propositions to empirical confirmation or disconfirmation. This enterprise is altogether necessary and legitimate, but it does not address the challenge Foucault poses to the writing of history.[2] His most telling challenge to conventional historiography may well be on the level of an articulation of history with critical theory that resists reductive operationalization. His specific form of articulation is a disturbing, even a disorienting mode of thought that cannot be confined within any one discipline. This mode of thought has important inter- and cross-disciplinary dimensions but, in its most extreme overtures, it goes beyond these initiatives and becomes de- and transdisciplinary. The obvious implication is that existing disciplines are inadequate in the investigation of significant problems having both intellectual and socio-political dimensions. Whether any approach of a disciplinary nature would be 'adequate' from Foucault's perspective remains an open question.

Particularly in his own use of language, Foucault also raises the question of the relation between the historian and his or her object of investigation. His discursive practice places in jeopardy the tempting position of transcendental spectator *vis-à-vis* the past – a position Foucault himself seems to assume in his more positivistic moments.

---

2 The latter point has been made, among others, by Allan Megill in *Prophets of Extremity: Nietzsche, Heidegger, Foucault, Derrida* (Berkeley, 1985). See also David R. Shumway, *Michel Foucault* (Boston, 1989), and the discussion of various approaches to interpreting the book in the essays appearing in *History of the Human Sciences* 3 (1989).

In addition, there are indications in *Histoire de la folie* that Foucault's own attempt to reconstruct periodization in terms of epistemological breaks was questionable even at the very time he appeared to assert and defend it. Foucault, on a manifest level of narration in *Histoire de la folie* and on a more explicit theoretical level in *The Archaeology of Knowledge*[3] poured new and more heady wine into rather old bottles, for he retained standard period concepts (antiquity, the Middle Ages, the Renaissance, the classical age, the age of positivism) but tried to give them a deep-structural foundation. His actual practice in his study of madness, however, would imply the need for a conception of temporality in terms of intricate and variable processes of repetition with change – at times decisive or traumatic change – a conception that his stress on epistemological breaks either oversimplified or obscured, for it dissociated more or less traumatic breaks from repetition and construed the former in isolation and the latter in intemporal terms.

In these respects, *Histoire de la folie* may repay rereading, especially insofar as it suggests different possibilities with respect to history and criticism than those that have become prevalent in the appropriation of Foucault. So-called new historicists have tended to focus on the later Foucault, particularly the Foucault of *Discipline and Punish*, and at times have taken his later thought in questionable directions, particularly through one-dimensional, 'symptomatic' readings of artifacts with respect to prevalent or dominant social discourses as well as through a rather indiscriminate concept of power as the key to a functionalist analysis of society and culture. In his *Philo-*

---

3 Michel Foucault, *The Archaelogy of Knowledge and the Discourse on Language*, trans. A.M. Sheridan Smith (1969; New York, 1972).

sophical Discourse of Modernity, Jürgen Habermas has elaborated a critique of Foucault's rendition of Nietzsche's will-to-power dynamics, his functionalism, and what Habermas calls his crypto-normativism (that is, his explicit rejection of norms or conflation of them with objectionable normalization, combined with an implicit, unargued reliance on an alternative normativity). But Habermas is content to dismiss Foucault's study of madness as a mere romantic reversal of modern rationalizing tendencies, and other aspects of his argument are doubtful.[4] Moreover, the recent turn of gay activists to Foucault provides a different perspective on certain of his tendencies. For example, David Halperin argues that what gay men confront 'is not only – and perhaps not ultimately – specific

---

4 Jürgen Habermas, *The Philosophical Discourse of Modernity,* trans. Frederick Lawrence (Cambridge, Mass., 1987). By crypto-normativism, Habermas means Foucault's tacit reliance on norms and values for which he explicitly leaves no room or provides no basis. A similar point was made earlier by Michael Walzer, 'The Politics of Michel Foucault,' in David Hoy, ed., *Foucault: A Critical Reader* (New York, 1986). Among the more doubtful aspects of Habermas's argument, I would mention the following: a restriction of hybridized or liminal forms to a safely marginalized status, an underplaying and even a largely negative understanding of forces that contest discursive rationality (including such forces as laughter and parody), an insistence on the parasitic nature of fiction *vis-à-vis* 'normal' discourse, an unqualified defence of predominantly monogeneric forms, and an assumption that the only viable alternative to de-differentiation, blurring, and levelling is strict if not rigid boundary maintenance between genres and disciplines such as philosophy, literature, and literary criticism. Habermas at times affirms the desirability of more creative tension and interaction among discursive forces, but many of his own propensities severely restrict or even undercut that affirmation. He does not, for example, allow for the importance and validity of well-articulated, multigeneric uses of language – uses that cogently and provocatively combine analytically distinguishable forms. Whether certain multigeneric uses of language such as Foucault's are convincing or provocative is open to discussion, but such uses should not be ruled out *a priori.* Instead the specific uses or articulations should be debated.

agencies of oppression, such as gay-bashers or the police' but rather 'pervasive and multiform strategies of homophobia that shape public and private discourses, saturate the entire field of cultural representation, and, like power in Foucault's formulation, are everywhere.' Moreover, 'the discourses of homophobia ... cannot be refuted by means of rational argument' and 'can only be resisted' strategically 'by fighting strategy with strategy' because 'homophobic discourses are not reducible to a set of statements with a specifiable truth-content that can be rationally tested. Rather, homophobic discourses function as part of more general and systematic strategies of delegitimation.'[5] Of course the question suggested by Habermas still remains: is a counter-strategy of delegitimation of dominant or mainstream norms (or normalization) sufficient, or must we elaborate in theory and practice an alternative normativity that regulates relations in more desirable ways? Halperin provides no answer to this question. Moreover, he devotes relatively little attention to *Histoire de la folie* and focuses primarily on the later Foucault. Still, his argument alerts us to the possibility that certain critical analyses of Foucault, notably by 'straight' liberals, may have unintended implications, at times including homophobic ones.

In *Histoire de la folie,* Foucault's approach to historical understanding seems to be both structural and hermeneutic – tendencies that the later Foucault would criticize.[6] The approach seems structural in its idea of periods defined through what Foucault elsewhere labels *epistemes*:

---

5 David Halperin, *Saint Foucault: Towards a Gay Hagiography* (New York and Oxford, 1995), 32–3.
6 On this point, see Hubert Dreyfus and Paul Rabinow, *Michel Foucault: Beyond Structuralism and Hermeneutics,* 2nd ed. (Chicago, 1983).

deep structures of organization that integrate a given time, or at least an area or region of discourse and practice at a given time, and separate it from a prior or subsequent period through an epistemological break. *Histoire de la folie* also contains hermeneutic tendencies in the attempt to interpret the experience of madness at a given time and over time. As Hubert Dreyfus and Paul Rabinow have pointed out, Foucault later tends to distance himself from both structuralism and hermeneutics as specific historical practices. For him they are related to the dubious constitution of the human being as object and subject of discourse. Structuralism and hermeneutics seem to be flip sides of the same coin. The former takes the human being as object of analysis and seeks the rules or laws that inform the functioning of the object; the latter takes the human being as subject of experience and discourse and investigates the nature of meaning assumed to be created by the human being. The later Foucault would like to situate inquiry beyond structuralism and hermeneutics as symptoms of the object-subject dualism. A genuinely thought-provoking dimension of Foucault's effort in this respect is a critique of what may be termed species-imperialism and anthropocentric creationism: the centring of everything on the human being (or, in typically gender-specific terms, 'man') construed as the creator or constructive generator of all meaning and value in the world.[7] Equally provocative is Foucault's rearticulation of power, authority, and discourse in a manner suggestive at

---

7 Anthropocentric or secular creationism may be a (perhaps unintended) consequence of radical constructivism and a rashly generalized conception of performativity. Unfortunately Foucault himself does not take the critique of humanism in the direction of an inquiry into the issue of animal rights. On this crucial issue, see especially Peter Singer, *Animal Liberation*, 2nd ed. (New York, 1990).

times of a concept of hegemony attuned to a sophisticated analysis of the interaction of language and institutions or of artifacts and prevalent discursive practices.[8] But at other times Foucault's effort seems to culminate in a rash rejection of humanism and an obliteration instead of a repositioning or rearticulation of the role of the subject as situated agent in a larger discursive and practical field – a field that he or she does not entirely master but in which he or she may act more or less responsibly. The more hyperbolic, 'death-of-the-subject' extreme emerges with variations in Foucault's seemingly neutral ultrapositivism, his quasi-mystical, passive rapport with language at least as an object of lyrical invocation and almost erotic desire, and his gallows functionalism erected on the concept of power.

In *Histoire de la folie*, this 'death-of-the-subject' extreme is checked by hermeneutic tendencies as well as by a more or less consistent effort to interpret problems in terms of the interaction of discursive and institutional forces in such settings as the insane asylum or the doctor's office.[9] But Foucault's most daring and controversial move is to attempt to get beyond a simple subject-object dualism in a valorization of a tragic and cosmic frame of reference. Indeed, in his own beguiling and at times mystifying use of language, Foucault attempts, in a double movement, both to trace a break between reason and unreason and to renew the 'tragic' connection between them. This stunning bid for a renewed 'dialogue' between reason and

---

[8] This important dimension of the conceptuality in *L'Histoire de la folie* may be more comprehensive and compelling than Foucault's stress on an indiscriminate concept of power or power-knowledge.
[9] As I have noted, this side of Foucault's practice is comparable to Tocqueville's.

unreason, marked by a strongly performative use of language, is perhaps Foucault's most radical linguistic gesture in this book – a gesture that may not be equalled in his later writing. What that dialogue might be – even whether it is a dialogue in any fathomable sense – remains and perhaps must remain an obscure, contestable, yet enticing matter. But somehow the renewed 'dialogue' would seem to relate, at least as a promise or a threat, to Foucault's use of language in this text – a sometimes uncanny use that is at best uncomfortably housed within existing disciplines such as philosophy, literary studies, or history.

In the 1961 preface to his book (omitted in the 1972 edition), Foucault tells us that he wants to write not the history of established discourses such as psychology or psychiatry in their own terms. He wants instead to write the history or to trace the archaeology of what they silenced, repressed, or excluded in constituting themselves and the institutions that house them such as the clinic or the doctor's office. Like other historians of the sciences, he criticizes progressive, in-house histories of disciplines that take the present state of the discipline as representing the truth and then tell the gratifying, triumphalist tale of how the truth was won. But Foucault, when viewed from the perspective of a more conventional and professional history of science, at times goes beyond the pale in untelling the teleological tale. For Foucault, teleological narratives and even the more conventional histories of science that depart from them may repress or exclude the very repressions and exclusions that various disciplines enacted to become what they are. They also tend to objectify the 'voice' of the other that was repressed or excluded to the exterior of discourse as a precondition of the 'positive' establishment of what became dominant discursive and institutional forms. In other words, the 'voice' of the 'other' poses no challenge to the discourse of either the science in question or to the historian or analyst of that science – even independent of the question of how that challenge should be met. Recapturing that voice for Foucault does not imply a simple return, or analogical relation, to the past. But it may require opening ourselves and our culture to disconcerting challenges by reactivating past potentials or lost occasions in the present and future through unheard-of transformations of discourse and practice.

Here we may note in passing that Foucault provides little space, in any conventional sense, for the 'voices' of unreason and madness. Except for the largely allusive use of literary sources, there are, for example, no quotations from those classified as radically 'other' over time – quotations that might conceivably be displaced from their more conventional function as mere inert evidence in support of assertions or hypotheses and made to raise questions for the discourse that tries to decipher or interpret them. At least in one sense, the voices of the 'mad' pose no resistance for Foucault himself. Nor does Foucault explicitly pose the problem of critical historiography in terms of the relation between accurate reconstruction and dialogic exchange. Instead his typical procedure is to attempt to evoke or be radically open to the voices of the 'mad' – or at least their broken and groping exchange with sanity or normality – in his own tortured prose. This prose might perhaps be characterized as an internally dialogized, indeed split monologue or narrativized soliloquy in which it is at times difficult to tell when Foucault is speaking in his own voice or infiltrating and merging with the voices of others. Indeed, as I suggested earlier, we might even argue that his approach at times eventuates in a disconcerting, riven monologism, that is, an involuted discourse internally open to radical difference but unable to recognize the other as a distinct other with a distinguishable voice. The result approximates a generalized free indirect style in the mobile relation of the narrator to objects of narration – what might perhaps be seen as an analogue of the 'middle voice' in discourse.[10] At certain points Foucault's discourse seems somewhat delirious – for example in the sections translated as 'Passion and Delirium' and 'Aspects of Madness.' Here is but one brief example: 'Madness designates the equinox between the vanity of night's hallucinations and the non-being of light's judgments' (English edition, 111). In generalizing a free indirect style and, even more so, in his delirious lyricism, Foucault is furthest from a recognizable historical approach to problems.

Jacques Derrida's essay on Foucault in *Writing and Difference* does not address the issues of free indirect style and discursive delirium, but it does raise a number of complex issues.[11] In general I think Derrida's essay should be read not as a nihilistic rejection (as it is for Carlo Ginzburg)[12] or even as a standard criticism of Foucault's effort. It is better read as a radical yet sympathetic rereading that

---

10 For a discussion and defence of a discursive analogue of the middle voice in the historical representation of traumatic limit events (specifically, the Holocaust), see Hayden White, 'Historical Emplotment and the Problem of Truth,' in Saul Friedlander, ed., *Probing the Limits of Representation: Nazism and the Final Solution*' (Cambridge, Mass. and London, 1992), 37–53. For a critical analysis of this initiative, see, in the same volume, Martin Jay, 'Of Plots, Witnesses, and Judgments,' 100–1, and my *Writing History, Writing Trauma* (forthcoming).
11 'Cogito and History of Madness,' in *Writing and Difference*, trans. with an intro. and additional notes, Alan Bass (1967; Chicago, 1978).
12 See Carlo Grinzburg, *The Cheese and the Worms*, trans. John and Anne Tedeschi (1976; Baltimore, 1980).

repositions the elements of Foucault's interpretation.[13] Especially in the essay's initial section, Derrida engages in what would seem to be a transcendental critique (in the Kantian sense) by insistently interrogating – in the disconcerting form of open questions – the very conditions of possibility of Foucault's project. How, he asks, can Foucault even attempt to write a history of madness, in its pristine or savage state, instead of restricting himself to the more historically intelligible enterprise of tracing one or more of the temporal figures of madness? Does Foucault's effort not amount to the paradoxical if not mad project of trying to write the history of historicity or the history of the very conditions of possibility of history? Derrida goes on to address in detail the issue of Foucault's interpretation of a specific passage in Descartes's first *Meditation*, arguing that Descartes cannot be read simply as a sign of the times and intimating that we must somehow relate textual exegesis or close reading, delimited historical interpretation in terms of periods or structures, and the *longue durée* of the tangled history of metaphysics, including its disorienting incentive epitomized in the evanescent moment of radical hyperbole.

For my own specific purposes, one of the most haunt-

---

13 I would interject in passing that I have a different reaction to Derrida's essay on Paul de Man, 'Like the Sound of the Deep within a Shell: Paul de Man's War,' *Critical Inquiry* 14 [1988], 590–652. In that essay there is, in my judgment, a questionable rewriting of the past. One difficulty is that Derrida seems to use the essay on Foucault as a model and to read the young de Man, especially the author of a manifestly anti-Semitic article of 4 March 1941, as if he were as complex and internally self-questioning as Foucault or Descartes. Particularly in the article on the Jews, however, de Man enacts the kind of stereotyping and scapegoating scenario that is open to criticism rather than to the kind of deconstruction that makes use of the internal tensions of a text to place it in question. Indeed, one problem with a stereotypical, scapegoating text is that it largely excludes or denies internal tensions and self-questioning.

ing questions Derrida raises – a question Foucault does little to respond to in his trenchantly polemical and irate rejoinder – is that of the position from which Foucault can write a book such as *Histoire de la folie*. In a limited sense, Derrida raises the questions of narrative voice and perspective. Foucault does not want to side with the dominant form of modern rationality which he, in a manner not too distant from the early Frankfurt school, sees as one-dimensionally instrumental and repressive. But he cannot simply side with the mad who, in modern civilization, are for him silent or silenced – more precisely, silent or fragmented because of an effective process of historical silencing. For Foucault the discourse of the 'mad' is no longer recognized as a language to be engaged in dialogue. Derrida argues that Foucault's uncomfortable position is that of someone who creates an internal disturbance within the dominant reason – a reason from which there would seem to be no simple departure or exit short of madness itself (if indeed there is such a thing as 'madness itself'). For Derrida Foucault is a kind of *agent provocateur*.

In passing, however, Derrida suggests a somewhat different point that deserves more reflection than he devotes to it. He intimates that the performative dimension of Foucault's style may evoke the pathos of a broken dialogue (hence the perhaps impossible or blankly utopian desire for a renewed dialogue) between reason and unreason. Derrida touches on this point with reference to the way in which silence, which cannot be said, seems to be 'indirectly, metaphorically made present [*rendu présent indirectement, métaphoriquement, si je puis dire*]' by the pathos of Foucault's book (37). Silence for Derrida is not mere muteness but essential for the articulation and rhythm of language. In this sense, one may go on to argue that Foucault at his most provocative writes neither from the side of the mad nor from that of the sane but from the problematic margin or border (the undecidably 'in-between' area) that divides the two. A liminal status on this margin, which allows or constrains a hybridized, internally divided voice, is particularly tenuous in the modern world as Foucault understands modernity, for modernity has been largely successful in reducing unreason to pathological madness if not at times to mere muteness. What lies beyond the margin may appear to be not text at all but empty space or an abyss. In some obscure fashion, Foucault would apparently like that torn and ragged margin to expand or even to explode in affirmatively changing society and culture.

I would also note in passing that the debate between Derrida and Foucault concerning the interpretation of a passage in Descartes's first *Meditation*, on which Foucault focuses in his reply, functions in the manner of Freudian displacement for both commentators: it is presumably the small object in which very large matters of interpretation are invested. The passage from Descartes reads:

> But it may be that although the senses sometimes deceive us concerning things which are hardly perceptible, or very far away, there are yet many others to be met with as to which we cannot reasonably have any doubt. And how could I deny that these hands and this body are mine, were it not perhaps that I compare myself to certain persons, devoid of sense, whose cerebella are so troubled and clouded by the violent vapors of black bile, that they constantly assure us that they think they are kings when they are really quite poor, or that they are clothed in purple when they are really without covering, or who imagine that they have an earthenware head or are nothing but pump-

kins or are made of glass. But they are mad [*amentes*], and I should not be any the less insane [*demens*] were I to follow examples so extravagent.

Now let us assume that we are asleep ... [and so on through dreaming up to the fiction of the evil demon]

A feature of this passage may make it impossible to decide whether Derrida or Foucault offers the better interpretation, to wit, the fact that it is unclear whether Descartes is speaking consistently in his own voice. Foucault simply assumes that he is and that his voice merges with that of the age. In his reply to Derrida (included as an appendix to the 1972 French edition), Foucault resorts to sarcasm to dismiss the possibility that Descartes may not be speaking in a unified voice. Derrida argues that Descartes, in a more or less regulated or controlled but not absolutely mastered movement of increasing hyperbole, begins by rendering the perspective of a naive, common-sensical interlocutor. I would suggest that this interlocutor is not simply a 'yokel' in the world of naive rustics, as Foucault intimates in his attempt to fend off Derrida's reading, but is to some extent a voice internalized by Descartes. In other words, Foucault refuses to see, in Descartes, internally dialogized modes of discourse that mark Foucault's own use of language but at times in more uncontrolled and opaque forms. Derrida does, however, acknowledge that Descartes as philosopher and presumably in his own voice comes to exclude madness in order to provide a firm foundation for reason – but only after raising the possibility of radical disorientation on a level that undercuts the opposition between reason and unreason through the fiction of the evil demon.

In his reply, Foucault argues – and I think that these are two of his most telling points – that Derrida misses Descartes's attempt to disqualify the status of the madman as subject and misinterprets the fiction of the evil demon which, for Foucault, is merely a safe, methodological feint and a fully mastered exercise. Yet it is curious that Foucault, in a passage of *Histoire de la folie* located in a chapter subsequent to the sections he debates with Derrida, makes an argument very close to Derrida's concerning the significance of the evil demon. (The debate focuses on three pages at the beginning of Part I, Chapter 2, '*Le Grand Renfermement*,' and the following passage may be found at the end of Part I, Chapter 5, '*Les Insensés*.' Neither passage is included in the English edition.)

> If contemporary man, since Nietzsche and Freud, finds deep within himself the point of contestation with respect to all truth, and is able to read in what he now knows of himself the indices of fragility where unreason threatens, on the contrary the man of the seventeenth century discovers, in the immediate presence of his thought to itself, the certitude in which reason announces itself in its first form. But that does not mean that classical man was, in his experience of truth, more distant from unreason than we can be ourselves. It is true that the Cogito is absolute beginning; but one must not forget that the evil demon [*le malin génie*] is anterior to it. And the evil demon is not the symbol in which are resumed and systematized all the dangers of the psychological events which are the images of dreams and the errors of the senses. Between God and man, the evil demon has an absolute meaning; it designates the peril which, well beyond man [*bien au delà de l'homme*], could prevent him in a definitive manner from reaching truth: a major obstacle, not of such a spirit but of such a reason. And it is not because truth which takes its illumination from the Cogito finally masks the shadow of

the evil demon that one should forget its perpetually menacing power: up to and including the existence of the external world, this danger will hang over Descartes's advance [*ce danger surplombera le cheminement de Descartes*]. How in these conditions can unreason in the classical age be reduced to the scale of a psychological event or even to the scale of human pathos? By contrast it forms the element in which the world is born to its own truth, the domain within which reason will have to answer for itself. (195–6)

How, one might ask, can Foucault after this passage interpret Descartes solely as a figure of exclusion? For from its complicated and somewhat obscure argument, involving (in the manner of Husserl) a rejection of psychologism and affirming what would seem to be a quasi-transcendental, tragic absolute, we may at least conclude that unreason is still a cosmic force in the classical age, and Descartes is divided concerning the question of whether to respond to its peril through a massive act of exclusion. It is also tempting to conclude that the great debate between Derrida and Foucault at times generates more heat than light and that each protagonist resorts too readily to the tactic of accusing the other of relying on scapegoating mechanisms of exclusion.[14] In any event,

---

14 In *French Philosophy of the Sixties: An Essay on Antihumanism* (1985; Amherst, Mass., 1990), Luc Ferry and Alain Renaut tend to repeat this accusatory gesture by sending both Foucault and Derrida packing. In a discussion that vies with Foucault and Derrida in opacity, they argue that neither Foucault nor Derrida gets 'to the essence of the matter' (86). Their mistake, concerning the understanding of madness in the seventeenth century, is that 'they both read the *Meditations* with the preconceived idea of madness as hallucination, as the inability to distinguish between sensory information and an image. Now, for all intents and purposes, the idea of madness as hallucination is a nineteenth-century concept' (87). The problem here is that Ferry and

Foucault does not speak in a fully unified voice or from one exclusive position in *Histoire de la folie*. He assumes at least three tensely interacting and overlapping positions or narrative voices with varying relations to one another. One complex position or voice is, as I have already intimated, close to the difficult, highly problematic marginal status, and – perhaps expectably – it tends to be relatively submerged in the text. But it is nonetheless insistently audible, and it has a performative, interventionist impetus. From this position, the marginal, at best paraprofessional narrator views history as the scene of a repeated struggle between more dominant forces and tendencies repressed by them – what might be termed hegemonic and counterhegemonic forces. We have in other words a Nietzschean or Heideggerian model of temporality as displacement or repetition with change, as seen from the problematic margin. (Here Foucault and Derrida are in the closest proximity to one another.) A telling phrase related to this first 'position' is 'torsions in the same anxiety.' Over time we have repeated but different – at times searingly different – torsions in the same anxiety which is, of course, not an identical anxiety in a narrow, logical sense. Earlier repetitions of the same anxiety seem for Foucault to have been more successful in continuing the dialogue between contending forces, and the modern 'torsion,' particularly in its positivistic form, was most effective in splitting or dissociating reason and madness while subjecting the latter to the hegemonic, disciplinary, and at times falsely complacent rule of the former. But, as

---

Renaut conflate dream with hallucination, offering no analysis of the waking dream and its relation to madness over time and no evidence for the assertion that the idea of madness as hallucination (waking dream?) is a nineteenth-century concept.

what might seem to be various modalities of the return of the repressed, countervoices have existed throughout the modern period – the voices of those such as Hölderlin, Nietzsche, and Artaud. Foucault is attentive to these countervoices, but he often invokes their names in a litany of transgression instead of critically analysing their texts. Foucault would apparently like to join his voice to theirs in a clamouring chorus that might convert the margin or the underground into a force with a significantly different relation to the principal text of rationality. Here as elsewhere in his work Foucault provides little thematic or regulative idea of what form this new dialogue might take and what broader social, political, and institutional implications it might have. Nor does he discuss the dubious kind of departure from rationality – or rather the perverse combination of formal rationality and substantive irrationality – that everything in his work would lead one to assume he would severely criticize (perhaps as the distorted and extremely violent return of the repressed), for example, the kind manifested in Nazi policy towards the Jews and other oppressed groups.[15] Instead, his relation to a desirable dialogue remains allusive and at times prophetic. The prophetic voice in Foucault is perhaps at its

---

15 In view of his political and philosophical concerns, it is surprising that Foucault did not make the Holocaust an important object of reflection. Until relatively recently, the Holocaust has often been a significant *impensé* in the texts of major French intellectuals, particularly those indebted to such figures as Nietzsche, Heidegger, Blanchot, and Bataille. For attempts to address problems related to the Holocaust, see Philippe Lacoue-Labarthe, *Heidegger, Art and Politics: The Fiction of the Political*, trans. Chris Turner (1987; Cambridge, Mass., 1990), and Jean-François Lyotard, *The Differend: Phrases in Dispute*, trans. George van den Abbeele (1984; Minneapolis, Minn., 1988). See also my *Representing the Holocaust: History, Theory, Trauma* (Ithaca and London, 1994) and *History and Memory after Auschwitz* (Ithaca and London, 1998).

most forceful in *Histoire de la folie*, but even in its later incarnations, the torsions it effects in the same anxiety tend to remain allusive or even apocalyptic and decidedly cryptic. What is at most suggested in Foucault's use of language in this book is one discursive form such a renewed dialogue might take, at least in an initial, broken, ambitious but perhaps at times mystifying and mystified form – the form of Foucault's own writing. One might argue that the broader (possibly intractable) problem, from this first position, would be to trace, even to enact, the changing yet repetitive 'torsions in the same anxiety' *and* to work through them to a renewed dialogue of voices that would address such problems as responsible agency in social relations, desirable alternative normativities, and viable political organization.

A second narrative voice or position in the text seems itself symptomatically to reinforce or replicate the basic, hierarchically organized split between the same and the other. It is the safe position of the scientific structuralist who, from an Olympian distance or indeed as transcendental spectator, indulges in what Sartre termed *l'esprit de survol*. He views history from on high in terms of discontinuous breaks eliminating communication over time and allowing only for objectifying classification and putative explanation. (Here Foucault is closest to one important current in *Annales* historiography.) Dissociated periods are presented as synchronic structures, frozen in a moment of time. Change from one period to another remains a mystery. And the historian is situated *hors jeu*. From the perspective of the more stabilized if not fixated second position, change or discontinuity (identified with temporality or historicity) is dissociated from repetition, and repetition itself is ultimately immobilized in an eternal or intemporal form. One gets in brief a stereotypical,

Neoplatonic idea of idealized and universalized repetition and an equally stereotypical idea of history as autonomized change of particulars (with synchronic periods as intervening structural or quasi-typological variables). Thus:

> While the return of unreason has the aspect of a massive repetition, connecting with itself outside of time, the awareness of madness is on the contrary accompanied by a certain analysis of modernity, which situates it from the start in a temporal, historical, and social context. In the disparity beween the awareness of unreason and the awareness of madness, we have, at the end of the eighteenth century, the point of departure for a decisive movement, that by which the experience of unreason will continue, with Hölderlin, Nerval, and Nietzsche, to proceed ever deeper toward the roots of time – unreason becoming, *par excellence*, the world's *contratempo* – and knowledge of madness seeking on the contrary to situate it ever more precisely within the development of nature and history. It is after this period that the time of unreason and the time of madness receive two opposing vectors: one [unreason] being unconditioned return and absolute submersion; the other [madness], on the contrary, developing according to the chronicle of a history. (English edition, 212)

One should nevertheless observe that, given the generalized free indirect style in which Foucault often writes, it is difficult to tell whether the views expressed in the above paragraph may be attributed to him or are his understanding of a frame of reference emerging at the end of the eighteenth century – or both. At times, moreover, the second (positivistic) voice merges with the first liminal or hybridized one and intensifies the anxiety of a broken dialogue. For example, Foucault's usage is not completely fixed or univocal in the text, and madness is not consistently specified as the simple, modern, reduced, and dissociated form or displacement of 'unreason.' The usage of '*folie*' and '*déraison*' is in general not consistent.

A third narrative position might be interpreted as an extreme protest against scientific constraints – a protest so extreme that it bursts beyond the marginal position to engender a tortuous, flamboyant, chiaroscuro lyricism that may either enchant or drive the reader crazy, or both. Here we seem to have a more direct discursive emulation or poetic mimicry of unreason in exorbitant, at times deliriously lyrical interludes. These interludes threaten to overcompensate for scientism, to spill uncontrollably beyond the margins and, in the modern context, to be mad and maddening. (This voice of extreme reversal is the principal one Habermas hears in Foucault or even in Derrida. It is related to a hyperbolic aesthetic of the sublime and in Foucault to a notion of the void or abyss at the origin of language – what might be seen as a preoccupation with, perhaps a fixation on, trauma accompanied by a powerfully dithyrambic form of post-traumatic writing.)

A further problem related especially to the second and third narrative positions (the structural-positivistic and the lyrical) is the way in which Foucault seems to see texts and other events either as scientific instantiations or as fleetingly lyrical illustrations of structures. In one sense, an event or artifact, including a text, may be related to a structure in a manner analogous to the relation between event and covering law in a positivistic conception of science. An artifact is simply an instance of a structure or some combination of structures. In another sense, references to artifacts may function less in a documentary or literal fashion than as poetic allusions or passing lyrical hints. In both the positivistic and the lyrical senses (which may curiously reinforce one another), we get little close investigation or reading of texts and other artifacts and their more problematic relations to structures, codes, or epistemes. At times suggested but insufficiently explored or even repressed is the way in which texts and other phenomena may not simply illustrate but also test and contest structures that to some significant extent inform or constrain them.

Foucault in general rarely inquires into a text, artifact, or other event as a complex scene of repetition of structures or contexts that may also vary them, at times not simply with symptomatic but with critical or even transformative effects. This more complex and perhaps internally self-questioning relation of text to contexts is one modality of 'torsions in the same anxiety' from which Foucault tends to keep his distance, at times (as in his response to Derrida) affiliating it with a politically diversionary and pernicious 'little pedagogy.' An exclusive, abstracted focus on texts or other artifacts in studied isolation from past and present contexts may devolve into such a pedagogy, especially when deconstruction becomes a misleading rationale for an ahistorical and projective reading technology that compulsively reiterates the aporetic impasses of language in all-consuming, conceit-laden, and at times extremely precious or mannered terms. But this is not a necessary direction for deconstructive analysis. It may take on more critical and political dimensions as a way of treating texts and other events from some variant of the first complex and problematic narrative position or internally dialogized voice that Foucault explores in *Histoire de la folie* – a voice that he rarely applies to the reading of texts or other artifacts. Foucault tends to use texts and artifacts as symptomatic documents of structures or – possibly with more critical and transformative implications – as passing allusions, and his references to them, while at times elliptically brilliant or even incandescent, tend to remain allusive. (One gets two or three lines on *Don Quixote* or a glancing aside on Nietzsche. Still, these allusions are open spaces where we may glimpse possible relations between artifacts and prevalent sociocultural structures or processes not limited to symptomatic reinforcement or instantiation.) At times Foucault is content simply with invoking names in an incantatory litany of transgression. The analysis of the passage from Descartes's first *Meditation* to which Derrida responds is one of the most sustained readings in Foucault's book, and it is only three pages long. (In a stunning performative inconsistency, Foucault's reply to Derrida, where he indicts a problematic of reading, contains one of his own most detailed and brilliant readings of a segment of a text.) Foucault's resistance to the problematic of reading may at times have a politically strategic rationale. (There are, after all, more pressing and important things to do.) But his attitude also deprives him of the occasion for an extended micrological investigation of the intricate interaction among symptomatic reinforcement, critical reworking, and possibly transformative implication in the relation between artifacts and contexts – an interaction that might be the discursive and analytic analogue of the micropractices or forms of intervention and resistance that he often defends in politics, especially in his occasional pieces. One might also suggest that such an investigation is a necessary but not sufficient dimension of historical criticism that must also involve structural and contextual analysis of the type Foucault adumbrates but does not relate consistently to a broader, self-critical model of research and practice.

Thus far my discussion has been largely analytic. I would now like to turn to Foucault's text and examine the story he tells in *Histoire de la folie*, at times intervening in his narrative to indicate related discussions or possibilities that supplement, complement, or contest his account.

In the preface to the book there is a fleeting, enigmatic allusion to Greece: 'The Greeks had a relation to something that they called *hubris*. This relation was not merely one of condemnation; the existence of Thrasymachus and Callicles suffices to prove it, even if their language [in Plato's *Republic*] has reached us already enveloped in the reassuring dialectic of Socrates. But the Greek logos had no contrary' (English edition, ix).

In this elusive passage, pre-Socratic Greece seems to be invoked as the scene of a dialogue between reason and unreason, with hubris in the role of unreason. (Hubris is of course generally understood as excessive, overweening arrogance, typically involving extreme transgression.) The notion that the Greek logos had no contrary would seem to indicate that, at least prior to the figure of Socrates, the Greek world was a cosmos in which reason and unreason were not dissociated but viably and tensely related in a manner we can at best approach in obscurely invocatory gestures. With Socrates the putative older interaction is lost and a tyrannical, one-dimensional logic dominates. This brief passage indicates Foucault's obvious indebtedness to Nietzsche's *Birth of Tragedy from the Spirit of Music*, which he in a sense rewrites in *Histoire de la folie*. The fact that this important intertextual relation remains largely implicit perhaps facilitates the tendency to repeat the equivocations of Nietzsche's account, its unstable weave of 1) a linear narration of discontinuous structures or stages, 2) a complex, uneven narrative of repetition with more or less traumatic change, and 3) periodic lyrical interludes. In Nietzsche the reason/unreason pair is discussed in terms of the Apollonian and the Dionysian. And in Nietzsche as in Foucault one line of the narrative presents a rather traditional story. Once upon a time in pre-Socratic Greece there was a creative dialogue or agon between reason and unreason. Then Socrates came along and this 'tragic' dialogue was lost or repressed. Reason became a one-dimensional tyrant, and unreason was reduced to mere subjectivity and emotional expressiveness. The apparent goal is to recapture the lost dialogue.

But in Nietzsche as in Foucault a more complex storyline complicates the tale and situates the pre-Socratic scene as an enabling critical fiction. It offers an account of time as marked by a repeated struggle between more or less dominant and submerged forces. In the modern period, a one-sided reason tends to predominate, and it both provokes irrational outbursts and functions to repress a different kind of interaction with unreason (or the Dionysian) that discourse, including Nietzsche's own use of language, may nonetheless re-enact or reinvent in however broken, obscure, and partial a form.

Foucault's evanescent reference to Greece in the preface may be read as a figure for the promise and the problems of his book. In the very next paragraph he leaps from Greece to the Middle Ages. In the medieval period there was some dialogue between reason and unreason in a cosmic context related to the role of religion.[16] Religion provided imagery for an exchange between reason and unreason. Later in the text, Foucault asserts that the mad were sacred above all because they 'participated in the obscure powers of poverty [*la misère*]' and thus benefitted,

---

16 Here I would reiterate that the 'death-of-God' motif and the importance of secularization have a role in Foucault that has not been sufficiently stressed.

as 'envoys from another world,' from medieval charity (76, French edition). Yet Foucault does not dwell on more intolerant and one-sided reactions to the 'mad,' for example, stoning or chaining. Nor does he treat more general attempts at domination and control in the Middle Ages that limited – at times severely – anything we might be tempted to see as a dialogue of reason and unreason. On a general level, we might of course refer to the obvious role of the church as an institutional structure, to the importance of feudal institutions, and to the role of scholasticism as a mode of thought.

To put it briefly, Foucault's treatment of the Middle Ages is idealized and sketchy, and along with the allusive reference to Greece it seems to function largely as a critical fiction in a paratactic argument or montage that juxtaposes stylized slices of history to make a critical point. Foucault stresses overmuch the exclusion of lepers and its relation to the treatment of the mad in the classical age. His more significant general contention is that madness later came to occupy the same space leprosy had earlier occupied in the imagination, in institutions, and in language. At times madmen were incarcerated in buildings that had formerly housed lepers. In this sense leprosy, with its rituals and taboos – and, one might add more insistently than Foucault, with its ability to induce ambivalent reactions of fear, pity, and fascination – was displaced onto madness. Here we have a clear instance in Foucault's account of a more repetitive temporality – of recurrence with change in contrast to either unbroken continuity or unproblematic epistemological breaks between periods. Another telling instance of transference or displacement rather than simple continuity or break is found when the medical man takes the place of the exorcist in the highly charged dénouement of Foucault's story.

A third period that Foucault discusses more extensively than Greece or the Middle Ages is the Renaissance. The Renaissance also inserted unreason into a cosmic framework and had for Foucault a tragic sense of its relation to reason. Foucault at least elegiacally valorizes the tragic and the cosmic in a critique of humanism. He pays little attention to responses to madness that are neither tragic nor narrowly humanistic (or positivisitic), and he does not take the critique of humanism in the direction of an inquiry into the relations over time of humans to animals and nature.

In the Renaissance, the madman for Foucault occupied a liminal or threshold position on the margin between this world and the Beyond. An important image that served as a medium of exchange between worlds was that of Christ's mad sacrifice on the cross – an image that was also important in the nineteenth century for figures such as Dostoevsky and Kierkegaard who, together with Nietzsche, may be seen as countervoices even in the midst of Foucault's intolerant age of positivism that effectively subordinated a dissociated unreason to a one-sided, tyrannical rationality. In the Renaissance, Shakespeare and Cervantes enacted a dialogue between reason and unreason, but Foucault's discussion of them is so brief that it is difficult to see how this dialogue took place. Of Cervantes Foucault writes: 'Just under the surface lies an enormous anxiety concerning the relationship, in a work of art, between the real and the imaginary' (29). Here we might recall Freud's discussion of the uncanny and its role in making problematic the opposition between the real and the imaginary. For Foucault the dialogue between reason and unreason is uncanny and strangely disconcerting, and it poses the problem of the return of the repressed.

Foucault places special emphasis on the role of painting in the Renaissance as an authentic medium of uncanny exchanges. Madness in Bosch is not purely human or dissociated from the world: it emerges as an image of the world itself, an *imago mundi* that unsettles the cosmos and disperses man. A crucial image in this respect is that of embarkation related to the ship of fools. The embarkation of the mad served a utilitarian function in getting rid of them. But for Foucault it also had a ritual meaning as a way of relating to them. The ship of fools might be seen as the embarkation of the mad in search of their reason.

Here two complementary questions have a sobering and possibly salutary effect: did the image of the ship of fools have any institutional embodiment or even a primarily ambivalent function in the Renaissance, and was there a full discontinuity between the Renaissance and the classical age of the seventeenth and eighteenth centuries with respect to it? Foucault is somewhat hesitant concerning the status of the image as more than a motif in literature and iconography, but he does assert that it existed as a social institution. According to Erik Midelfort there is but one clearly documented case of 'a madman's having been set adrift in a boat, and it is quite possible that the intention was to drown him' – an event that is difficult to interpret as an ambivalent dialogic encounter through an embarkation of the mad in search of their reason.[17] In addition, there is evidence of strongly marked ambivalence and a tragically cosmic – or at least other than exclusively anthropocentric – relationship to unreason on the other side of the putative divide in the age of classicism, as

---

17 See Erik Midelfort, 'Madness and Civilization in Early Modern Europe: A Reappraisal of Michel Foucault,' in Barbara Malament, ed., *After the Reformation: Essays in Honor of J.H. Hexter* (Philadelphia, 1980), 254.

Foucault at times indicates. Foucault after all borrows the image of embarkation from Pascal and mentions the importance of Diderot in the eighteenth century; more generally, he notes the persistence of some exchange between reason and unreason through the images of animality and the Fall. I have already intimated that Descartes's epochal position as an inaugural figure of classical exclusion is contested not only by Derrida's interpretation but by a passage in Foucault's own text. These considerations would support the contention that the period boundary between the Renaissance and the classical age is somewhat more permeable or indeterminate than Foucault explicitly seems to allow, particularly in his later concept of decisive epistemological breaks. Even within the terms of Foucault's argument, if there is a specificity of the classical age with respect to the problem of unreason and madness, it would seem to pertain primarily to the particular articulation of discourse and practice on an institutional level in the establishment of houses of confinement.

For Foucault there is one crucial, dissociative, hierarchical tendency in the Renaissance. It is found in humanism. The humanistic current, as found for example in the works of Erasmus, is interpreted rather reductively by Foucault as a domestication of madness, a reduction of it to frivolity and human foible. Erasmus's praise of folly was in reality a condemnation of it with praise that was too faint and humanistic. Active in *Histoire de la folie,* as I have noted, is a somewhat unguarded critique of humanism as an anthropocentric departure from a tragic, cosmic perspective – a critique that places species imperialism in radical question but also threatens to obscure the issue of responsibility or answerability. Here I would like to mention at least two other views of the Renaissance that, in more qualified terms, partially converge with Foucault's or at least reinforce his tendency not to see the Renaissance exclusively or even predominantly as the age of humanism. Mikhail Bakhtin stresses the dialogic with reference to an institution and a process that receive little explicit attention in Foucault – carnival and the carnivalesque.[18] But Bakhtin does not simply reject humanism or focus on the tragic. Instead, he emphasizes the festive interplay of seeming opposites, including reason and unreason, in the carnivalesque. Here it might be argued that there is a supplementary and mutually contestatory relation between Foucault's and Bakhtin's emphases and that the problem is to investigate the interaction of the tragic and the festive in a phenomenon such as carnival, including the way in which carnival limits humanistic values through the problematization of ordinary roles and ethical norms. For Bakhtin, the fool's cap as well as the carnival mask might be taken as a symbol of 'unreason,' for example, in the grotesque uncrowning of the higher faculties and an assertion of the 'lower bodily stratum.' Laughter as the nonlinguistic choral accompaniment to an exchange between reason and unreason is not fully under the control of the subject. Given the relative decline or repression of carnival as a viable social institution in the modern period, anything like a dialogue between reason and unreason tends for Bakhtin, as for Foucault, to be reduced, domesticated, and distorted, but it may nonetheless take on powerful discursive and artistic forms, for example, in the work of Dostoevsky. It may also appear in more sadistic and masochistic variants that Bakhtin

---

18 See esp. M.M. Bakhtin, *The Dialogic Imagination*, ed. Michael Holquist and Caryl Emerson (Austin and London, 1981).

tended to ignore, for example, in quasi-sacrifical forms of victimization and quests for regeneration through violence. Indeed, within carnivals there is the problem of the relation between the sacrificial or quasi-sacrificial (including scapegoating and the acting out of prejudice) and the life-affirming, rejuvenating forces Bakhtin stressed.

A second fruitful supplement to Foucault on the Renaissance is Frances Yates.[19] Yates stresses a phenomenon to which Foucault, curiously, pays little explicit attention – although his own work might at times be interpreted as an underground attempt to rehabilitate certain of its tendencies in an inhospitable modern context. I am of course referring to Hermeticism. For Yates, Hermeticism relied on an at times syncretic cosmic symbolism, and it explored the destructive and regenerative role of forces often seen in one-sided fashion as negative or irrational, for example, chaos. It presented in a positive or at least a richly ambivalent light the Magus as a creative figure whose power might challenge divinity. A figure such as Giordano Bruno was for Yates commonly seen as hubristic and excessively arrogant – a wild man if not a madman. Yates argues that Bruno was condemned and burned at the stake by the Church not because of his premature scientific rationalism but because he posed a rather different kind of threat in terms of his heterodox Hermetic tendencies with complicated ties to science. Of course, a so-called heretic is a heterodox individual interpreted in a necessarily reduced and limited way from an orthodox position.

In another of his books, *The Order of Things: An Archaeol-*

---

19 See esp. *Giordano Bruno and the Hermetic Tradition* (Chicago, 1964). Yates's views remain contestable in the historical profession.

ogy of the Human Sciences,[20] Foucault provides a very obscure discussion of sixteenth-century thought in terms of the role of similitudes – what others might interpret as metaphoric thought. He disorients the reader by perhaps intentionally focusing largely on marginal types and does not even discuss Bruno. In contrast to *Histoire de la folie*, in which he singles out humanism for criticism, in *The Order of Things* Foucault sees all prose as sharing a certain episteme. Yates, in comparison, discusses well-known Renaissance figures in perhaps deceptively clear prose and an endearingly self-effacing style (an approach that may oversimplify – or give the reader an inadequate sense of the difficulty and challenge of – certain problems). She also elucidates the role of Hermetic symbolism in milder forms in humanists such as Ficino and provides some basis for an understanding of the range of discursive options in the Renaissance. And she argues that Hermeticism may have been a prevalent if not dominant trend in certain intellectual elites in the sixteenth century. In a fashion that parallels one dimension of Foucault, Yates sees Descartes and Cartesianism as driving Hermeticism underground but not entirely eliminating it in the classical age. It tends to return as the repressed in constricted, distorted, and at times militantly opposed forms, for example, in Rosicrucianism. I would add that a more or less acceptable critical history of repressed Hermetic and carnivalesque forces – at times in complex combinations – in the modern period has yet to be written.

The next period Foucault addresses is the so-called classical age, the titular focus of his book. Here he works with

---

20 Michel Foucault, *The Order of Things: An Archaeology of the Human Sciences*, trans. Alan Sheridan (New York, 1970). First published in French as *Les Mots et les choses: Une Archéologie des sciences humaines* (Paris, 1966).

the equation that links the Renaissance with embarkation and the ship of fools in contrast to the classical age, with its emphasis on confinement and the house of confinement. During the classical period the mad were deprived of freedom and put behind bars or walls – materially excluded from society. For Foucault, the creation of the house of confinement was a decisive institutional change related to newer ways of disciplining people, especially through internalized controls within the guilty conscience. Foucault asserts that in the middle of the seventeenth century, within a period of several months, one out of a hundred people in Paris was confined. In what might perhaps be seen as a subdued Marxist gesture, he mentions the role of an economic crisis at the time, but he argues that as an economic measure, confinement was a failure. The basic explanation for it lay not in economics but in murkier ritualistic, moral, and political considerations.

The great confinement puzzled later observers. The 'reformers' of the post-classical, positivistic period were particularly shocked by the fact that in the classical house of confinement the mad were incarcerated with the criminal, the poor, and the profligate. The classical age gathered all of these heterogeneous representatives of unreason together in the same place – a place earlier inhabited literally or figuratively by lepers.[21] For Foucault, the one common element that men of the classical age saw in these figures revealed the real function of their confinement. This common element was their inability to

---

21 Midelfort also argues that Foucault's thesis concerning the decisively epochal status of the classical house of confinement can be questioned in terms of the relation of such houses to earlier monasteries and not only to leprosaria. This relation would also help account for the mingling of various types in the same establishment.

conform to the work ethic of a bourgeois social order. The Republican ideal of civic virtue, shared on one level by Robespierre, Rousseau, and Bentham, sought an ideally transparent union of morality and the state, the work ethic, and the confinement of deviants. In this dimension of his analysis, Foucault seems very close to Max Weber, and the overall process he appears to trace is one of secularization, disenchantment, and the decline or displacement of sacred values. Yet for Foucault similar processes occurred in Protestant and Catholic regions, although he does not investigate the role of the Counter-Reformation in bringing about a convergence. Foucault also underscores the role of the work ethic in presenting work as punishment and a means of atonement for a guilty, fallen humanity. But, in spite of its repressive side, such an ethic also indicated the existence of a narrow channel for a dialogue with unreason in terms of the Fall and the animality or bestiality of man. Among forms of unreason madness was exalted as a scandal and ostentatiously displayed, for example, in the exhibition of the mad to onlookers on Sundays.[22]

Significant for Foucault was the fact that madness in the classical age was not subordinated to medical problems but manifestly conjoined with ritual, juridical, and political concerns. The construction and medicalization of madness as a specifically mental illness is for Foucault a modern, suspect phenomenon. He insists that the medi-

---

22 In his desire to indicate some vestige of the tragic in the classical age, Foucault does not question this prejudicial conception of animality or bestiality, which easily functions in a dubious 'humanistic' register by covertly projecting extreme human possibilities onto animals and thereby helping to justify the subordination of all 'creation' to putative human interests. Beasts are not bestial, but humans may be, notably in their treatment of each other and animals more generally.

cal man first entered houses of confinement as a representative of public order – an exorcistic ally of the police and not primarily a representative of scientific knowledge or psychotherapy. In the late eighteenth century there was a great fear of leperlike contagion spreading from houses of confinement. The doctor was summoned to allay anxiety when people were panicked by the corruption, pollution, and tainted exhalations they feared were emanating from houses of confinement.

In the early nineteenth century, the age of positivism begins in earnest. This is the next structural form at an archaeological level in the relation of reason and unreason or perhaps the next torsion in the same anxiety, and here we witness further dissociation and splitting. Madness is dissociated from other forms of unreason, analytically isolated and localized as an object of positivistic knowledge and socio-political control. Foucault's hyperbolic response may well reduce the complexity of modern phenomena in favour of a rather one-sided polemical conception of them. (He also takes this tack in *Discipline and Punish*, especially towards the end of the book, with the fantasia of the carceral society.) Foucault reacts strongly against what he sees as the ideologically motivated and mystified history of the modernizing process as a story of increasing freedom, in which 'reformers' such as Pinel and Tuke play the heroic role of revolutionary liberators of the mad.

For Foucault the so-called liberation of the insane from the classical houses of confinement was a more effective confinement of them and a denial of what they had to say. In this respect (and despite their marked differences of focus and approach), for Foucault as for Tocqueville, the French Revolution may have fostered forces that were more 'reactionary' than the old régime. The new, post-

Revolutionary asylum took away the literal bars of the classical house of confinement, but it set up new bars in the conscience of the madman and made him experience his transgression predominantly if not exclusively as abject guilt, subjection, and inarticulate, unintelligible, even silent deviance.

Samuel Tuke was a Quaker who used religion to impose moral ideas on the mad. Unlike Tuke, Philippe Pinel stripped away the forms of religion and further secularized morality and reason. But they shared an authority that did not derive from science, a way of treating the madman as a child or minor, and the modelling of the asylum on the bourgeois family. The madman could speak only by returning to a socially defined voice of reason. More generally, for Foucault the positive science of psychology arose on the basis of political, social, and moral practices. Through these practices, the mad could be studied as objects in a seemingly objective way only because they had been objectified and reduced to silent objects of a dominant gaze (*regard*) and discourse of the other. Such a science could take itself as autonomous only when it had thoroughly repressed and denied its own founding mechanisms – mechanisms that critical historical research may nonetheless excavate and subject to critical scrutiny. The sciences of man for Foucault were founded on the secularization, disarticulation, and rearticulation of what had been a cosmic context, and their 'objectivity' is derived from nonscientific and contestable practices. Here Foucault is offering a new rendition of the old story tracing a movement from religion to science (for example, Max Weber's tale of disenchantment). But he is doing it with a hyperbolically, at times reductively, critical twist and trying to disclose the genealogy of forms of knowledge and power whose historical origins are often occluded or repressed. In the process, he inquires critically into the assumptions or presuppositions of existing disciplines and practices. For Foucault, perhaps the most significant aspect of the asylum in the age of positivism was the 'apotheosis of the medical personage.' Drawing in part on the prestige of science, the medical man was an authority figure with the intimidating power of the father, the judge, and the law. Here one might open a parenthesis and note the importance of Freud's intervention in an area that Foucault does not discuss. Freud recognized the importance of the authority of the doctor that could not be accounted for on totally objective or 'rational' grounds, and he related it to the question of transference. Transference also indicated how the analyst was implicated in the 'object' of study in a manner that could not be entirely mastered but that nonetheless posed the problem of critically working through transferential displacement instead of denying or indulging in it. Here an extended quotation from Freud's *Autobiographical Study* is apposite:

> My patients, I reflected, must in fact "know" all the things which had hitherto only been made accessible to them in hypnosis; and assurances and encouragements on my part, assisted perhaps by the touch of my hand, would, I thought, have the power of forcing the forgotten facts and connections into consciousness. No doubt this seemed a more laborious process than putting them into hypnosis, but it might prove highly instructive. So I abandoned hypnosis, only retaining my practice of requiring the patient to lie on a sofa while I sat behind him, seeing him, but not seen myself ... (51)
> In every analytic treatment there arises, without the physician's agency, an intense emotional relationship between

the patient and the analyst which is not to be accounted for by the actual situation. It can be of a positive or of a negative character and can vary between the extremes of a passionate, completely sensual love and the unbridled expression of embittered defiance and hatred. This transference – to give it its shortened name – soon replaces in the patient's mind the desire to be cured, and, so long as it is affectionate and moderate, becomes the agent of the physician's influence and neither more nor less than the mainspring of the joint work of analysis ... It must not be supposed, however, that transference is created by analysis and does not occur apart from it. Transference is merely uncovered by analysis. It is a universal phenomenon of the human mind, it decides the success of all medical influence, and in fact dominates the whole of each person's relations to his human environment. We can easily recognize it as the same dynamic factor that the hypnotists have named "suggestibility," which is the aspect of hypnotic *rapport* and whose incalculable behavior led to such difficulties with the cathartic method. When there is no inclination to a transference of emotion such as this, or when it becomes entirely negative, as happens in *dementia praecox* or paranoia, then there is no possibility of influencing the patient by psychological means.[23]

Foucault neither treats the importance of transference in psychoanalysis nor investigates the import of the concept for the relationship between the historian or critic and his or her 'object' of study, including the unacknowledged role of transference in his own account. Instead, he sees Freud as an equivocal figure in the history of mad-

---

23 Sigmund Freud, *An Autobiographical Study*, trans. James Strachey (New York, 1963), 79.

ness. In a sense Freud is acceptable to Foucault to the extent that he resembles Nietzsche. (This view is insufficient insofar as Freud's notion of 'working through' moderates Nietzschean hyperbole without simply denying it.) For Foucault Freud renewed the possibility in medicine and psychology of a dialogue with the mad at least by allowing a monologue of the mad, to which he attentively listened. But he nonetheless retained and intensified the alienating role of the doctor as an authority figure if not a hidden god.[24]

For Foucault the true voices of unreason in the modern period went underground in art and literature, and they lacked a sustaining sociocultural background. The unmoored voices of unreason in an obscure dialogue with reason seemed to come not out of the cosmos or even out of a more delimited cultural context but out of the void. Here Foucault refers to such iconic figures as Nietzsche, Hölderlin, Artaud, and Sade. He tellingly contrasts the paintings of Bosch and Goya. In Bosch, unreason is a sub-

---

24 In the Appendix of 1972, 'La folie, l'absence d'oeuvre,' Foucault changes his tack and sees Freud more in Foucault's own terms. Freud presumably did not restore to madness a language that had been silenced for centuries. Instead he 'made words go back to their source – until they reached that white region of auto-implication [or self-referentiality] where nothing is said' (580). I would note that, from a psychoanalytic perspective, the three narrative positions or voices I discussed earlier may be interpreted in the following way: the first position – that on the margin or threshold from which history is explored as the scene of a repeated struggle between more or less dominant and submerged forces – might be seen as a problematic attempt to work through the problems Foucault treats; the second position – that of the scientific structuralist – involves denial of our transferential relation to the past and an attempt to achieve the position of a transcendental subject or spectator; and the third position – that of a lyricist emulating or mimicking the voices of madness – acts out the problems that are being discussed. In the course of the book, these positions or voices interweave in complex ways, and they periodically tend to be obliterated in that traumatic return, black hole, or 'white region of auto-implication where nothing is said.'

terranean force of the cosmos; in Goya (at least in certain paintings), unreason erupts from an abyss. In Goya's *Witches' Sabbath*, for example, we have, in Foucault's words, 'glances shot from nowhere and staring at nothing.' This is, I think, one of the brilliant allusions in Foucault that sheds condensed and heightened illumination on the artifact. There is no eye contact in the painting: glances are indeed shot from nowhere and stare at nothing.

Foucault ends his book with a notoriously opaque, lyrically evocative, intriguingly disorienting discussion of the relation between art and madness in the modern world. Art and madness are in the closest proximity yet separated by a radical divide: the work of art is ripped from madness, and the onset of madness marks the end of work in art. But both art that is precariously positioned on the edge of an abyss or torn from the temptation of madness and the artist who goes mad indict modern civilization. In this fulminating, neo-baroque climax to his history of madness Foucault also indicts modern civilization in the name of an alternative that remains elusive, an obscure underground or a lost dialogue that he, however darkly, would like to see become a groundswell.

In conclusion I shall try to render explicit my intention in focusing on a relatively close reading and analysis of Foucault's study of madness. As I intimated earlier there has been a tendency in recent criticism to periodize Foucault's work and usually to single out a later phase as most fruitful for contemporary research. Frequently this phase is the one in which Foucault moves to a concept of power-knowledge – a phase epitomized in *Discipline and Punish*, which in many respects has been a proof-text or touchstone for the new historicism. The concept of power-knowledge presumably marks an advance if not an epistemological break *vis-à-vis* an earlier phase wherein Foucault, taking a 'linguistic turn,' focused on internal analyses of discourse or at best of discursive practices construed in overly narrow 'epistemological' terms. My intention is not to reverse perspectives or to deny either the important aspects of Foucault's later work or the limitations of the earlier texts. But I do think that applying periodization to his thought is as problematic and restrictive as his own use of periodization in the study of the past. Virtually all of Foucault's later work is at least prefigured in the full version of *Histoire de la folie*; the abridgements in the shortened version that Foucault himself authorized may function (if they were not intended) to obscure the extent of that prefiguration or, more precisely, that proleptic intimation that would nonetheless enable significant changes over time.

In more positive terms, I would argue that there is still much to be derived from critical exchange with such a difficult, challenging, and disturbing text as *Histoire de la folie*, where Foucault at times places in question what are often identified as restrictive traits of his 'epistemological' or 'discourse-analysis' period. In this text he indicates directly, indirectly, or even by the deficiencies of his account the role of a conception of time in terms of displacement or repetition with change (at times traumatic change). And he shows how processes of repression or exclusion and those of normalization, regulation, and the deployment of power are not necessarily incompatible. (Indeed in certain contexts they may be mutually reinforcing.) He may also be closer at times to a more comprehensive notion of hegemony as a tool of critical genealogical analysis in the exchange between past and present – a notion that tends to be obscured in his later and more reductive stress upon power as a universal solvent. (In the work before his death, where the problems of subjectivity and of ethicopolitical norms are posed with new insistency and insight, the turn to a plain style brings both gains in accessibility and losses with respect to the daring project in writing that is perhaps epitomized in *Histoire de la folie*.) To put the point another way, the post-68 Foucault sometimes appears to centre thought around a rather indiscriminate concept of power or power-knowledge that is the unmoved mover of a gallows functionalism. From such a perspective, everything in the 'system' (notably including artifacts of 'high' culture) functions at least in a symptomatic way, agency is not simply obscured but at times obliterated, contestation becomes moot, and resistance tends to be immediately recuperated or 'refloated' to energize the 'system' of power-knowledge.[25]

---

25 Nancy Fraser recognizes the empirical and conceptual usefulness of Foucault's later understanding of power but reinforces Habermas's critique in observing: 'Whether we take him as suspending every normative framework, or only the liberal one, or even as keeping that one, he is plagued with unanswered and perhaps unanswerable questions. Because he fails to conceive and pursue any single consistent normative strategy, he ends up with a curious amalgam of amoral militaristic description, Marxian jargon, and Kantian morality. Its many valuable empirical aspects notwithstanding, I can only conclude that Foucault's work is normatively confused ... Foucault writes as though he were oblivious to the existence of the whole body of Weberian social theory with its careful distinctions between such notions as authority, force, violence, domination, and legitimation ... Clearly, what Foucault needs, and needs desperately, are normative criteria for distinguishing acceptable from unacceptable forms of power.' *Unruly Practices: Power, Discourse and Gender in Contemporary Theory* (Minneapolis, Minn., 1989), 31–3. Of course one may argue that Foucault is intentionally and insistently employing a delegitimating strategy for which such distinctions as that between power and authority break down, but the question remains whether such a strategy is cogent and effective. From a different perspective, which stresses the complex elucidatory, symptomatic, and contestatory role of a view of power often diagnosed as paranoid, see Eric L. Santner's discussion of Foucault in the context of a study of Daniel Paul Schreber, *My Own Private Germany: Daniel Paul Schreber's Secret History of Modernity* (Princeton, N.J., 1996),

Forces of resistance have a somewhat different status in *Histoire de la folie,* even when they are compelled to go underground. And the book may serve to raise questions about the relation of the critic or historian and the object of study that are still of pressing concern. It may even sensitize us to features of the later Foucault that do not entirely conform to a generalized if not indiscriminate concept of power and a gallows functionalism.

One important question that arises from a reading of *Histoire de la folie* is whether we can recognize the appeal of Foucault's evocation of a mutually tempting and contestatory relation between discursive forces even if we assume a critical distance from certain of its features. Foucault focuses on a crucial problem often marginalized or excluded in liberal discourses that emphasize mainstream institutions and processes such as those discussed by Tocqueville. And, in addressing these processes, Foucault seems either to bracket liberal concerns or to engage in a radical delegitimation of them. Yet the result is a rather vague crypto-normativism (in Habermas's term) in which alternative norms, to the extent they are present, remain so embedded as to be obscure if not indecipherable. At times the alternative even seems to be a blank, anarchistic

---

esp. 83–96. In what may perhaps be seen as a gesture within the spirit of Foucault's own history of madness, Santner writes: 'Schreber discovers that power not only prohibits, moderates, says "no," but may also work to intensify and amplify the body and its sensations. Put somewhat differently, Schreber discovers that symbolic authority in a state of emergency *is* transgressive, that it exhibits an obscene overproximity to the subject: that it, as Schreber puts is, *demands enjoyment.* Schreber's experience of his body and mind as the site of violent and transgressive interventions and manipulations, which produce, as a residue or waste product, a kind of surplus enjoyment, is, I am suggesting, an index of a crisis afflicting his relation to the exemplary domain of symbolic authority to which his life was intimately bound, namely the law' (32).

or even anomic utopia, which is allusively invoked in apocalyptic tones. The question here is whether Foucault's interest in marginalized or excluded groups and issues (including the politics of everyday life) can be related to a transformed liberalism concerned both with the restructuring of 'mainstream' institutions (the family, education, the workplace, the state) and with the constitutional protection of minority and human (even other than human) rights – including those of groups Foucault discussed. Foucault did not offer an extensive treatment of possible alternative normativities or polities that had a direct bearing on the present, and he did not explicitly take up the question of the role of intermediary groups in a reconstituted society and polity – groups that might bring everyday life into contact with politics, including representation at the level of the state. But, if we consider this issue, a crucial question is which intermediary groups should be given political representation as mediating links between the individual and the state. Could a status as an institutional unit of political representation (rather than a status as lobby or pressure group) be granted to constituencies made up of gays, prisoners, or even the 'mad' – or could such different groups be represented politically only as participants in other activities?[26]

Aside from near delirous lyricism and rather uncontrolled use of free indirect style, perhaps the primary mode in which the temptation and threat of 'madness' arise in Foucault's own writing is in terms of a post-tragic, compulsive, hyperbolic insistence on the abyss or void –

---

26 The politically relevant traditional role of court jester was at times played by someone seen as 'mad.' It should be noted that the diagnosis of 'madness' has been a convenient way for oppressive regimes to silence, delegitimate, or get rid of dissidents.

the traumatic disruption of the speculatively dialectical quest for identity and totalization – a disruptive insistence conveyed in both agonized and playful movements of language. (Here of course Foucault is far from being alone in a daring practice that threatens to be isolating or monological – a practice in which one engages in a 'sublime,' paradoxically nondialogic 'dialogue' beyond dialogue with a radically different other.[27]) In *Histoire de la folie* we can see Foucault lyrically acting out, positivistically situating, and ambivalently relating to that temptation and threat as well as pointing backward to a transforming, tragic cosmos in an untimely gesture made at times with a cataclysmically violent sense of urgency. Both in this text and elsewhere in Foucault, the recurrent danger is the tendency to sacrifice an attempt to bring about an interaction between legitimate limits and hyperbolic transgression in deference to an unrestrained aesthetic of the transgressive, traumatizing, quasi-transcendent sublime.[28] The dubious political analogue of this aesthetic combines

---

27 For a recent exploration of this motif (indeed leitmotif), see Jacques Derrida, *The Gift of Death*, trans. David Wills (1992; Chicago and London, 1995). Derrida discusses and traces his own relations to Levinas, Kierkegaard, and the Biblical account of Abraham and Isaac, and he insists on the notion that every other is radically other (or altogether different – *tout autre est tout autre*). He also extensively investigates the question of sacrifice and stresses the role of the gift (of death) in it. He does not address the problems of victimization and regeneration through violence in sacrificial processes. Nor does he cogently relate the quasi-theological notion of radical or absolute alterity to commonality, communication, and shared commitments which, to some viable degree, would seem necessary in ethics and politics.

28 The converse danger in a thinker such as Tocqueville is to sacrifice the interaction between limits and challenges to them in defence of an abstract, overgeneralized affirmation of limits that leads one to inveigh against, obscure, or obviate the significance of the traumatic, the radically transgressive, and the revolutionary (including of course the role of intellectuals who are identified as the bearers of these tendencies).

seeming nostalgia for a lost 'tragic' past, total condemnation of modernity except for scarcely audible echoes or evanescent lightning flashes of that past, and blind, perhaps apocalyptic hope for a radically different, indeterminate future. This all-too-familiar pattern obviates the need for more specific critical analysis of modern phenomena and lends itself too easily to a politics of cultural despair. The admittedly problematic yet more promising possibility Foucault leaves us with is that of specific modes of resistance and work provocatively exploring the interaction between contending forces in language and life. My own view here is that – at least on a discursive level – we must be open to certain risks of transgressive hyperbole that test limits (and simultaneously limit the possibilities of dialogic exchange) but not become compulsively fixated on these risks and surreptitiously or dogmatically constitute them as the *telos* or hidden agenda of language. Instead, we should investigate and explore their disorienting relation to other forces, including those attendant upon transformed normative frameworks, in a larger discursive and practical field. In this respect, the question is how to elaborate a notion of normative, critical, self-critical (or practical) reason, allowing for affect and bound up with socio-political processes of working through problems – a substantive (not narrowly one-sided or technical) reason that is open to a mutually challenging interplay between limits and certain 'excessive' challenges to them.

── 4 ──

Reconfiguring French Studies

In the first chapter, I focused on problems of reading as they bore on historiography. I made reference to critical and literary theory insofar as it was pertinent to these problems. In this concluding chapter, the balance of interest shifts somewhat. Historical understanding is still at issue, but an important focus is the study of literature and other art forms. The overriding concern, however, is to further a mutually challenging interaction between history and these areas in a broader conception of French studies that also makes room for other disciplinary concerns, notably those of philosophy and critical theory. And the institutional questions that arise to some extent bear on various departments and programs, not only the traditional French department. One might well argue that history departments should be transformed at least to allow greater opportunities for the hiring of faculty and the training of graduate students who go beyond the conventional research paradigm in order to engage questions not generally encompassed by it, including the relations of research, critical theory, and the close reading of artifacts (including documents). One might also argue for a significant place for music, film, and visual studies in both historiography and a reconfigured French studies – a development that is already well under way.

The problem of French studies confronts French departments directly on a departmental and disciplinary level and implies significant changes in orientation for many present and, especially, future practitioners of the field. For this reason it may be met at least initially with suspicion, anxiety, and even hostility, for there is a possible threat to the genuine intellectual convictions as well as to the hard-earned, existing 'cultural capital' of many members of French departments. The obvious problem is how acquired skills and deep-seated investments in certain critical and analytic approaches (such as poststructural orientations and *explication de texte* or the close reading of literature) may be situated in a broader conception of the field that allows for a diversity of interrelated, thought-provoking, at times mutually questioning, perspectives.[1]

---

[1] See the special issue of *Diacritics* 28 (1998), edited by Jonathan Culler and Richard Klein and entitled *Doing French Studies*. The editors write in their preface that 'if there is a single substantial theme that runs through [all the contributions to the volume], it may be the mundane concern that Tom Conley calls "wondering what can be done to invigorate one of the richest of all literary canons." How does that canon respond to the kinds of questions and issues that the unravelling and dissolution of boundaries – including those of France itself – have made possible? And should French studies, in the end, be conceived as the integration of the numerous interdisciplinary trajectories that depart from or traverse this canon or as a more distinctively specific practice for the study of everything French that is structured like a language?' With reference to the latter question, one may wonder whether a decision is called for or whether instead a vital dimension of the internal dynamic of the field would be the mutually challenging interaction between the two possibilities, often in the work of the same person. The contributions include an essay by Klein entitled 'The Object of French Studies – *Gebrauchkunst*' – an essay devoted to a sustained and forceful theoretical reflection (a reflection in certain ways reinforced by the other largely

The prospect of French studies confronts historians to a lesser extent on a departmental or even disciplinary level and more directly as individuals orienting or reori-

---

theoretical piece in the volume, Sandy Petrey's 'When Did Literature Stop Being Cultural?'). Klein, in a gesture intimating that something old is new again, seems to decide the question posed in the preface in favour of 'a distinctively specific practice' with a delimited object. He takes as a model of French studies Leo Spitzer's *explication de texte* of a Sunkist orange juice advertisement. The seemingly restrictive, even ironic, implication is that French studies should be the close reading of commodified culture or what Klein refers to as *Gebrauchkunst* (use-art): 'that is to say, artifacts of civilization which serve some interest or use but which are formed by aesthetic procedures and mechanisms. Like advertising (or propaganda), *Gebrauchkunst* can be distinguished from, say, art or literature by virtue of the way it subordinates its aesthetic aims to commercial or political ends' (8). This kind of analysis might indeed find a place in French studies, but (despite the recent importance of the focus on commodified and, especially, consumer culture in cultural studies) it would hardly seem paradigmatic of the field, especially if one takes seriously Culler and Klein's comments in the preface. The direction Klein spells out for French studies is hardly something he wants to be dominant or perhaps even prevalent in French departments, which he (in union with Sandy Petrey) apparently does not want to see transformed into departments of cultural studies. Among the many notes he strikes, however, Klein includes this promising one: 'For Spitzer, French studies is not a matter of doing either literature or history, or of doing a little of each, but of finding ways, critically, to articulate them together' (10). It is not to dismiss the significance of at least certain of the thought-provoking articles in this special issue either to wonder to what extent they effect this articulation or to observe that they differ at best marginally from articles that might appear in any issue of *Diacritics*. It might be argued that these articles do not go far enough, in theory or practice, in contributing to a needed reconfiguration of French studies. Alternatively work already being done – even what is by now more standard or prevalent work (including modes of post-structuralism) – might be seen to realize what is best in French studies, thus implying a strong reaffirmation of existing practices in the field. The special issue includes arguments and analyses that would lend support to both views, thereby indicating that the field of French studies is contested. The object of critical reflection may be not to end that internal contestation but to provide it with the most fruitful and engaging directions possible.

enting their teaching and research.[2] It would confront history departments on a general or collective level with respect to such issues as the types of graduate students to admit, the kinds of courses to encourage, and the possible selection of a French historian having a 'French studies' approach in contrast, say, to a more circumscribed eco-

---

2 It would take a separate essay to chart the vicissitudes of the study of France within history departments and among professional historians. There is still insufficient communication (or even mutual curiosity) between those in French and history departments, and the very project of French studies may be the occasion for greater interaction, whether through a thoroughly cooperative French studies program (even department) or through joint appointments. (Given the stronger professional self-consciousness and the rarity of joint appointments in history departments of those without degrees from history departments, joint appointments would probably be more likely in the case of historians in departments of French or French studies.) The work of certain historians, such as Roger Chartier, Robert Darnton, and Pierre Nora, has become rather well known among colleagues in French departments. But it is probably still the case that relatively few historians of France read seriously the work of those in French departments. Professional historians tend to think that those trained in French departments (usually meaning a training in language and literature, perhaps along with varieties of critical theory) have an insufficient knowledge of historical contexts, a restricted familiarity with the work of professional historians, a penchant for a manneristic style, and little if any training in archivally based research. Moreover, the great majority of historians have had little sympathy for the currents of critical theory for which French departments have been crucial conduits. Those in French departments often think that historians do not have sufficient competence in either close reading or critical theory, but – especially with the recent turn in literary studies towards historicization – they may appreciate historians' extensive knowledge of context, if only as background to the study of literature and other art forms. Still, it is, I think, becoming increasingly evident that a key problem of French studies is to transform these perceptions and to bring about a greater interaction and imbrication of contextual knowledge, research, close reading, and theoretical sophistication. I also think there is a willingness at present to give attempts to bring about this transformation at least the benefit of the doubt. A step in the right direction is made by encouraging graduate students in French and in history departments to do extensive crossover work and to interact with one another in colloquia and other venues. The next step would be for French and history departments to consider seriously the

nomic, political, or social orientation.[3] (In practice, such a historian would probably have an intellectual-cultural or sociocultural orientation.) Aside from the broad question of allowing for initiatives that go beyond a restricted research model, the immediate question for a history department would be the overall representation and prominence of approaches close to French studies and its concerns. The *Annales* school has of course had an important influence on the study of France (and to a lesser extent on the study of other areas) within history departments (as well as, to some extent, within French departments), and its recent movement in the direction of cultural history – or at least to an understanding of cultural history as more than an epiphenomenon (or 'third tier') of history after the presumably more fundamental levels of economic and social history – has facilitated a movement among certain historians in a direction compatible with French studies.[4] And individual historians (or

---

possibility of appointing a person trained primarily in the other discipline or department but of course having crossover competence and skills. Until relatively recently, it may have been implausible for someone to acquire this type of competence – given the difficulty of emergent critical theories, the demands of historical training, and the rudimentary state of extensive interchange between relevant disciplines and perspectives. But it may now be possible for graduate students to put together programs of study that interrelate and, in important ways, viably integrate pursuits such as close reading, training in archival research, and a judicious, argumentative assimilation of (in contrast to total or unquestioning immersion in) critical theory.

3 For example, the work of historians Leora Auslander and Jan Goldstein would be a boon to any French studies program. Their work is of course important for their colleagues in history at the University of Chicago, but it does not define the profile, or probably even provide an orienting pole, for the department as a whole.

4 On this question, see Philippe Carrard, *Poetics of the New History: French Historical Discourse from Braudel to Chartier* (Baltimore and London, 1992). I would note that, although the conception of the relevant social-scientific theories and theorists changes over time, the concern with the relation of

history to the social sciences, at times correlated with a de-emphasis of the significance of narrative, has been a hallmark of the *Annales* in France (as well as of the Bielefeld 'school' in Germany). A concern with the relation between history and the social sciences is crucial, but a primary if not exclusive orientation in the direction of the social sciences often implies a devaluation of literary studies, rhetoric, and (perhaps to a lesser degree) philosophy as relevant for the self-understanding or conduct of historical inquiry (as well as of philosophers and literary theorists as pertinent interlocutors for historians), and it constitutes philosophy and literature largely as *objects* of historical and social-scientific analysis. The unfortunate result is often limited insight into the work and play of philosophical and literary texts or the way they respond – at times critically – to social categories and assumptions, however probing and complex may be the analysis of their social insertion in a collective representation, structure, field, or network. (The mutual reliance of history and the social sciences was in certain respects accentuated by the 1994 change in the title of the journal *Annales ESC [Economies Sociétés Civilisations]* to *Annales HSS [Histoires, Sciences Sociales]*.) In view of the importance of literature and literary theory in French departments, this approach to culture and cultural history limits the pertinance of the *Annales* orientation (and may generate a suspicion of its advocates) with respect to a reconfigured French studies. Recently this orientation may be changing to allow a broader conception of inter- and cross-disciplinarity in which there is a critical, discriminating opening to the role of philosophy and literary theory as sites that, along with the social sciences, are relevant to a reconceptualization of (or 'critical turn' in) history. For the editors' attempt to rethink the journal's approach, see 'Histoire et sciences sociales. Un tournant critique?' in *Annales ESC* 43 (1988), 291–3 and '*Tentons l'expérience*,' in *Annales ESC* 44 (1989), 1317–23. See also *Annales ESC* 48 (1993) on '*Mondes des arts*' and *Annales HSS* 49 (1994) on '*Littérature et histoire*.' For a harsh critique of any turn in the *Annales* that would stress theoretical reflection or discourse analysis – much less a mutually thought-provoking interaction with philosophy and literary studies or an openness to the idea that disciplines on some significant level must be essentially contested undertakings in which debate about self-definition (or 'crisis') is never resolved – see Gérard Noiriel, *Sur la 'crise' de l'histoire* (Paris, 1996). Relying in good part on the unlikely combination of Pierre Bourdieu and Richard Rorty, Noiriel affirms both pragmatism (devoid of any philosophical defence [175n]) and a primary orientation towards social science for the analysis and affirmation of autonomous historical practices in the study of society (putatively in the tradition of Marc Bloch's understanding of the historian's craft). Noiriel's perspective to a significant extent falls within a disciplinary 'identity-politics' mould conjoining a 'scientific' project, collective disciplinary solidarity (including norms and practices of admissibility), and autonomy – a mould that would render the role of history in a French studies program extremely problematic. Noiriel also seems blind to the

Reconfiguring French Studies 175

social scientists) of France may play a leading role in initiating or leading programs in French studies.[5] But it remains the case that the greatest, most clear and present departmental and disciplinary (in partial contradistinction to intellectual) challenge posed by French studies is to French rather than to history (or, more generally, social science) departments.[6]

---

contradiction between his idealistic desire for an exemplary historical profession that embodies solidarity, democracy, and equality and a definition of that profession in narrow terms that would perforce exclude those not sharing his conception of it. Put in other terms, he seems unwilling to recognize the extent to which a critical insight he applied to the study of nationalism and immigration might also apply to the discipline of history without depriving it of all coherence: that an exaggerated if not intolerant idea of national unity or autonomy induces an inability to recognize the extent to which the French population and culture were and are the result of multiple inputs, including those of immigrants at times perceived as unwelcome outsiders. See *Le Creuset français. Histoire de l'immigration* (Paris, 1988).

5 This is the case with my colleague at Cornell, the noted historian of France Steven L. Kaplan. One may also mention scholars in the social sciences at other universities who play an important role in French studies programs, for example, Ezra Suleiman at Princeton.

6 Important bases for a movement towards an expanded conception of French studies exist already in both faculty and approaches to problems in French departments, and one might maintain that such a movement already has significant momentum, although there is considerable resistance as well as debate about an acceptable formulation of a reconfigured conception of the field. The diversity of approaches in French studies at present may be indicated by the following partial list of more or less 'senior' scholars in the field currently having (to the best of my knowledge) an affiliation with a French department or analogous administrative unit (such as a department of Romance Studies): Emily Apter, Ora Avni, Leo Bersani, R. Howard Bloch, David Carroll, Ross Chambers, Antoine Compagnon, Tom Conley, Shoshana Felman, Nelly Furman, Suzanne Gearhart, René Girard, Sima Godfrey, Lionel Gossman, Jean-Joseph Goux, Mitchell Greenberg, Marianne Hirsch, Denis Hollier, Marie-Hélène Huet, Joan DeJean, Alice Jardine, Alice Kaplan, Richard Klein, Lawrence D. Kritzman, Françoise Lionnet, Jeffrey Mehlman, Françoise Meltzer, Nancy K. Miller, Toril Moi, Valentin Mudimbe, Stephen Nichols, Linda Orr, Sandy Petrey, Gerald Prince, Michael Riffaterre, Kristin Ross, Susan Rubin Suleiman, Richard Terdiman, and David Wills. Even though this list (no doubt skewed by my own interests

Still, the problem of reading is interdisciplinary, in that it relates – at times by stimulating debate and mutual questioning between – distinct disciplines, as well as cross-disciplinary, in that it cuts across disciplines, both receiving different inflections in them and occasionally suggesting ways of reconceptualizing them. Pursuing the problem of reading in different registers may destabilize the boundaries between disciplines and even suggest better, possibly more interactive, relations between (or articulations of) them that allow for greater cooperation and provocative exchange. Moreover, to some extent, problems in French studies parallel those in older and more highly developed area studies programs (in which historians and social scientists have extensiveiy participated). It would make sense for those interested in French studies to investigate closely the ways in which area studies programs have confronted dif-

and acquaintances) might be lengthened or revised, a careful reading of the works of those mentioned in it would provide some pragmatic idea of the possibilities and limits of reconfiguring French studies at the present time. Indeed, one commitment probably shared by all members of French departments concerns the importance of close reading itself, and it can be a cause of contention between them and advocates of cultural studies. See the comments of Richard Klein and Sandy Petrey in the special issue of *Diacritics* 28 (1998). Klein, with evident disagreement, quotes Lawrence Grossberg, one of the advocates of cultural studies, as asserting: 'although there is no prohibition against textual readings [in cultural studies], they are also not required' (quoted, 8). Within the context of a 'traditional' French department, the analogue of Grossberg's comment would be a Christian asserting that it is optional to believe in Christ. For my colleague Richard Klein, as for many others in the field of French, the proponent of French studies who is not more like Leo Spitzer than like Lawrence Grossberg threatens to be a philistine at the gates. It may be both too obvious and too simple to add – as both Klein and Grossberg might agree – that the point is to get beyond these antagonistic perceptions and any realities to which they may in part refer.

ficulties and opportunities.[7] Unlike many area studies programs, however, French studies is not developing in the cold-war context and may thus have greater intellectual and curricular (along with fewer financial) opportunities open to it. It nonetheless faces issues related to

---

[7] The distinction, often functioning as a binary opposition, between the West and 'the rest' has had great historical and institutional power, both for those who see themselves as within the West and for its 'others.' The distinction has also been crucial in the conception and organization of departments and disciplines in the academy. Disciplines studying the West often have the Westerner (or things Western) as both subject and 'canonical' object of study. French studies has been included in this category – often at the high end of 'snob appeal.' Disciplines studying 'the rest' continue to privilege the Westerner as subject conducting inquiry but one area or another of 'the rest' as object of study (with the 'other' often objectified and denied a voice as dialogic interlocutor). Area studies programs have typically been included in the latter category, and former French colonies have at times been objects of study in such programs. (More recent 'ethnic' studies programs – such as African-American, Asian-American, Native American, and Latino/a studies – have attempted to recognize the voices of putative 'others' and struggled with problems of self-conception, identity politics, and institutional organization, often torn between the need for relative autonomy and the desirability of not being ghettoized or isolated in the academy. Jewish studies began as a relatively ghettoized area but has recently not had a self-image as an ethnic studies program.) One may readily deconstruct the opposition between the West and the rest by showing how each seeming opposite has internalized and often phantasized the other. This procedure is important. It helps to bring out the ambivalences, equivocations, and contradictions in subjected populations (for example, in both demonizing and idolizing the West or aspects of it) that have to be worked through both internally and in relation to the dominant Western powers. Moreover, it highlights points of convergence or of beneficial interaction with 'the West' that groups in postcolonial societies might want to affirm in their own voice (for example, with respect to women's rights). It also points to the massive ambivalences, equivocations, and contradictions in the West (the civilizing mission, manifest destiny, the white man's burden, a place in the sun, and so forth) as well as indicating the more fruitful role of self-questioning, for example, in the critique of ethnocentrism, colonialism, and imperialism or in the attempt to introduce a strong dialogic dimension into disciplines such as anthropology and history whereby 'others' are indeed recognized as having voices that may challenge our assumptions and values, including

colonialism and postcolonialism that have posed problems for other programs.[8]

At present the exchanges between historians and literary critics or critical theorists may seem too limited or

---

those embodied in research practices. But the opposition – or even a nonbinary distinction – between the West and 'the rest' should also be the object of more thoroughgoing critique that, while recognizing the historical and current importance of such an opposition, nonetheless attempts to dismantle it and to develop newer concepts and institutions that provide different articulations of relations and open different possibilities of interaction. One limited initiative in this direction is the attempt to take the francophone out of area studies and include it in French studies – but in a nonimperial, nonassimilationist manner bound up with a basic rethinking and reconfiguration of French studies itself. This attempt should be related to a broader effort to rethink both ethnic studies programs and programs not seen as ethnic studies for the questionable reason that their objects are Western European (or originally from Western Europe) even if they address problems such as immigration and the nature of highly composite populations (such as those of France, Germany, or the United States). The investigation of globalization and its relation to nationalism, capitalism, and group identities provides one important basis for this broader effort. On the latter problem, see Bill Readings, *The University in Ruins* (Cambridge, Mass. and London, 1995), and my discussion of this book in 'The University in Ruins?' *Critical Inquiry* 25 (1998), 32–55. (Certain of the problems touched on in this note were addressed by my colleague, Naoki Sakai, in a lecture entitled 'Dislocation of the West: On the Status of the Humanities,' given at Cornell University on 2 February 1999.)

8 For approaches to French studies sensitive to these issues, see Kristin Ross, *Fast Cars, Clean Bodies: Decolonization and the Reordering of French Culture* (Cambridge, Mass., and London, 1995) and the contributions to *MLN* 112 (September, 1997): *Camus 2000*, ed. Marc Blanchard. See also Nelly Furman, 'French Studies: Back to the Future,' in the annual publication of the Modern Language Association, *Profession 1998*, 68–80. Furman stresses the role of a reconfigured French studies in furthering not only linguistic but what might be termed cross-cultural literacy or competence in learning to read the signifying practices of other cultures and the way they resemble or differ from those of one's own culture. (Cross-cultural literacy should be distinguished from the attempt, through unmediated identification, to become French or even *plus français que les français* – an attempt that produces the cultural 'resident alien' and typically rests on disimplication from one's own culture conjoined with uncritical embrace of all things French. I would nonetheless add that attempting to acquire a near-native-speaker's fluency

insufficiently challenging and thought-provoking.⁹ History remains to a significant extent an epistemologically conservative, highly professionalized discipline at times overly preoccupied with boundary maintenance as well as

---

(*not* to be identified with a Parisian accent) in French is, in my judgment, a *sine qua non* of a member of a French or French studies department or program.) The further development of French studies beyond a traditional 'language-and-literature' paradigm need not be centred on a delimited (and perforce exclusionary) idea of history or cultural studies. Both within French studies and between it and other disciplines or fields, one might well complement the attempt to arrive at a flexible, nondogmatic agreement on the curricular basics of cross-cultural literacy with cooperation in achieving such goals as expanding the field of inquiry (notably in the direction of the francophone), engaging more sustained or even different forms of dialogic exchange, posing revitalizing challenges to scholars and teachers as well as to students, creating newer forms of diversity, facilitating better combinations of methods (for example, close reading, critical theory, and meticulous historical – including archival – research), and perhaps generating more convincing modes of articulation among approaches. Ideally, the admininistrative issue of whether there should be a formal department (or at least program) of French Studies to replace or supplement existing units should not be seen in terms of departmental status as an end (or an anxiety-producing threat) in itself but settled on the basis of what best serves these larger goals – a question that may receive different answers in different contexts.

9 Advocates of French studies may be criticized (at times unfairly) both from a 'traditional' French-department perspective and from that of historians. Hence they may be treated as dilettantes by both historians and members of French departments. 'French-studies types' may not be able to quote Baudelaire by heart or know the colour of Emma's dress at her first meeting with Charles Bovary at *les Bertaux*. In other words, they may seem to lack the intimacy with closely read, indeed internalized texts that is the hallmark of members of a 'traditional' French department, including those employing poststructural modes of reading. Moreover, they may seem to want to move beyond the 'language-and-literature' paradigm, often in a historicist direction, without having the training and skills of the professional historian. See, for example, the unsympathetic, indeed harshly critical, review of the book often taken as the paradigm case of a French-studies approach, Kristin Ross's *Fast Cars, Clean Bodies*, by the historian Richard Kuisel in *The American Historical Review* 101 (1996), 859. Kuisel concludes by asserting: 'Ross spoils her study by indulging her imagination. Historians can ignore this book.' Ron Fantasia offers a more balanced assessment of the book's interest for

intellectual and disciplinary autonomy.[10] (If my experience in organizing and participating in events is typical – and I think it is – one concrete sign of this state of affairs is that relatively few historians, especially outside the subfield of intellectual and cultural history, are motivated to attend lectures and conferences that do not have a direct and obvious bearing on their own delimited research and teaching interests in history but might be argued to have broad, albeit at times controversial, humanistic import – including events that involve such widely known figures as Jacques Derrida, Jürgen Habermas, Fredric Jameson, Julia Kristeva, Claude Lanzmann, Cornel West, or Hayden White. This reluctance leads to only limited participation in the larger public sphere of the academy and is particularly evident with respect to forums or approaches involving critical theory even when it addresses historiographical problems.) Nonetheless, historians have undertaken critical investigations of the existing state and history of historiography either with an open-minded, at times transformative intent or with the preconceived goal of validating existing practices and warding off 'incur-

---

social scientists: 'Although not all the linkages or relationships are convincing, Ross's book is filled with provocative insights, and it provides a more engaging picture of French postwar modernization than does most other work on the subject. More importantly, this book will prod its readers to think widely across seemingly disparate fields – and for this reason needs to be read within ours' *Contemporary Sociology* 25 [1996], 156.

10 In these respects, history is curiously like analytic philosophy. The latter's strongest interdisciplinary connections are not with literary and visual studies (or history) but with fields such as cognitive psychology and possibly classics. In the American academy continental philosophy has to some extent migrated into intellectual history and areas of literary and cultural studies (notably German studies, French studies, and comparative literature).

sions' from other disciplines or approaches.[11] Some have even adopted techniques from literary criticism or seen critical theory as relevant to both historical self-understanding and practice; a few have either tried to reorient historiography or 'deconstruct' it in the interest of newer intellectual and institutional formations, for example, rhetorical studies that derive their primary inspiration from the work of literary critics.[12] The early Hayden White was a leading figure in the latter movement that was carried further (albeit in somewhat different directions) by his students Hans Kellner and Sande Cohen.[13] These initiatives have at times gone too far in assimilating history to rhetoric and poetics, especially when the latter are narrowly construed in terms of projective (or meaning-endowing) tropes or presumably fictive narrative structures, to the detriment of recognizing both a less restricted conception of rhetoric and the importance of truth claims and research in historiography on the level

---

11 See Keith Windschuttle, *The Killing of History: How a Discipline Is Being Murdered by Literary Critics and Social Theorists* (Paddington, NSW, 1996). For a more modulated account, which includes an appreciation of the contributions of other disciplines to historiography, see Peter Novick, *That Noble Dream: The 'Objectivity Question' and the American Historical Profession* (Cambridge, 1988), as well as the debates it has generated. See esp. J.H. Hexter, Linda Gordon, David Hollinger, Allan Megill, Peter Novick, and Dorothy Ross in *The American Historical Review* 96 (1991), 673–708.

12 For a broad survey of various initiatives in historiography, see the critical but sympathetic account of Robert Berkhofer, Jr, *Beyond the Great Story: History as Text and Discourse* (Cambridge, Mass., and London, 1995). Of course we cannot identify literary studies and critical theory, although the former has been an especially hospitable site for the latter.

13 See Hans Kellner, *Language and Historical Representation: Getting the Story Crooked* (Madison, Wisc., 1989), and Sande Cohen, *Historical Culture: On the Recoding of an Academic Discipline* (Berkeley, 1986). See also the essays included in Brian Fay, Philip Pomper, and Richard T. Vann eds., *History and Theory: Contemporary Readings* (Malden, Mass. and Oxford, 1998).

not only of references to events but also of larger narrative and interpretive or explanatory structures. More difficult to classify – or to apply in any unmediated manner – are complex, nuanced efforts to further self-understanding across disciplines and to elaborate a sustained interaction between historiography, literary studies, and critical theory that is both attuned to differently inflected problems of reading or interpretation and open to broader issues in the relation of signifying practices and disciplines.[14]

One intellectual challenge posed by figures such as Tocqueville and Foucault is that their work cannot be claimed by, or squarely situated in, any single discipline or department. In addition to the points made in the Introduction about their differential reception, I would observe that, with some notable exceptions in the case of critics concerned with the relations between history and literature

---

14 I would situate my own contributions in this category, at least in terms of their manifest intent and ambition. A qualified, historicized defence of hyperbole might be made in bringing into prominence considerations that are arguably underrepresented or downplayed in a discipline at a given point in its history. (Such underrepresentation was the position of a concern for even the broadest conception of rhetoric in historiography before the mid-1980s.) Moreover, hyperbole is especially defensible when it is explicitly framed as hyperbole and does not participate in an abstract movement of excess, obscure the problem of limits, or lead to an unchecked, systematic one-sidedness. On these issues, see the first chapter as well as references in it to my previous work, especially *History and Criticism* (Ithaca and London, 1985), chap. 1 ('Rhetoric and History'), and my early (1978) appreciation and critique of White's work in 'A Poetics of Historiography: Hayden White's *Tropics of Discourse*,' included in *Rethinking Intellectual History: Texts, Contexts, Language* (Ithaca and London, 1983), 72–83. See also my *Writing History, Writing Trauma* (forthcoming). For what I find to be a limited, rather theory-averse exchange about history and fiction, see the 'AHR Forum: Histories and Historical Fictions' that includes a presentation by Margaret Atwood and responses by Lynn Hunt, Jonathan D. Spence, and John Demos, *The American Historical Review* 103 (1998), 1502–29.

(for example, Stephen Bann, Lionel Gossman, and Linda Orr), literary critics (aside perhaps from the area of American studies) have not taken Tocqueville as a significant reference point. Literary critics' relative lack of interest in Tocqueville is unfortunate since the recent widespread turn to problems of social and political theory has at times been conjoined with an approach to these problems that may be too restricted because of the reliance on an overly circumscribed set of references – Foucault, Derrida, Lacoue-Labarthe, Jameson, Spivak, Laclau, and Mouffe being prominent among them. However important the contributions of these figures may be, basic thought about political and social theory, especially if it is concerned with crucial institutional and practical issues, must obviously be more thoroughly grounded in the tradition of classical theory as it informs the work of contemporary social and political theorists.[15] Tocqueville is a central figure in the tradition of political and social theory, and his work is particularly important for a re-evaluation of liberalism and democratic theory. This is especially the case if one believes (as I do) that the liberal tradition requires a rereading and selective recuperation, notably with respect to constitutionalism, minority rights, and related issues – issues that should be carefully distinguished from economic liberalism in terms of a capitalistic market economy. One may argue that important communitarian or qualified socialist initiatives be counterbalanced by political and social liberalism – including not only tolerance for but an affirmation of the value of

---

15 Even the very important *Feminists Theorize the Political*, ed. Judith Butler and Joan W. Scott (New York and London, 1992), not all of whose contributors are in departments of literature, lists in its index twenty-three references to Foucault, twenty-nine to Derrida, but none to Tocqueville.

certain differences – without defending all aspects of capitalism, although one may see a significant role for a market mechanism in a mixed economy.[16]

In contrast to Tocquevillle, Foucault has recently become a common reference point for literary critics as well as for other practitioners of humanistic and social science disciplines, including history, continental philosophy, and critical theory more generally. Texts such as *Discipline and Punish* or *The History of Sexuality* are more easily operationalized for research projects both in the history or sociology of disciplines and in the new-historicist reading of literary texts.[17] They are also most obviously available for articulation with other important critical-theoretical approaches, such as psychoanalysis and feminist criticism as well as social constructivism. In these respects, they are of continued importance and provide significant pointers for research and criticism even when one does not agree with all of their dimensions or emphases. Yet they may also be too readily assimilated into relatively standard attempts to conjoin history and literary studies – whether on the part of historians or literary critics – that often fall back on unproblematized notions of

---

16 One may also ask how ecological issues and animal rights may be accommodated in liberal and socialist perspectives – issues that had little explicit place in either Tocqueville or Foucault.

17 Relying on a non-Derridean conception of the text that identifies it with the written word rather than with the instituted trace in general, even Edward Said somewhat misleadingly writes: 'Derrida is concerned only with reading a text, and ... a text that is nothing more than what is in it for the reader ... Derrida's criticism moves us *into* the text, Foucault's *in* and *out*.' *The World, the Text, and the Critic* (Cambridge, Mass., 1983), 183. For a discussion of the failed 'dialogue' between *Annales* historians and Foucault (which the author himself also instantiates), see Gérard Noiriel, 'Foucault and History: The Lessons of a Disillusion,' *Journal of Modern History* 66 (1994), 547–68.

context as their means of articulation.[18] I have focused on Foucault's 'History of Madness' because of my belief that its importance has been underemphasized, especially in the recent past, and that it poses some of the greatest, at times most thought-provoking challenges to disciplinary assumptions and to the projects of reading and writing across the disciplines. It is a text that resists operationalization and, even when it prompts disagreement with certain of its tendencies, remains a source of renewed reflection about basic issues – notably those concerning boundary setting and maintenance – in history, literary criticism, and critical theory. Indeed disagreements with it may help us to clarify and better define our very understanding of these issues.

I have intimated that part of the problem in French studies is the relation between French departments and other areas of the university concerned with things French, including history departments. The traditional focus of French departments has been on literature and language; a more recent concern has been critical theory. A crucial question is whether and how French departments – without losing (indeed strengthening) the concern with critical theory (not in the abstract but especially in its bearing on specific problems of reading and

---

18 One of the most broadly informed, theoretically circumspect attempts to conjoin history and literary studies that makes limited use of new-historicist, Foucauldian work is Gabrielle Spiegel's. See her methodological essays, 'History, Historicism, and the Social Logic of the Text in the Middle Ages' (1990) and 'History and Postmodernism' (1992), in Keith Jenkins, *The Postmodern History Reader* (London and New York, 1997), 180–203, 260–73. See also the contestable use made of her earlier essay by Lawrence Stone, 'History and Postmodernism' (1991), *The Postmodern History Reader*, 255–9. I would also make special mention of the work of Ruth Leys, especially her forthcoming book that provides a critical genealogy of the concept of trauma.

research) – might be linked with more broad-based institutional units that combine the study of literature with the study of culture and history. Indeed, an important if not primary role for French departments in the recent past has been to serve as a conduit in the Anglo-American world for theoretical currents issuing from continental Europe and especially from metropolitan France. Among the more prominent have been structuralism, post-structuralism, deconstruction, and variants of feminism. The 1960s, 1970s, and 1980s witnessed the emergence of a remarkable series of critical theories that provided both the framework and the intellectual ferment in terms of which students of French literature and culture reread texts and even addressed broader interpretive issues. The situation in the 1990s might by contrast be seen as marked by a theoretical lull and a process of stocktaking that both reveal a flagging of interest or at least of enthusiasm and provide the occasion for new opportunities to rethink French studies. Among these opportunities is the possibility of a sustained, mutually provocative relation between history, critical theory, and literary studies as well as the departments that are their primary loci in the academy.

Although theoretical currents, with the partial exception of feminism, ethnic studies, and gay and lesbian studies, may no longer be impelled by the immediacy and dynamism that typified them in the recent past, one should not construe the critical activity they inspired as a mission that has been accomplished. Older approaches to French studies that were questioned by these currents have not disappeared, and it is still important to subject to scrutiny certain ideological assumptions those approaches at times harboured. Indeed certain assumptions may be regenerated in some contemporary, post-theoretical, if not atheoretical or even antitheoretical, conceptions of French studies.[19] These ideological assumptions include unproblematic identity (notably including both national and disciplinary identity), belief in basic or even unbroken historical continuity, and often blind gendering or racializing of terms or relations.[20]

---

19 Even certain contributions to the informative and valuable *French Cultural Studies*, ed. Jill Forbes and Michael Kelly (Oxford, 1995), manifest older tendencies in new garb by relying on contextualism as explanatory and providing little close, critical reading of texts and other phenomena. The approach of contributors at times resembles older, synoptic narrative forms of cultural history and tends to ignore the implications of recent critical theories for the study of culture and history. At the opposite end of the spectrum, Sandy Petrey's response to the spectre of French studies is thought-provoking in its defence of close reading and its antipathy to superficial forms of 'cultural studies,' but it is overly general in its dismissive reaction to attempts to broaden the field beyond the focus on elite literature. (See 'French Studies/Cultural Studies: Reciprocal Invigoration or Mutual Destruction?' in *The French Review* 68 [1995], 381–93.) Petrey signals snob appeal as one reason for students' earlier interest in things French, and he asserts that there is no distinctive reason to study France instead of other areas if one is interested in a far-ranging conception of culture. Both points may be admitted but not seen as convincing reasons for a negative reaction to a broad-based understanding of French studies, particularly one that is self-critical and insistently poses the question of reading. See also Petrey's related article, 'When Did Literature Stop Being Cultural?' in *Diacritics* 28 (1998), 12–22, where he reinforces his earlier expressed views. In his contribution to the special issue of *Diacritics*, Petry writes: 'My conviction is that productive transformations will come not through changing what we teach but changing how we teach it. The interdisciplinary orientation of cultural studies will infuse new life into French Studies only if our programs respect what gives them their strongest identity, their most influential research topics, and their greatest appeal to students, namely their definition as programs in language *and literature*. Literature continues to deserve the central place it has long occupied in French Studies because nothing else can give us the focus without which interdisciplinarity becomes another word for dilettantism' (22). The question is whether one can expand the focus without simply shifting it radically or blurring it.
20 For an insightful analysis of gendered assumptions in such otherwise 'progressive' figures as Miles Davis, W.E.B. DuBois, C.L.R. James, Leadbelly, and Paul Robeson, see Hazel Carby, *Race Men* (Cambridge, Mass., 1998). In certain ways, this study might serve as a model for work on related problems in

They may at times involve a stark opposition of practice to theory (for example, in historical research and writing) and denigrate the importance of theory in both creating a space for and critically testing (as well as being tested by) practice.[21] They may also rest on the historicist assumption that contextualizing a text or other phenomenon is not simply necessary for situating and critically analysing but fully adequate and explanatory in coming to terms with it.[22] But they may, on the contrary, also be guided by the neoformalist assumption that elite literature is autonomous and thus amenable to study in purely 'literary' terms that abstract it from its conditions of production, circulation, and reception. The question avoided by such complementary and mutually reinforcing assumptions is the manner in which prominent tendencies in recent critical theory may be fruitfully transformed, rather than repressed or denied, in the light of developments in the field. The latter are signs of a growing realization that students of French in general and members of French departments in particular face new challenges and opportunities. A vital question is how an active response to literature or other art forms – a response that

---

a field such as French studies. Carby's approach may be contrasted with that of Simone de Beauvoir who, on a certain level, may be argued to have reproduced the 'masculinist' prejudices of French culture evident in such important figures as Jean-Paul Sartre and Claude Lévi-Strauss. (See *The Second Sex*, trans. H.M. Parshley [New York, 1961].)

21 The denigration of theory and the preponderant or even exclusive valorization of practice often accompany the idea of history as a craft and the invidious distinction between the 'working' historian and his or her 'other' (who often remains unnamed).

22 Despite its value, Pierre Bourdieu's focus on the 'field' in the interpretation of literary texts may function to rehabilitate relatively unproblematic contextualism in another guise. See his *Rules of Art: Genesis and Structure of the Literary Field*, trans. Susan Emanuel (1992; Stanford, Cal., 1995).

engages literature and art as literature and art – may be articulated in a nonreductive fashion with informative and intellectually challenging modes of contextual or historical analysis that monitor response and keep it from going to the extreme of projective reprocessing, unsituated subjective impression, or narcissistic opacity (which may take condescending, 'in-group' form).[23] This question at the very least involves an understanding of how art

---

23 I have already indicated the possibility of a qualified defence of hyperbole. But the problems of extreme projection, subjective impressionism, and narcissistic opacity are especially pressing when one attempts to write the history – or more generally give an account – of experience. The turn to experience has been widespread in recent historiography (including the concern with memory), and perhaps its most prominent example in literary criticism is the movement towards autobiography (or perhaps auto-ethnography). Experience (or response) cannot be reduced to subjectivity, but subjectivity is an important dimension of experience (and an element of response). One problem is how to write a history or, more generally, give an account of subjectivity that is not itself simply subjective. Here a minimal problem is to elaborate one's own subjective experience into a more objective form that can convince – or at least engage in mutually critical dialogue with – others familiar with the material of the historical and critical applicability and cogency of an approach involving (but not necessarily confined to) subjective response. (I noted in Chapter 1 that such an undertaking requires a re-examination of the problem of empathy in understanding – empathy that is not tantamount to projective identification but instead involves recognition of and is open to the challenges posed by the other as other.) One criterion of success (albeit not the only one) is the ability to convince informed colleagues and interlocutors that a particular approach is indeed insightful and illuminating (or at the very least worth taking seriously) with respect to material under investigation. This demand is especially pressing if one takes neither the route of narrowly technical analysis nor that of straightforward contextualization that does not engage on any significant level the problem of inquiring into, and responding to, the object of study itself. Music is an area in which these problems arise with great acuteness, for music may be understood as an articulation of subjectivity whose historical and critical analysis is particularly challenging (especially if one does not simply fall back on a reliance on program notes, libretti, and comparable textual material but attempts to give music itself a crucial role in its interaction with this material).

may be argued to come to terms with historical pressures or opportunities and how it is in turn received, appropriated, read, used, and abused (notably including the manner in which it is discussed among members of a profession or discipline as well as the ways in which it is disseminated to students and a broader public).

I would like to draw attention to or recapitulate some of the newer challenges that are being posed to the field of French studies and whose implications for it are still being sorted out. These challenges do not amount to a laundry list insofar as they interact to form a constellation in which each problem or tendency requires coming to terms with the others.

First is the important movement or turn from the French to the francophone. Here we encounter intricate problems of colonialism and postcolonialism. We also confront the need for a far-reaching, fundamental reinscription and decentring of the metropole in the attempt to relate the familiar authors and topics of French literature to issues and writers in francophone areas and cultures as well as to less familiar, even 'noncanonical' dimensions of canonical authors and topics themselves. (Hence, for example, the attention paid recently to Flaubert's 'orientalism,' Baudelaire's experience of Creole culture, or Sartre's gendered language.)[24] In other words,

---

24 See, for example, the prognosticative, influential discussion of Flaubert in Edward Said, *Orientalism* (New York, 1978) as well as the discussion in Richard Terdiman, *Discourse/Counter-Discourse: The Theory and Practice of Symbolic Resistance in Nineteenth-Century France* (Ithaca and London, 1985). See also Françoise Lionnet, 'Reframing Baudelaire: Literary History, Biography, Postcolonial Theory, and Vernacular Languages,' in *Diacritics* 28 (1998), 63–85. On Sartre, see the early analyses in Margery Collins and Christine Pierce, 'Holes and Slime: Sexism in Sartre's Psychoanalysis,' in Carol C. Gould and Marx W. Wartofsky, eds, *Women and Philosophy: Toward a Theory of Liberation* (New York, 1976), 112–27, and Dominick LaCapra, *A Preface to Sartre* (Ithaca

we may have to question not only a reified canon but the very concept of canonicity, including the issue of how to justify paying special attention to certain texts or problems. Such inquiry implies the attempt to rethink the problem of textuality in its relations with a field of artifacts, discourses, and practices not restricted to literature although certainly not excluding it. This is a vast, difficult, even daunting undertaking that may require re-education in basic ways, insofar as the ability to investigate a novel set of problems was not part of our earlier formation. For certain forms of research and analysis, it may even require learning languages other than standard French and English, for example, Arabic (and its Maghrebi dialects), Tamazigh (the language of Berbers), or complex dialects, 'Creolizations,' and variations of French (including *joual* in French-speaking Canada). There is even a sense in which French literature – like all formerly national literatures – must become a form of comparative literature if it is to be understood in other than narrowly parochial and ideologically freighted terms. We are thus confronted with a task that goes well beyond the kind of formation traditionally required of teachers and students of French. Indeed it imposes demands even on younger scholars who

---

and London, 1978). For a more recent discussion, see Toril Moi, *Simone de Beauvoir: The Making of an Intellectual Woman* (Oxford and Cambridge, Mass., 1994). My discussion in Chapter 2 of certain dimensions of Tocqueville's thought, such as his views on Algeria, may also be seen in the light of recent emphases on less familiar dimensions of canonical authors related to the interest in the francophone. Foucault's writings would also repay study from this perspective. (His history of madness is of course Eurocentric in focus, but his approach might have implications for work on other regions. See, for example, Stephen Clingman, 'Beyond the Limit: The Social Relations of Madness in Southern African Fiction,' in Dominick LaCapra, ed., *The Bounds of Race: Perspectives on Hegemony and Resistance* (Ithaca and London, 1991), 231–54.)

are not content simply to apply prevalent modes of, say, deconstructive, Foucauldian, or Lacanian analysis to new topics or textual objects with the relatively anodyne admixture of a little historical background information culled from secondary sources. And it is a task that cannot be satisfied by the nonetheless necessary attempt to rethink on a theoretical level such concepts as historicity, context, translation, hybridization, and reference.

A second challenge is to come more cogently to terms with the demands of cross-disciplinarity that cannot be reduced to mere interdisciplinarity. As I have already suggested, by interdisciplinarity in its more limited sense I mean the addition or juxtaposition of two disciplines such as literary criticism and historiography. The typical site of interdisciplinarity is the team-taught course based on the mistaken assumption that if you take an empirically based, conventionally trained historian and a literary critic – preferably one with some degree of theoretical sophistication – and put them in the same room with a class for a semester, something significantly different and better will emerge – that one plus one will at least equal two. But without both learning thoroughly – and rearticulating some of – the presuppositions and assumptions of disciplines, what tends to emerge may be less than two and perhaps even less than one.

Cross-disciplinarity is different from additive interdisciplinarity in that it explores problems that cut across existing disciplines, and it may lead to an unsettling and rearticulation of disciplinary lines, possibly even giving rise to newer objects of study and disciplinary formations, or at least to newer emphases, concentrations, and specializations. Obvious but demanding types of cross-disciplinary problems involve the interactions of texts, intertexts, and contexts, of scholarship on unmarked or 'straight' topics and attempts to 'queer' the canon, and of close reading and historical understanding or sociocultural analysis. At the very least, taking these problems seriously means taking the opening to philosophy that has characterized recent critical theory and extending that opening to other texts and discursive practices.[25] History as a consequence cannot be restricted to the history of philosophy or of metaphysics, although the relation of this history to other problems is important and, as Jacques Derrida has taught us, its role and its results easily pass unperceived.[26]

A third challenge involves the movement or expansion of the field of interest from literature to culture, society, and history, including francophone cultures, societies, and histories. With this shift the civilization course is no longer a makeshift delegated to an overly gullible, unguardedly good-natured, insufficiently high-powered, or otherwise theory-impaired colleague. It becomes a truly demanding undertaking that epitomizes the entire problem of expanding the field from a study of literature

---

25 Here the closest affinities of members of French departments will probably be with intellectual and cultural historians who take the problems of close reading and textuality seriously rather than simply subsuming them under (or taking texts or artifacts merely as instantiating evidence for) broader categories, currents, and contexts such as individualism, subjectivity, experience, nationalism, globalization, and so forth. The latter tendency remains the emphasis of most historians. The point may be not to eliminate different emphases (or the skills they require) but to bring them into more sustained and mutually thought-provoking interaction and to encourage their fruitful articulation.

26 Derrida argues that the assumptions most explicit in the work of noted philosophers often tend to operate in more implicit and unexamined ways in other areas, such as the social sciences or even ordinary language. See, for example, 'Structure, Sign, and Play in the Discourse of the Human Sciences,' in *Writing and Difference*, trans. with an intro. and additional notes by Alan Bass (1967; Chicago, 1978), 278–94.

in the restricted sense to a concern with culture in a broader anthropological, theoretical, and historical sense. And it requires sustained, mutually challenging interaction between members of departments of literature, history, and other relevant humanistic and social science disciplines. In other words the civilization course or text becomes an exemplary site for an attempt to rearticulate and reframe the field of French studies and critically to explore the demanding problem of the interaction among theory, criticism, historiography, ethnography, and the study of literature or other forms of art – a problem that may deceptively be taken as a solution and called cultural studies.[27] This move to a broader conception of

---

27 Perhaps the most prominent form of cultural studies in the Anglo-American academic world stemmed from the so-called Birmingham school that included such important figures as E.P. Thompson, Raymond Williams, and Richard Hoggart. It justifiably stressed the importance of popular culture as well as the integration of cultural and social analysis, and its orientation was Marxist or at least leftist. For some practitioners in the United States, it represents the *echt* tradition in relation to which more eclectic forms are declensions. See, for example, the Introduction to Lawrence Grossberg, Cary Nelson, and Paula Treichler, *Cultural Studies* (New York, 1992) – a book that served for a while as the 'bible' of cultural studies. (Its selections do not all conform to the Birmingham-school paradigm.) Anglo-American cultural studies has at times been characterized by monolingualism, presentism, a rather indiscriminate valorization of popular culture (often conflated with mass culture), a conception of close reading as optional but not necessary for cultural studies, and a relative lack of interest in 'high' culture, cross-cultural interaction and comparison, or theoretical self-reflection. (It should be noted, however, that the critique of presentism need not lead to a defence of a study of the past in and for itself. It should be related to a combination of objective reconstruction and dialogical exchange that provides the genealogy of present discourses and practices, thereby placing one in a more informed position to critically appraise and, if warranted, attempt to change them.) Lauren Berlant, however, cautions against oversimplified conceptions of cultural studies and warns of a backlash motivated by 'a displaced expression of discomfort with work on contemporary culture' 'Collegiality, Crisis, and Cultural Studies,' in *Profession 1998*, 107. She offers this characterization of cultural studies that brings out its ambitiousness, diffuse-

culture, including popular and mass culture, does not imply an abandonment of practices of careful, close reading of literary texts and artifacts of 'high' culture. Nor does it justify a facile identification of all popular or even mass culture with kitsch or *Gebrauchkunst* – an identification that obscures both the value and complexity of certain kinds (or aspects) of popular (even mass) culture and the role of kitsch or non-aesethetic concerns (such as self-serving prestige, cachet, or symbolic capital) with respect to 'high' culture and fine art. This move does, however, entail an interest in the rhetorical analysis of nonfictional texts, a less restrictive idea of the literary and its interaction with the nonliterary, and a rethinking of what is required of close reading, especially in relating a text to a

---

ness, and utopian hope: 'Dedicated to engaging with and writing the history of the present, cultural studies seeks to address and explicate the geopolitical specificity of cultural forms and practices; to describe not only the hierarchical mechanisms that produce identities of all kinds but also the contexts for agential practice, resistance, and experience articulated around those mechanisms; to track in particular peoples' ordinary lives the effects of discursive and institutional practices of domination, subordination, and hegemony; to appraise technologies of intimacy, longing, aversion, and ecstasy; and to historicize political spaces and forms like bodies, schools, cities, nations, and transnational corporations' (106). An ambitious book, with certain affinities to cultural studies, that might (if properly supplemented, especially for the recent past) be considered as a candidate for a textbook in courses in modern French studies – a book that deserves to be translated and better known – is Maurice Crubellier, *Histoire culturelle de la France XIXe–XXe siècle* (Paris, 1974). For initiatives related to French studies, see also Denis Hollier, ed., *A New History of French Literature*, (Cambridge, Mass. and London, 1989), Lawrence D. Kritzman, ed., *Auschwitz and After: Race, Culture, and 'the Jewish Question' in France* (New York and London, 1995); H.R. Kedward and Nancy Wood, eds., *The Liberation of France: Image and Event* (Oxford and Washington, D.C., 1995); and Jean-Joseph Goux and Philip R. Wood, eds., *Terror and Consensus: Vicissitudes of French Thought* (Stanford, Cal., 1998). For some critical responses to cultural studies, see the contributions to *MLN* 112 (April 1997): *Cultural Studies, Ideologies*, ed. Werner Hamacher, Matt Hartman, and Jan Mieszkowski.

larger field of discursive and nondiscursive forces both in the past and in the present. No doubt the attempt to combine close reading with broader sociocultural and historical analysis brings the risk of mutual disruption as well as the hope of articulation between these practices. But disruption may itself be instructive in that it questions certain overly choreographed or patterned practices (for example, what are by now deconstructive, Foucauldian, or Lacanian set pieces or even finger exercises) and enables a clearer if disconcerting awareness of the limits of practices as well as of difficulties in the effort to combine them cogently. It also reveals the limitations of conventional narratives that stylistically produce harmonizing or normalizing effects, especially when such narratives are addressed to crisis-ridden, indeed traumatic occurrences. It may indicate the need to allow trauma to register in our accounts of certain problems as well as to engage the difficult issue of how to work through such problems in a manner that neither blindly repeats them nor blandly reinstates 'reasonableness' (or the pleasure principle) by deceptively smoothing over asperities and denying difficulty. Moreover, the very interaction between articulation and mutual disruption in the relation of practices, such as close reading and sociocultural or historical analysis, is the challenging dynamic of any newer undertaking that is not indentured to premature codification or totalizing myths and methodologies (including conventional, harmonizing, pleasure-bearing, closure-seeking narrative).[28]

---

28 It should go without saying that not all narrative is conventional or fetishistic in the sense of denying the possibly traumatic nature of the events that called it into existence. The question is the extent to which narrative in historiography, especially when it avoids an encounter with theoretical problems and seeks a premature (re)turn to the 'pleasure principle' or even an 'upbeat' ending, tends to be conventional and to overly mitigate, repress, or

It is also a reason why a prevalent mode of recent discourse is the exploratory critical essay, with important books often being collections of essays.[29]

---

deny difficulties in representation that are especially acute with respect to extreme, traumatic events. It is significant that Martin Broszat, in arguing for an attention to certain aspects of daily life (*Alltagsgeschichte*) during the Nazi period that presumably would more fully historicize and contextualize the Holocaust, was concerned with the fact that a focus on the Nazi genocide blocked 'the pleasure in historical narration' (*die Lust am geschichtlichen Erzählen*). See his '*Plädoyer für eine Historisierung des Nationalsozialismus*,' *Merkur* 39 (1985), 375, as well as the exchange of letters between Broszat and Saul Friedlander (*New German Critique* 44 [1988], 85–126) and the discussion in Eric L. Santner, 'History Beyond the Pleasure Principle,' in Saul Friedlander, ed., *Probing the Limits of Representation: Nazism and the Final Solution*' (Cambridge, Mass. and London, 1992), esp. 148–9.

29 I am not advocating incoherent mixtures of types of assertion or a freewheeling slippage in discursive registers, for example, between the metaphysical (or meta-metaphysical) and the historical, as sometimes occurs in deconstructive approaches to events such as the Holocaust or in 'trauma theory' when a historically specific limit-event or trauma is subsumed under, or construed as a mere instance of, a general or structural condition (such as the 'wounding' aporia, 'originary' violence, the traumatizing encounter with the 'real,' or an implication in an unresolvable linguistic predicament). Slippage at least threatens to occur, for example, when Derrida, commenting on the significance of the date in Paul Celan's poetry, makes an abrupt or unmediated passage to the aporia between the singular and its iteration or repetition, thus identifying the wound as the seemingly universal effacement of singularity in the aporetic relation: 'Given that all experience is the experience of a singularity and thus is the desire to keep this singularity as such, the "as such" of the singularity, that is, what permits one to keep it as what it is, this is what effaces it right away. And this wound or this pain of the effacing in memory itself, in the gathering-up of memory, is wounding, it is a pain rewakened in itself; the poetic in Paul Celan is also the thing of this pain.' 'Passages – from Traumatism to Promise,' in Jacques Derrida, *Points ... Interviews, 1974–1994*, ed. Elisabeth Weber, trans. Peggy Kamuf and others (1992; Stanford, Cal., 1995), 378. (A point that tends to be blunted in Derrida's reflection is that 20 January – a date on which Celan insisted – was the date of the Wannsee conference at which plans for the 'final solution' were finalized.) One may argue that there is an important nexus among trauma, aporia, and unworked-through problems, but the point then becomes not simply to universalize (and etherealize) or compulsively repeat this nexus but to relate its transhistorical conditions to an attempt to specify its histori-

The attempt to combine close reading with broader sociocultural and historical analysis also requires the self-critical attempt to acquire perspective on, and provide genealogies of, current theoretical orientations that are sometimes taught as a primary language, applied indiscriminately as universal solvents, and related to earlier texts or theories in a highly selective, overly participatory, and even projective manner. Taking seriously a theoretical orientation (such as deconstruction, psychoanalysis, or Foucauldian analysis) means working to some extent within its terms, but one may have critical distance from those terms without simply objectifying them or believing they are totally explicable through contextualization. Indeed, acquiring some perspective on an orientation may lead to its redirection or supplementation in order to account better for ignored or marginalized issues. Here, as one significant example among others, we may point to what was until recently a very restricted relationship to Georges Bataille in both Derridean deconstruction and Foucauldian analysis.[30] In Derrida's essay on Bataille, 'From a Restricted to a General Economy,' the focus is on the critique of Hegel, while in Foucault's 'Preface to

---

cal and poetic insistence and come to terms with it. (One may also argue that all experience is not the experience of a singularity but involves the role of templates that adapt or mold the singular to types and thus render it memorable, although this process is possibly what is referred to by Derrida's elusive formulation concerning the immediate effacement of singularity.) The critical role of historical inquiry is to test public memory and prevent the process of adaptation from going to the point of unacceptable distortion, for example, that of Holocaust negationists or 'revisionists.' See also notes 42 and 51, below, as well as the discussions in the principal text to which they refer.

30 Steven Ungar has tried to raise questions concerning the relationship to Blanchot in recent French thought. See his *Scandal & Aftereffect: Blanchot and France since 1930* (Minneapolis, Minn., 1995).

Transgression,' Bataille becomes a pretext for a dithyrambic yet disconcertingly abstract paean to excess or transgressive thought at the limit of language in what seems to be a displaced supplement to the *Histoire de la folie*.[31] The relation to Bataille is one important instance of the larger problem involving the reworking by recent theoretical tendencies of the canon of French literature and culture, including the demotion or exclusion of certain authors (such as Jean-Paul Sartre or Albert Camus, not to mention an earlier figure such as Tocqueville) and the promotion of others (such as Bataille or Maurice Blanchot). It is also an indication of the relation of recent theory to politics – a relation that has, until recently, often been allusive and indirect.[32]

---

31 See Jacques Derrida, *Writing and Difference*, 251–77, and Michel Foucault, *Language, Counter-Memory, Practice: Selected Essays and Interviews*, ed. with an intro. by Donald F. Bouchard, trans. Donald F. Bouchard and Sherry Simon (1963; Ithaca and London, 1977), 29–52.

32 See the attempt to counteract this tendency and to link post-structuralism with historical and political analysis in David Carroll, *French Literary Fascism: Nationalism, Anti-Semitism, and the Ideology of Culture* (Princeton, N.J., 1995). See also Richard Beardsworth, *Derrida and the Political* (London and New York, 1996) where the political import of Derrida's work is seen primarily in the spectral terms of keeping faith with the aporia and with the radical promise of otherness. Here the political threatens to become an endlessly suspensive Messianic gesture in which one seems able only to reject positions and not provide any guidance – however tentative and undogmatic – concerning more desirable options, particularly with respect to institutions. For a sympathetic yet critical appreciation of Derrida's *Spectres of Marx: The State of the Debt, the Work of Mourning, and the New International* (1993; New York and London, 1994), which points to the deficiencies of Derrida's economic, social, and political analyses, see Moishe Postone's essay-review in *History and Theory* 37 (October 1998), 370–88. For a critique of post-structuralism, including deconstruction, from a perspective close to that of Habermas, see Peter Dews, *Logics of Disintegration: Post-Structuralist Thought and the Claims of Critical Theory* (London and New York, 1987). For a more sympathetic critique, see Peter Starr, *Logics of Failed Revolt: French Theory After May '68* (Stanford, Cal., 1995). See also Jürgen Habermas, *The Philosophical Discourse of Modernity* (1985; Cambridge, Mass., 1987), chap. 7. For a recent

In neither Derrida's nor Foucault's essays is there a sustained confrontation with the explicitly political dimensions of Bataille's thought, including his complex and shifting attempt to come to terms with fascism. This deficit may be symptomatic of the widespread avoidance, at least until relatively recently, of a significant engagement with Nazism, fascism, and the Vichy regime in both French critical theory and the historiography of the *Annales* school. With the partial exception of Lyotard, one by and large looks in vain for this engagement in the series of French thinkers who helped shape the approach to problems in our French departments – and to the names of Derrida and Foucault, one may add those of Lévi-Strauss, Lacan, Barthes, Girard, and Kristeva (*Pouvoirs d'horreur* notwithstanding). Indeed, when *Pouvoirs d'horreur* is reread today, what seems most striking is the aestheticizing and perhaps even apologetic approach it takes to Céline's anti-Semitic and *fascisant* tendencies, whose treatment is, in any case, largely subordinated –

---

critique, see Gillian Rose, *Mourning Becomes the Law: Philosophy and Representation* (Cambridge and New York, 1996). Rose writes: 'Post-modernism in its renunciation of reason, power, and truth identifies itself as a process of endless mourning, lamenting the loss of securities which, on its own argument, were none such. Yet this everlasting melancholia accurately monitors the refusal to let go, which I express in the phrase describing post-modernism as "despairing rationalism without reason." One recent ironic aphorism for this static condition between desire for presence and acceptance of absence occurs in an interview by Derrida: "I mourn, therefore I am"' (12). I do not agree with all aspects of Rose's analysis and critique, but I recognize the force of her concern about an insistence on impossible mourning that continually loops back into inconsolable melancholy, thereby providing little room for even limited processes (including political processes) of working through problems. See the independently developed discussion of mourning and melancholy in my *Representing the Holocaust: History, Theory, Trauma* (Ithaca and London, 1994), *History and Memory after Auschwitz* (Ithaca and London, 1998), and *Writing History, Writing Trauma* (forthcoming).

rather than problematically related – to stylistic considerations.³³ One also wonders why Foucault did not even attempt to relate fascism and Nazism to the argument of his history of madness, especially in light of his insistent valorization of a cosmic and tragic world in contrast to what he saw as the domination of one-sided rationality and moralizing normalization in modernity, with more disconcerting forces confined to an underground inhabited only by isolated, towering thinkers and writers such as Nietzsche, Hölderlin, and Artaud. In one prominent place Foucault did refer to fascism – his preface to *Anti-Oedipus* – it is in the extremely polemical and indiscriminate sense prevalent in the late sixties, a sense that lacks historical specificity.³⁴ A more critical confrontation with

---

33 See Julia Kristeva, *Pouvoirs d'horreur: Essai sur l'abjection* (Paris, 1980), trans. as *Powers of Horror: An Essay on Abjection* by Leon S. Roudiez (New York, 1982). See page 160 of the French edition, where Kristeva asserts that Céline's 'ambivalent, derisory adherence to Nazism is inexplicable [l'adhésion, elle-même ambivalente, dérisoire, au nazisme ne s'explique pas]' and that his anti-Semitism is derived from a biographical need for identity (rather than, say, ideological commitment related to his textual practice, including his penchant for hyperbole and scatological invective).

34 Gilles Deleuze and Félix Guattari, *Anti-Oedipus: Capitalism and Schizophrenia*, trans. Robert Hurley, Mark Seem, and Helen R. Lane with a preface by Michel Foucault (1972; Minneapolis, Minn., 1983), xiii. Foucault's brief analysis of Nazism in the first volume of *The History of Sexuality* is more pointed and thought-provoking: 'Nazism was doubtless the most cunning and the most naïve (and the former because of the latter) combination of the fantasies of blood and the paroxysms of a disciplinary power. A eugenic ordering of society, with all that implied in the way of extension and intensification of micro-powers, in the guise of an unrestricted state control (*étatisation*), was accompanied by the oneiric exaltation of a superior blood, the latter implied both the systematic genocide of others and the risk of exposing oneself to a total sacrifice. It is an irony of history that the Hitlerite politics of sex remained an insignificant practice while the blood myth was transformed into the greatest blood bath in recent memory' (*The History of Sexuality*, vol. I, trans. Robert Hurley [1976; New York, 1980], 149–50). The allusion to fantasy, dream, and myth in the Nazi genocide might be related

fascist dimensions of the past seems to have arrived belatedly – in fact, at a time when it may unfortunately have functioned (and may continue to function) to some extent as a diversion from the equally pressing and more immediate demands of working through problems of colonialism and postcolonialism, notably with respect to Algeria.

Thus far I have referred to the francophone, cross-disciplinarity, and the sociocultural. A fourth challenge is posed by the need for specificity in relating interacting disciplines and critical theory to problems and phenomena. One frequent tendency in recent theory has been an emphasis on self-referentiality or on a meta-level of analysis that generates its own complexities and aporias and seems to defer, denigrate, or even dismiss as regional or relatively inconsequential any more specific engagement with history, institutions, and politics. When historical issues, past contexts, or particular social or political problems are discussed, the result is at times an unmodulated indirectness and allusiveness that has a suggestive role in the treatment of literature and art but may be of more limited value in other areas.[35] There may also be a rela-

---

to a ritual anxiety about contamination by the other and a quasi-sacrificial quest for purification and redemption through violence. In the last chapter, I noted the difficulties with respect to normative issues in many of Foucault's principal texts. Although his later texts do not resolve these difficulties, there are pronounced ethical and political concerns in Foucault's *Use of Pleasure: The History of Sexuality Volume Two* (1984; New York, 1986) and *The Care of the Self: The History of Sexuality Volume Three* (1984; New York, 1986), as well as in occasional pieces. See, for example, *Politics, Philosophy, Culture: Interviews and Other Writings 1977–1984*, ed. with an intro. by Lawrence D. Kritzman (London and New York, 1988). The political motif is pervasive in Derrida, *Points ... Interviews, 1974–1994*.

35 I think relatively unmodulated allusiveness and indirectness are at times problems in the writing of Derrida and those influenced by, or emulating, him.

tively unchecked projective reprocessing or active rewriting of these issues, contexts, and problems in which the justifiable desire to redeem from them that which we now deem questionworthy for us is not countered by a sensitivity to the voices and concerns of the past or of other cultures and the ways in which they may pose genuine challenges to us and our concerns.[36] The deconstruction of metaphysics has in this sense often remained within a meta-metaphysical orbit. This mode of thought involves a recurrent confrontation with the undecidable, the aporetic, the abyssal, the unnamable, the un(re)presentable, the abject, the traumatic, or the 'real' – more generally with that which delimits any desire for totalization or adequacy and may disorient any quest for meaning and significance.[37] There is an urgency or 'appeal' (*appel*) in this approach that should not be dismissed or denied, especially in its sustained concern for the residual, marginal, abjected, or excluded. But there is a major problem when it becomes prepossessing or obsessive to the point

---

36 I argued earlier that Foucault's *Histoire de la folie* is equivocal in this respect. In it the narrator undergoes the threat and temptation of 'madness' and at times speaks or writes in an internally dialogized voice, as the broken dialogue between reason and unreason is evoked, acted out, and to some extent worked over if not worked through. But the dialogization tends to remain internal, and the difference of the other as a distinct other is not recognized, for example, through the provision of quotations and commentaries. And (as noted earlier) at times one even suspects the genesis of a new monologism that is internally split or 'schizoid' but involuted and not responsive to the voices of others – a monologism that is most disturbing and forceful in an abyssal, hyperbolic, involuted, self-consuming, 'sublimely' nonsensical form of writing.

37 This mode of analysis has been prevalent in post-structural literary criticism. To a significant extent it has been displaced into recent trauma theory, at times in challenging and thought-provoking ways. It has also been subjected to forceful criticism by figures as diverse as René Girard, Jürgen Habermas, Fredric Jameson, and Edward Said.

of displacing or devaluing other problems that can neither be fully assimilated to nor assimilate it. When the extreme point of preoccupation or even of obsessive fixation is reached, the results are dubious and the outcome may not be theory but theoreticism – that is to say, theory that feeds primarily if not exclusively on itself and ideologically reprocesses its objects without being tested or pointedly questioned by them. In theoreticism, theory is not simply ahistorical but actively, at times quasi-transcendentally, distanced from history and prone to a misleadingly abstract construction or redefinition of it – say, as undecidability, aporia, radical contingency, pure performativity, 'originary' violence, trauma, movement of the material signifier, or missed encounter with the 'real.' (This redefinition may, of course, paradoxically present itself as determining the 'authentically' historical.) Specific historical configurations may be reduced to mere illustrations or contingent, regional instances of massive, world-historical or transhistorical forces that are presumably disclosed by – as well as inscribed in – the movement of theory itself.[38]

---

38 Here one may juxtapose the enigmatic, pyrotechnic concluding lines of Derrida's essay on Bataille and Foucault's *Histoire de la folie*: 'Thus, there is the *vulgar* tissue of absolute knowledge and the mortal opening of an *eye*. A text and a vision. The servility of meaning and the awakening to death. A minor writing and a major illumination. / From one to the other, totally other, a certain text. Which in silence traces the structure of the eye, sketches the opening, ventures to contrive "absolute rending," absolutely rends its own tissue once more become "solid" and servile in once more having been read' (Jacques Derrida, *Writing and Difference*, 276–7). 'Ruse and new triumph of madnesss: the world which believed it could measure madness, justify it through psychology, must justify itself before madness, since in its effort and its debates, it measures itself by the excess [*démesure*] of works such as those of Nietzsche, Van Gogh, Artaud. And nothing in itself, especially nothing it is able to know about madness, assures the world that it is justified by these works of madness' (Michel Foucault, *Histoire de la folie à*

As I intimated, we cannot dismiss the foregoing features insofar as they are components of thought insistently engaged with the problem of its own limits, but we can raise questions about – or even contest – their dominance or obsessive role and try to counteract them in significant ways. I find these features to be quite prevalent in the relatively recent past – for example, in somewhat different ways in *aspects* (I strongly emphasize 'aspects') of the work of Jean-François Lyotard, Paul de Man, Jacques Derrida, and recent 'trauma theorists' (notably Shoshana Felman).[39] (His undeniable qualities notwithstanding, Slavoj Žižek's recent overnight success and the intense spate of rather uncritical Žižekomania are in part symptoms of the prevalence of these features.) All of the above-mentioned figures or tendencies have, to a greater or lesser extent, been important in the formation of current French studies, and the rethinking of the latter may well require a careful, discriminating critique of them that does not simply exclude them from new canons or modes of interpretation and eliminate their more cogent or genuinely thought-provoking dimensions. Even more inaccurate would be the inference that the upshot of my comments is either an indiscriminate, reductive contextualism or a

---

l'âge classique [1961; Paris, 1972], 557). These passages warrant close reading in terms of their situation and role in the texts in question, but they also convey a sense of rather unmoored theoretical movement or the submergence of the historical in the transhistorical or world-historical.

39 In the last chapter, I discussed such features in Foucault's thought. But certain aspects of *Histoire de la folie*, conjoined with Foucault's turn to genealogy and archaeology, renew our conception of critical historical inquiry, especially in the excavation of contemporary assumptions that are rendered problematic through a reconstruction of their contingent origins and displacements over time. Moreover, Foucault's insistence on the interaction of historical inquiry and critical thought counteracts the conventionalization of historiography and its separation from sustained theoretical reflection.

carte-blanche defence of an accessible, common-sensical, occasionally uplifting, complacent outlook that inveighs against stylistic difficulty, dismisses recent critical theory as obscurantist or nihilistic, and reverts to conventional procedures of inquiry or even to a born-again positivism. Indeed the problem, in my judgment, is to combine a strong defence of critical theory with a selective, tentative, and nondismissive analysis and critique of certain questionable features (such as theoreticism or a general dismissal of liberalism and humanism). In the present context I shall simply discuss briefly certain figures or tendencies I have mentioned – a discussion intended as little more than an inadequate provocation and an invitation to further debate.

Lyotard's *Le Différend* constituted a forceful challenge at the time it appeared, notably with respect to Auschwitz and all that it entailed.[40] Moreover, one may recognize the value of notions such as nomadism, hybridity, and diasporic movement, developed by Lyotard and others, such as Deleuze and Guattari, especially when the challenge they pose to assertions of pure identity, integralism, and ethnic or national rootedness does not eventuate in indiscriminate disdain for group solidarities or an equally indiscriminate celebration of difference, hybridization, and nomadism.[41] Especially noteworthy are the argu-

---

40 Jean-François Lyotard, *The Differend: Phrases in Dispute*, trans. Georges Van Den Abbeele (1983; Minneapolis, Minn., 1988).
41 On these problems, see Paul Gilroy, *The Black Atlantic: Modernity and Double Consciousness* (Cambridge, Mass., 1993). Despite its theoretical limitations in rethinking basic concepts and its propensity at times to rely on the notion that a term (such as 'double consciousness') may solve problems rather than indicate their insistence, Gilroy's analysis serves as a welcome reminder that inquiry cannot be focused on literature alone or on texts in the literal sense. He brings out the importance of music in 'black' cultures – an importance that can be attributed to other cultural forms and signifying practices as

ments (prominent in Lyotard) that what remains to be 'phrased' always exceeds what can at any time be put into language and that the absolute is radically transcendent or barred from access and thus cannot be realized or directly represented. (A comparable move may be found in Lacan's 'barring' of the Other or Derrida's critique of the transcendental signified.) These arguments gain in force when they do not lead in their turn to an exclusive aesthetic of the sublime, an overblown dismissal of all representation, or an 'all-or-nothing' logic that remains repeatedly suspended between an impossible desire for the absolute and a dismissive or perfunctory idea of sublunar possibilities in history and social life. Moreover, the valid insistence on the dangerous allure of the desire for totalization should not induce a view of institutions as precipitates of the evil demon; it should rather assist in posing the problem of the possibilities of institutions as sites of normatively guided life in common as well as their limitations with respect to demands they cannot fulfil.

The more dubious sides of Lyotard's reformulation of Kant and his stress on the un(re)presentable and the sublime become apparent in his *Heidegger and 'the jews.'*[42] In it he tends to turn away from specificity and to evacuate history by construing the Holocaust as a total caesura or trauma in which everyone (victims, witnesses, perpetra-

---

well. Gilroy stresses the interaction among American, European, African, and other sociocultural forces in the figures he discusses. For example, he criticizes a narrowly literary or American-centred treatment of Richard Wright and notes in passing: 'What would it mean to read Wright intertextually with Genet, Beauvoir, Sartre, and the other Parisians with whom he was in dialogue?' (186).

42 Jean-François Lyotard, *Heidegger and 'the jews,'* trans. Andreas Michel and Mark S. Roberts, foreword by David Carroll (1988; Minneapolis, Minn., 1990).

tors, revisionists, those born later) seems to be reduced to an ultimately levelling silence. He even tends to identify the (lower-case) 'jews' with a hyperbolic '(an)aesthetics' of the sublime and his own postmodern understanding of its analogues or accompaniments: trauma, *écriture*, alterity, nomadism, the un(re)presentable, *Nachträglichkeit*, not-forgetting-there-is-the-Forgotten, and so forth. To the extent that actual Jews are at issue in the account, it is only in a dehistoricized and oversimplified manner that generalizes a limited understanding of the Diaspora and discounts such phenomena as Zionism. Jews lose their own history in order to become the pretext for a paradigm of the nomadic outsider in general. And the (lower-case) 'jews' tend to become mere markers for postmodern motifs. Lyotard even runs the risk of unintentionally repeating in his own voice the Nazi project of purveying stereotypes of Jews as antiaesthetic, ugly, nomadic, rootless, and so forth, but now valorizations are reversed so that what was negative becomes positive or at least affirmative as the un(re)presentable. In the process Auschwitz tends to become converted into a decathected or affectless paradigm of the 'differend' that subverts speculative dialectics and representational aesthetics – in brief, a trope or Trojan Horse for postmodernism in Lyotard's understanding of it.

Lyotard thus proffers his version of trauma theory in which victimization tends to be rashly generalized, representation demonized, and history confounded with a rather indiscriminate notion of trauma.[43] Such a view tends to obviate a more careful and differentiated

---

43 Shoshana Felman develops a version of trauma theory in her contributions to the book she co-authored with Dori Laub, M.D., *Testimony: Crises of Witnessing in Literature, Psychoanalysis, and History* (New York, 1992). A somewhat different inflection is found in Cathy Caruth, *Unclaimed Experience: Trauma, Narrative, and History* (Baltimore and London, 1996).

account of these problems. Moreover, there is something misleading if not ludicrous in the prevalent idea that the basic problem with fascism and Nazism was dialectical sublation, totalization, and an aesthetic ideology, particularly when the latter are not convincingly related to other factors that may at times complicate their role. A desire for totality and for beautiful wholeness (or a well-ordered society on the model of a classical garden) did play an important role in Nazi ideology. But it was not the only – or even at times the most active – component of that ideology. At the very least, it was complicated and counteracted by other factors. Among these factors, I would mention ritual and deranged sacrificial forces as well as the role of a negative sublime, a desire for unheard-of transgression, and a fascination with violence and death that shatter totality and considerations of beauty – factors that were at play in certain versions of fascism and Nazism. (Heinrich Himmler's 1943 speech at Posen, delivered to upper-level SS officers, may be taken as a *locus classicus* for the role of these factors.)[44]

Whatever one may argue about his particular analyses, the following comments of de Man lend themselves to theoreticism:

> Literary theory can be said to come into being when the approach to literary texts is no longer based on non-linguistic, that is to say historical and aesthetic, considerations or, to put it somewhat less crudely, when the object of discussion is no longer the meaning or value but the modalities of production and of reception of meaning and of value prior to their establishment the implication

---

44 On these issues, see my *Representing the Holocaust: History, Theory, Trauma* and *History and Memory after Auschwitz*. See also James M. Glass, '*Life Unworthy of Life*' (New York, 1997).

being that this establishment is problematic enough to require an autonomous discipline of critical investigation to consider its possibility and its status ... If these difficulties are indeed an integral part of the problem then they will have to be, to some extent, a-historical in the temporal sense of the term ... Such difficulties can be read in the text of literary theory of all times, at whatever historical moment one wishes to select ... Nothing can overcome the resistance to theory since theory is itself this resistance.[45]

One may well try to argue for a different understanding of temporality in terms of displacement that is conflated neither with teleology nor with sheer chronology, and much in de Man is of great assistance in this attempt. One may also affirm both the value of resisting reductive contextualism and the importance of stressing philosophical concerns. But it is difficult to see what concept of historicity would not involve temporality. Moreover, the idea that theory is the insuperable resistance to theory would seem to lend itself to theoreticism that resists being tested by the results of research or specific inquiry into problems, including historical problems.

De Man's statements may invite a cavalier attitude towards history and a reprocessing of past texts and phenomena in terms of an abstract, compulsively repetitive reading technology oriented to the disclosure of aporia. Moreover, the above-quoted lines would seem to imply that the specific historical circumstances of a text's writing or its reception over time make relatively little if any difference for the mode and results of analysis, even in terms of a dialogic exchange with the past that would critically note such an exchange's diverse and divergent proclivities

---

45 Paul de Man, *The Resistance to Theory*, trans. Wlad Godzich (Minneapolis, Minn., 1986), 7, 12, and 19.

and be sensitive to its limitations – limitations that were crucial for de Man. On the basis of de Man's statement, we might not have a recurrent pleasure of recognition but may well have a repeated anxiety or agony of nonrecognition and sublime or uncanny disorientation. Indeed, analysis might amount to a kind of *unheimlich* manoeuver to force the bone of history from one's theoretical throat.

The aporia may be seen as marking the site of a trauma that has not been worked through and thus must be returned to, but we may also conteract the compulsive acting out of a repetition compulsion with the attempt to work through problems to the extent they can be worked through. Such an attempt would at the very least require the distinction between historical traumas (such as the French Revolution, the Holocaust, or the Algerian war) and structural trauma that has a transhistorical import (and has been variously figured as original sin, primal crime, castration anxiety, the passage from nature to culture, the entry into the symbolic, 'originary' violence, the missed encounter with the 'real,' and so forth). The conflation of one with the other leads either to reductionism or hypostatization – to the notion that particular historical events cause all concern with certain problems (such as anxiety or aporia) or the equally dubious (indeed complementary or inverted specular) idea that historical events are mere illustrations of some ahistorical or transhistorical force such as structural trauma.[46] The problem

---

[46] On the problems referred to in this paragraph, see my 'Trauma, Absence, Loss,' *Critical Inquiry* 25 (1999), 696–727. For example, Slavoj Žižek opposes contextual reductionism with theoreticist hypostatization when he writes: 'All the different attempts to attach this phenomenon [concentration camps] to a concrete image ("Holocaust," "Gulag" ...), to reduce it to a product of a concrete social order (Fascism, Stalinism ...) – what are they if not so many attempts to elude the fact that we are dealing here with the "real" of our civilization which returns as the same traumatic kernel in all social systems?' (*The Sublime Object of Ideology*, [London, 1989], 50).

is rather to investigate both the mutual articulation of structural and historical trauma and what the process of working through (which is not tantamount to simple transcendence or total liberation) may accomplish with respect to them.

With reference to Derrida, I would initially point to one of his more sustained engagements with the problem of the historical appropriation and political use of an important reference point for deconstruction: his treatment of Nietzsche in 'Otobiographies.'[47] I think even this text, in which there is an attempt to acquire some critical distance on Nietzsche, is still in important ways indicative of the largely participatory and at times orphic appropriation of Nietzsche in recent French thought. This appropriation is valuable in its stress on the critical and self-critical dimensions of Nietzsche, but it is of limited use in enabling us to understand his more dubious tendencies (such as elitism, an antidemocratic animus, a relatively indiscriminate penchant for hyperbole, and a willingness to manipulate stereotypes or verbally sacrifice an individual or group for the sake of an ironic or acerbic witticism). It is also quite restricted in indicating how these tendencies were taken up historically and adapted to purposes that might have appalled Nietzsche. In 'Otobiographies' Derrida raises the important question of what in Nietzsche opened itself to appropriation by the Nazis, and he insists that this appropriation was not purely accidental. But this question tends to hover like a cloud over his discussion without being elucidated in – or exercising sufficient pressure on – it. No differentiated, specific understanding of what in Nietzsche invited or resisted Nazi uses and abuses is

---

47 Included in Jacques Derrida, *The Ear of the Other: Otobiography, Transference, Translation*, ed. Christie McDonald, trans. Peggy Kamuf (1982; New York, 1985).

offered; mention is made of the role of antidemocratic notions of education (*Bildung*) and the need for a leader (*Führer*) in an early work ('On the Future of our Educational Institutions') but that work was, to the best of my knowledge, not important to or used by Nazis. The level of engagement with historical and political issues by and large remains allusive, abstract, and empirically underdeveloped. Moreover, in 'Otobiographies,' Derrida permits himself the following more or less rhetorical question that is reminiscent of Heidegger at his most tendentiously world-historical, dubiously apocalyptic, and portentously vague: 'In a word, has the "great" Nietzschean politics misfired or is it, rather, still to come in the wake of a seismic convulsion of which National Socialism or fascism will turn out to have been mere episodes?' (31). Whatever there may be in the way of future seismic convulsions and their wakes, to refer to 'National Socialism or fascism' as 'mere episodes' is objectionable and may even lend itself, however unintentionally, to a normalizing view of the Nazi period and the Shoah.

The note I would like to end on is that of specificity, and here I would like not to take back but to reflect critically on certain of my own arguments, especially with respect to the important figures I briefly invoked. A more or less satisfactory analysis of any of the complex figures mentioned would require an extended, differential treatment and more space than I have alloted to them. Moreover, it is important to note that there have been various modes or uses of post-structuralism, within which there have also been, from early on, attempts to relate close reading to institutional, political, and historical problems.[48] It is deceptive either to have an undifferentiated

---

48 I would include some of my own work among these attempts.

view of post-structuralism or to think that its various currents can be correlated with a narrow strategy of reading or at best with an allusive relation to history, society, and culture. Nor should we believe that the road to redemption in French studies lies in abandoning critical theory or close reading and turning instead to *Annales* historiography or the sociology of Pierre Bourdieu, however much there is to be derived from them.[49] Here part of the answer may be to go back and reread texts of so-called post-structuralists to understand better the still unrealized potentials of their thought – for example, the ways in which important leads, such as Derrida's critique of ethnocentrism in *Of Grammatology*, may be elaborated and further specified.[50] It would also involve recognizing the extent to which post-structuralists engaged broader considerations by critically and self-critically implicating reading (and themselves) in an entire network of problems and issues. More subtle and qualified analyses of various, at times divergent, tendencies in different periods or dimensions of their activity and in particular texts would also be necessary. Such analyses would require inquiry into the thought-provoking manner in which their work, rather than leading away from historical and political questions, may instead help to rethink them in their very

---

49 As I intimated in the Introduction, Luc Ferry and Alain Renaut's *French Philosophy of the Sixties: An Essay on Antihumanism* (1985; Amherst, Mass., 1990) contains arguments concerning recent French thought (notably the work of Foucault, Derrida, Bourdieu, and Lacan) that deserve to be taken seriously, and they are to be commended for trying to bring that thought into critical contact with liberal, humanist traditions, including Tocqueville's work. But their extended discussions contain many questionable points and in general have the limitations one might perhaps expect in a brief treatment intended to provoke discussion and debate.

50 Jacques Derrida, *Of Grammatology*, trans. Gayatri Chakravorty Spivak (Baltimore, 1976), esp. Part I.

relation to problems of specificity and critical theory. With reference to Derrida, this inquiry would involve not only recognizing the importance of his direct involvement in GREPH and its role in contesting political attempts to reorient the educational system in narrowly technological and preprofessional directions. It would also entail placing greater emphasis on the institutional contexts and implications of the very texts and traditions that were objects of deconstructive analysis. For example, one might examine the institutionalization of the metaphysical tradition that Derrida deconstructs or look again at the significance of the sustained dismantling of the scapegoat mechanism in Derrida's texts – a mechanism that relies on clear-cut binary oppositions and attendant processes of exclusion and elimination. One might also investigate the relation between the painstaking, almost classically orchestrated deconstruction of metaphysics and the more allusive relation to certain historical problems – almost amounting in some instances to a haunting, allegorical survivor discourse – in the early texts as well as the relation between the more insistently experimental, disseminatory, at times seemingly associative dimension of later texts and the increased concern for particular historical, even local, contexts and problems, notably the Holocaust. To the extent that they withstand critical scrutiny, these proposed relations do not point unambiguously in any one direction and may indeed enact the economy of interacting losses and gains that Derrida has emphasized quite explicitly. Similar problems would arise with respect to the other figures. As I have observed, part of the interest in rereading the early Foucault, notably including his *Histoire de la folie*, is to counteract the overemphasis on aspects of his later work in the new historicism and the neo-Foucauldian history of disciplines – approaches that often conventionalize or operationalize Foucault by removing or downplaying his more controversial, indeed disorienting, yet provocative philosophical, political, and 'writerly' dimensions.[51] And there are still ways in which the critical and selective attempt to relate Derrida's and Foucault's concerns bearing on problems of reading, genealogy, and contextualization, beyond the delimited issues rehearsed in their famous debate, may be one promising avenue in the reconfiguration of French studies.

Here I would like to open a parenthesis to examine one area where Derrida seems to have had second thoughts – belated or afterthoughts – about his reading of Benjamin's 'Critique of Violence' (*Kritik der Gewalt*) with respect to issues raised by the Nazi genocide or 'final solution.' Derrida gave the first version of his essay on Benjamin at a conference at the Cardozo Law School. He presented a later version at the UCLA conference sponsored by Saul Friedlander that eventuated in the book *Probing the Limits of Representation: Nazism and the Final Solution*.' Derrida's lecture on Benjamin inaugurated this conference, including what became a footnote in the printed version of his essay that appeared in the *Cardozo Law Review* special issue on 'Deconstruction and the Possibility of Justice.' He also added a 'Post-scriptum' that is even more pertinent to the question of the relation of

---

51 As I noted in the Introduction, one can derive an idea of the emphases in the new-historicist use of Foucault from the choice of selections from Foucault in Paul Rabinow, ed., *The Foucault Reader* (New York, 1984). For Jan Goldstein's important and influential Foucauldian approach to the history of disciplines, see *Console and Classify: The French Psychiatric Profession in the Nineteenth Century* (Cambridge and New York, 1987). See also the collection of essays she edited, *Foucault and the Writing of History* (Oxford and Cambridge, Mass., 1994).

deconstruction to historical understanding, ethics, and politics.[52]

---

[52] Jacques Derrida, 'Force of Law: The "Mystical" Foundation of Authority,' *Cardozo Law Review* 11 (1990), 920–1045. See also my response to the original version of Derrida's essay, which did not include the footnote and the Post-scriptum, 'Violence, Justice, and the Force of Law,' *Cardozo Law Review* 11 (1990), 1065–78. With respect to Benjamin's defence of 'bloodless' divine violence and Derrida's assertion that, for Benjamin, 'the essence of Judaism ... forbids all murder, even in the case of legitimate defence' (1029), I observed: 'How can one be sure to stop violence short of killing, especially if it is a matter of revolutionary mass action? Even beyond pragmatic considerations, might not the individual or community take up the responsibility of violent killing in "true" war or even consider it a legitimate act of self-defence? These questions become particularly disturbing in the context of a messianic *politique du pire* wherein the rational estimation of the efficacy of means and a concern for consequences do not limit – or help to demystify – the allure of violence. Finally, it may not be entirely beside the point to notice that there are, quite literally, many ways to kill without bloodshed, one of which was perfected by the Nazis. In a very important sense, blood does not make all the difference' (1077). For a spirited defence of Derrida's approach, even without the two addenda, see Drucilla Cornell, 'The Violence of the Masquerade: Law Dressed Up as Justice,' *Cardozo Law Review* 11 (1990), 1047–64. (Cornell, however, does not seem to have taken certain considerations relating to the Nazi genocide as bringing as much weight to bear on Derrida's original essay as Derrida himself apparently did.) In an analysis of the relation of Benjamin and Carl Schmitt, Horst Bredekamp comments on Derrida's essay: '"Affinities" beween Benjamin and Schmitt have led Jacques Derrida to subject Benjamin's "Kritik der Gewalt" to a similar analysis in the name of "deconstruction," an investigation whose cryptic conclusions make the association appear downright harmless. Again and again, the comparison with texts by Schmitt is merely hinted at, causing the motive for the examination of Benjamin to remain vague. Only in one passage, where Derrida deals with the problem of time that arises in the moment of legislation, does he address the connection that was apparently constitutive of the "affinities" between Benjamin and Schmitt: "It is the moment when the justification of law hovers in the void or over the abyss, clinging to a purely performative act"' ('From Walter Benjamin to Carl Schmitt, via Thomas Hobbes,' *Critical Inquiry* 25 [1999], 265). Bredekamp, however, does not comment on the two addenda to Derrida's essay. Still, in his essay on Benjamin as elsewhere, Derrida has a problematic notion of 'originary,' performative violence whose precise status and import for historical understanding and ethicopolitical analysis or change are unclear.

In the footnote, Derrida observed of the earlier version of his essay on Benjamin that 'the horizon of Nazism and the final solution will appear only through signs or brief flashes of expectation and will be treated only in a virtual, oblique, or elliptical fashion' (977). This honest situating of his reading might be for some a sign of its limitation. In the 'Post-scriptum' his discourse takes a less elliptical turn, although it is framed as a problematic speculation concerning what Benjamin, had he lived, might conceivably have said about Nazism and the 'final solution.' What is most interesting about the 'Post-scriptum,'' however, may well be what Derrida himself says about Nazism and the 'final solution' and the manner in which he says it as well as reflects back on Benjamin's essay in terms and tones that are more pronounced or even more emphatic than those employed in the earlier version of his essay.

Derrida outlines four ways in which Benjamin might have approached Nazism and the 'final solution,' ways initially described in a sympathetic manner or even a free indirect style reminiscent of his approach in his original essay. Benjamin might have seen the Nazi genocide as: 1) 'the radicalization of evil linked to the fall into the language of communication, representation, information,' 2) 'the totalitarian radicalization of a logic of the State (and our [Benjamin's] text is a condemnation of the State ...),' 3) 'the radical but also fatal corruption of parliamentary and representative democracy through a modern police that is inseparable from it,' or 4) 'a radicalization and total extension of the mythical violence, both in its sacrificial founding moment and its most conservative moment' (1041). These four views (especially the first two) are represented in the literature on the Holocaust and may be questioned in various ways; Derrida himself, as we shall see, will, at a concluding point, question them in a forceful gesture that may perhaps also be read as a self-questioning if not a self-criticism.

Before he reaches that point, Derrida's exegesis executes a number of subtle and complex manoeuvres in which he seems to be expressing, as Benjamin's, views to which he is himself often close. He asserts that, to avoid damaging complicity, 'one must try to think [the uniqueness of an event like the 'final solution'] beginning with its other, that is to say, starting from what it tried to exclude and to destroy, to exterminate radically, from that which haunted it at once from without and within.' Here we might expect Derrida to turn to the problem of the scapegoated victims and of attending to their voices. His procedure is somewhat different. 'One must try to think it starting from the possibility of singularity, the singularity of the signature and of the name, because what the order of representation tried to exterminate was not only human lives by the millions, natural lives, but also a demand for justice; and also names: and first of all the possibility of giving, inscribing, calling and recalling the name' (1042). This approach may seem to begin etherealizing problems, at least insofar as the extermination of names and of the demand for justice are not insistently linked to people who cannot be reduced to mere 'natural lives.' (For their relatives and friends, not the possibility of singularity but the actual – at times, in the context of the Holocaust, difficult or even impossible – task of finding the names of specific dead people is crucial for processes of mourning.) Moreover, the turn to names would still seem too much within Benjamin's own dubious dichotomy between representation (which tends to be demonized) and a mystical or poetic language of pure appellation or naming – a language that would also be one of expressiveness.

Derrida seems to develop further his argument from within a certain Benjaminian perspective when he continues: 'From this point of view, Benjamin would perhaps have judged vain and without pertinence – in any case without a pertinence commensurable to the event, any juridical trial of Nazism and of its responsibilities, any judgmental apparatus, any historiography still homogeneous with the space in which Nazism developed up to and including the final solution, any interpretation drawing on philosophical, moral, sociological, psychological or psychoanalytical concepts, and especially juridical concepts (in particular those of the philosophy of right, whether it be that of natural law, in the Aristotelean style or the style of the *Aufklärung*) ... No anthropology, no humanism, no discourse of man on man, even on human rights can be proportionate to either the rupture between the mythical and the divine, or to a limit experience such as the final solution' (1042). Here we seem close to an extreme, perhaps Messianic counsel of despair that would reject limited understanding and necessary judgment in the name of the name (or in the name of pure expressiveness, impossible understanding, and absolute or divine justice that is always *à-venir* [to come]). Moreover, we would also seem to be distant from the basic principle of deconstruction that one must in some sense begin with the object to be understood or analysed and work through it in order to arrive at some other, significantly different perspective.

Derrida seems attentive to these last considerations when he notes that for Benjamin (as for Derrida) the point is not simply to renounce or demonize representation but to arrive at some viable 'compromise.' 'This does not mean that one must simply renounce Enlightenment and the language of communication or representation in favor of the language of expression. In his *Moscow Diary* of 1926–27, Benjamin specifies that the polarity between the two languages and all that they command cannot be maintained and deployed in a pure state, but that "compromise" is necessary or inevitable between them. Yet this remains a compromise between two incommensurable and radically heterogeneous dimensions.' Although the immediate, almost automatic leap to incommensurability may be questioned, special notice might be taken of the further point that this 'compromise' would be made 'in the name of the justice that would command one to obey at the same time the law of representation (*Aufklärung*, reason, objectification, comparison, explication, the taking into account of multiplicity and therefore the serialization of the unique) and the law that transcends representation and withholds the unique, all uniqueness, from its reinscription in an order of generality or of comparison' (1044). This language of necessary compromise is most relevant to both historical understanding and to ethics and politics addressed to this-worldly considerations of both justice and generosity. It is the language to whose threshold deconstruction continually brings us without perhaps sufficiently entering into the problem of articulating and elaborating it in a sustained manner.

In his final two paragraphs, Derrida may also be sensitive to the last-mentioned points, for he turns back to Benjamin's text with an uncommon combination of hesitation and decisiveness, perhaps even impatience:

> What I find, in conclusion, the most redoubtable, indeed (perhaps, almost) intolerable in this text, even beyond the affinities it maintains with the worst (the critique of *Aufklärung*, the theory of the fall and of originary authen-

ticity, the polarity between originary language and fallen language, etc.), is a temptation that it would leave open, and leave open notably to the survivors or the victims of the final solution, to its past, present or potential victims. Which temptation? The temptation to think the holocaust as an uninterpretable manifestation of divine violence insofar as this divine violence would be at the same time nihilating, expiatory and bloodless, says Benjamin, a divine violence that would destroy current law through a bloodless process that strikes and causes to expiate ... When one thinks of the gas chambers and the cremation ovens, this allusion to an extermination that would be expiatory because bloodless must cause one to shudder. One is terrified at the idea of an interpretation that would make of the holocaust an expiation and an indecipherable signature of the just and violent anger of God.

It is at this point that this text, despite all its polysemic mobility and all its resources for reversal, seems to me finally to resemble too closely, to the point of specular fascination and vertigo, the very thing against which one must act and think, do and speak, that with which one must break (perhaps, perhaps). (1045)

The double 'perhaps' is a (repeated) reminder that even the most careful deconstruction or critique, while setting up warnings against specular fascination, cannot be entirely 'uncontaminated' by its object and attain a state of purity or total rupture with it but must, in a spirit of self-criticism and self-questioning, work over and through it towards a significantly different articulation of problems and possibilities.

I have gone over Derrida's 'Post-scriptum' with some care (although certain important aspects of it were omitted, notably its indication of intricate relations, even 'vertiginous proximities' and 'radical reversals' (1040), in the relations between German and Jewish thinking just before the rise of Nazism) in order to give some idea of the movement of Derrida's thought with respect to a crucial historical, ethical, and political problem in relation to which his approach takes, albeit in a belated manner, some of its most thought-provoking turns – turns that also indicate directions in which his practice might be extended and conjoined with other practices and forms of analysis and argument.

The list of figures I have just evoked – Lyotard, Bourdieu, Foucault, Kristeva, Derrida – to which others might be added (Lévi-Strauss, Barthes, Lacan, Deleuze, and so forth) – is an index of a renaissance in French thought that seems to have crested. Many commentators have remarked that there are no replacements for this generation on the current intellectual and academic scene and that the age of giants seems to have been succeeded by one of epigones or at least of somewhat less imposing figures. Perhaps the very project of French studies bears witness to this change, for it may substitute a more genuinely collective undertaking for earlier ones that involved the often mimetic emulation of a 'master thinker' or the translation of his or her work into a *lingua franca* that might be appropriated and used by practitioners. (Indeed, a journal such as *Diacritics* has had as one of its most significant *raisons d'être* the socialization of deconstruction and other post-structural tendencies into a discourse that could be more or less differentially used by various contributors.) As I indicated earlier, the present problem in French studies is significantly different, and it may at the very least provide the occasion for more critical, judicious responses to earlier tendencies as well as for a nondoctrinaire attempt to better articulate whatever is valuable in them with other approaches such as historical inquiry and socio-political analysis.

Moreover, it would be deceptive to perceive the francophone as a monolithic bloc and to obscure the multiple, at times mutually contestatory, differences and differentiations within it. A monolithic perception of the francophone contributes to the ghettoization of its objects of study as well as its students, and it risks conflating its importance with a nominal concession to recent trends or political pressures. To make this observation is to insist on a distinction among, as well as complexities within, various and at times very different francophone areas or cultures – for example, the Caribbean, the Canadian, the North African, the West African, the Pacific island, the Southeast Asian, and so forth. But the point of this insistence is not merely to acknowledge or celebrate diversity that may engender a new set of particularized ethnic or nationalistic specializations and purified if not ritualized canons. It is rather to underscore the importance of working out newer articulations among francophone concerns and their relations to diverse tendencies in the metropole. This process would include an awareness and elucidation of the significant interaction between francophone and metropolitan currents and figures that, in turn, have various backgrounds and itineraries. Here one may simply mention in passing the use of Deleuze in Edouard Glissant's defence of Creole counterdiscourses or the role of Derrida's own Algerian background as it is mediated by a multiplicity of factors as well as the significance of his writing for, say, figures in North Africa (for example, Abdelkebir Khatabi). An obvious and important earlier example is, of course, Frantz Fanon with his Martiniquais background, his role in theorizing liberation movements, notably in Algeria, his relation to French intellectuals such as Sartre, and his redeployment of Marxism and psychoanalysis. Examples could be multiplied almost endlessly.[53]

The interactions between metropolitan France and its former colonies have been complex, often hegemonically skewed, and typically strained. Still, any understanding of francophone literature and culture should, I think, attempt not to isolate it but to explore its contested relations with the metropole and with figures and intellectual or cultural forces that are themselves not simply metropolitan but often internally complex, self-contradictory, hybridized, or riven. In addition, it is crucial to stress the interconnection of the study of both the metropolitan and francophone with the study of processes of globalization involving the colonial and the postcolonial. The turn to the francophone should in fact mean a turning of both the francophone and the metropolitan towards one another in order to elicit their tangled relations, their often lost opportunities, and their possibilities for the future. In any case, it would seem as unrealistic to propose a return to a purely canonical understanding of French literature as to postulate the viability of a purely francophone orientation. Problems raised by the objects of study and by their producers and readers would reveal the futility of such gestures.

By the same token, cultural studies, history, and forms of cross-disciplinarity are hardly uncontested or clearly bounded sites that one may appropriate in the attempt to supplement modes of close reading or provide a ready-made agenda for French studies. An attempt to deploy them requires us to investigate their development, 'inter

---

53 On these issues, see, for example, Françoise Lionnet, *Postcolonial Representations: Women, Literature, Identity* (Ithaca and London, 1995).

nal' debates, limitations, and diverse possibilities for analysis in order to be able to make a critical and self-critical use of them.[54] For example, one cannot simply appropriate Pierre Bourdieu, Roger Chartier, Robert Darnton, Pierre Nora, or Henry Rousso without a careful attempt to situate them in complex sociological and historical fields and to analyse critically what they do.[55] The stress on the role of the francophone, cultural and historical studies, and cross-disciplinarity thus does not provide a 'quick fix' or a simple alternative to modes of close reading. Rather it helps to raise in a distinctive way the problem of the interaction between reading and a complex set of problems. The constellation of forces and possibilities may shift significantly as a result, but we arrive at another problematization of the field of French studies with complex relations to formerly prominent theoretical approaches. This reproblematization is, I think, necessary if the field is to be vital and in a viable position to make a place for itself in a configuration of disciplines that is being redefined in the face of both intellectual and economic demands. French studies then emerges not as an enclosed area or a strictly bounded discipline but as a contested site on which important issues – literary, historical, and other – that bear on the French and the francophone may be explored.

---

54 These issues are central to the first chapter of this book.
55 The questionable effects of an appropriation of Bourdieu, at times unmediated by the close reading and critical analysis of texts, can be seen even in the important, impressive work of John Guillory, notably *Cultural Capital: The Problem of Literary Canon Formation* (Chicago and London, 1993).

Index

Abraham, 167n
Abrams, M.H., 55n
Alcoff, Linda, 61n
American Historical Review, 29, 57
Annales School, 113, 141, 173, 174n, 184n, 200, 214
Apter, Emily, 175n
Aristotle, 84, 220
Aron, Raymond, 7n, 8, 9n, 18, 73; *The Elusive Revolution: Anatomy of a Student Revolt*, 9n; *Main Currents of Sociological Thought*, 8n; *Opium of the Intellectuals*, 7n
Artaud, Antonin, 140, 161, 201, 204n
Aschheim, Steven E., 35–6n
Atwood, Margaret, 182n
Auerbach, Eric, 85n
Auslander, Leora, 179n
Avni, Ora, 175n

Baker, Keith Michael, 55n

Bakhtin, Mikhail, 58, 65, 71n, 152–3
Balzac, Honoré de, 46
Bann, Stephen, 183
Barthes, Roland, 46, 200, 223
Bataille, Georges, 51, 140n, 198–9
Baudelaire, Charles, 179n, 190
Beardsworth, Richard, 199n
Beaumont, Gustave de, 95n
Beckett, Samuel, 36, 44
Bell, Daniel, 18
Benjamin, Walter, 216–22; 'Critique of Violence,' 216–22; *Moscow Diary*, 221
Bentham, Jeremy, 156
Berkhofer, Robert, Jr, 116n, 181n
Berlant, Lauren, 194–5n
Bersani, Leo, 49–50n, 175n
Blanchot, Maurice, 51, 140n, 198n, 199
Bloch, Marc, 174n
Bloch, R. Howard, 175

Bloom, Harold, 44
Bonaparte, Louis Napoleon (Napoleon III), 102
Bosch, Hieronymus 150, 161
Bourdieu, Pierre, 75, 116n, 174n, 188n, 214, 223n, 226
Bradley, Owen, 76n
Braudel, Fernand, 23n, 173n
Bredekamp, Horst, 217n
Broszat, Martin, 197n
Bruno, Giordano, 153–4
Burke, Edmund, 79, 86, 108, 114
Butler, Judith, 5n, 116n; *Bodies That Matter: On the Discursive Limits of 'Sex'*, 5n; *Gender Trouble: Feminism and the Subversion of Identity*, 5n; *The Psychic Life of Power: Theories in Subjection*, 5n
Bynum, Caroline Walker, 55

Callicles, 146
Camus, Albert, 3n, 199
Carby, Hazel, 187–8n
Carrard, Philippe, 23n, 173n
Carroll, David, 175n, 199n
Caruth, Cathy, 208n
Celan, Paul, 197n
Céline, Louis Ferdinand, 200, 201n
Cervantes, Miguel de, 145, 149
Chambers, Iain, 116n
Chambers, Ross, 175n
Chartier, Roger, 23n, 172n, 173n
Chevalier, Louis, 30n
Christ, Jesus, 149
Clingman, Stephen, 191n
Cohen, Sande, 181

Collins, Margery, 190n
Coltrane, John, 46
Compagnon, Antoine, 175n
Conkin, Paul K., 54n
Conley, Tom, 170n, 175n
Connor, Steven, 50n
Cornell, Drucilla, 217n
Crapanzano, Vincent, 55n
Crubellier, Maurice, 195n
Culler, Jonathan, 88n, 170–1n; *Doing French Studies*, 170n–171n; *Flaubert: The Uses of Uncertainty*, 88n

Darnton, Robert, 31n, 54n, 172n, 226; *The Great Cat Massacre and Other Episodes in French Cultural History*, 31n, 54n; 'The Symbolic Element in History,' 54n
Davis, Miles, 187n
Davis, Natalie Zemon, 31n
de Beauvoir, Simone, 188n, 191n, 207n
DeJean, Joan, 175n
Deleuze, Gilles, 47n, 49n, 201n, 223–4; *Anti-Oedipus: Capitalism and Schizophrenia*, 47n, 201n; *A Thousand Plateaus*, 47n
de Man, Paul, 39–41, 43–4, 49, 53, 123n, 205, 209–11; *Allegories of Reading: Figural Language in Rousseau, Nietzsche, Rilke, and Proust*, 41n; *Resistance to Theory*, 40–1n, 209–11
Demos, John, 182n
Derrida, Jacques, 6n, 36, 39–44, 46, 49, 51, 52n, 58, 69, 124,

Index

132–8, 143–5, 151, 167n 180, 183, 184n, 193, 197–8n, 198–200, 202n, 204n, 205, 207, 212–24; *Aporias*, 41n; *Dissemination*, 52n; *The Ear of the Other: Otobiography, Transference, Translation*, 212–13; 'Force of Law: The "Mystical" Foundations of Authority,' 216–23; *Glas*, 46; *The Gift of Death*, 167n; 'Like the Sound of the Deep Sea within a Shell: Paul de Man's War,' 39–40n, 43–4, 133n; Memoires for Paul de Man, 39n, 41n; *Of Grammatology*, 43, 43n, 214; *Points ... Interviews 1974–1994*, 197–8n, 202n; *Specters of Marx: The State of the Debt, the Work of Mourning, and the New International*, 199n; 'Structure, Sign, and Play in the Discourse of the Human Sciences,' 43, 193n; *Writing and Difference*, 132–8, 198–100, 204n
Descartes, René, 6n, 133, 135–8, 145, 151, 154
Dews, Peter, 199n
Diacritics, 170–1n, 223
Diderot, Denis, 10n, 117, 151
Dilthey, Wilhelm, 55
Dostoevsky, Fyodor, 149, 152
Drescher, Seymour, 82n; *Dilemmas of Democracy: Tocqueville and Modernization*, 82n; *Tocqueville and Beaumont on Social Reform*, 95n; 'Why Great Revolutions Will Become Rare: Tocqueville's Most Neglected Prognosis,' 82n
Dreyfus, Hubert, 127n, 128
DuBois, W.E.B., 187n
Durkheim, Emile, 17, 120–1

Eley, Geoff, 116n
Erasmus, 151

Fanon, Frantz, 224–5
Fantasia, Ron, 179n
Felman, Shoshana, 52n, 175n, 205, 208n; 'Paul de Man's Silence,' 52n; *Testimony: Crisis of Witnessing in Literature, Psychoanalysis, and History*, 52n, 208n
Fénélon, François de Salignac de, 117
Ferry, Luc, 6–7n, 8, 8n, 9n, 115n, 138–9n, 214n
Flaubert, Gustave, 44, 52, 88, 190; *Madame Bovary*, 88n; *The Sentimental Education*, 52
Foucault, Michel, 3–20, 46–7, 58, 116n, 123–68, 182–5, 191n, 192, 196, 198–201, 202n, 203n, 204–5n, 214n, 215–16, 223; *The Archaeology of Knowledge and the Discourse on Language*, 125; *The Care of the Self: The History of Sexuality, Volume 3*, 202n; *Discipline and Punish: The Birth of the Prison*, 9, 10n, 125, 157, 162, 184; *The History of Sexuality, Volume I: An Introduction*, 13, 184, 201n; *Language, Counter-Memory, Practice:*

Selected Essays, 198–200; *Madness and Civilization: A History of Insanity in the Age of Reason*, 3–4, 6n–7n, 10n, 11, 19, 46–7, 123–68, 185, 199, 2–3n, 204–5n, 215–16; *The Order of Things: An Archaeology of the Human Sciences*, 10n, 14–15n, 153–4; *Politics, Philosophy, Culture: Interviews and Other Writings 1977–1984*, 10n, 202n; *The Use of Pleasure: The History of Sexuality, Volume Two*, 202n
Fourier, Charles, 112
Fraser, Nancy, 7n, 116n, 164n
Freud, Sigmund, 22, 45, 62, 70, 135, 137, 159–60; *Autobiographical Study*, 159–60; 'Mourning and Melancholia,' 22n; 'Remembering, Repeating, and Working Through,' 22n
Friedlander, Saul, 197n, 216
Fukuyama, Francis, 116n
Furet, François, 7n, 8, 18, 79n, 80–2, 85–6, 112
Furman, Nelly, 175n, 178n

Gauchet, Marcel, 8n
Gearheart, Suzanne, 175n
Geertz, Clifford, 54, 54–5n
Genet, Jean, 44, 207n
Gibaldi, Joseph, 56n
Gilroy, Paul, 206–7n
Ginzburg, Carlo, 133
Girard, René, 200, 203n
Glass, James M., 209n
Gobineau, Arthur, Comte de, 92, 94

Goethe, Johann Wolfgang von, 67
Goldstein, Doris S., 78n
Goldstein, Jan, 116n, 173n, 216n; *Console and Classify: The French Psychiatric Profession in the Nineteenth Century*, 216n; *Foucault and the Writing of History*, 216n
Gordon, Linda, 181n
Gossman, Lionel, 23n, 183
Goux, Jean-Joseph, 175n, 195n
Goya, Lucientes de, 161–2
Gramsci, Antonio, 88n
Greenberg, Mitchell, 175n
Grossberg, Lawrence, 176n, 194n
Guattari, Félix, 47n, 49n, 201n; *Anti-Oedipus: Capitalism and Schizophrenia*, 47n; *A Thousand Plateaus*, 47n
Guillory, John, 226
Guizot, François, 95n

Habermas, Jürgen, 7n, 36n, 76n, 116n, 125–7, 143, 164n, 165, 180, 199n; *Philosophical Discourse of Modernity*, 7n, 36n, 125–7, 199n; 'Taking Aim at the Heart of the Present,' 7n
Halperin, David, *Saint Foucault: Towards a Gay Hagiography*, 126–7
Hamacher, Werner, 195n
Harootunian, Harry, 116n
Hartman, Geoffrey, 116n
Hartman, Matt, 195n
Hartz, Louis, 8, 73

Hegel, Georg Wilhelm Friedrich, 53, 55, 57, 61, 64, 93, 198
Heidegger, Martin, 6–7n, 15n, 51, 124n, 139, 140n, 213
Helvétius, Claude Adrien, 117
Herr, Richard, 113n
Hexter, J.H., 181n
Higham, John, 54
Himmelfarb, Gertrude, 24n
Himmler, Heinrich, 209
Hirsch, Marianne, 175n
Hobbes, Thomas, 217n
Hoggart, Richard, 194n
Hölderlin, Friedrich, 140, 142, 161, 201
Hollier, Denis, 175n, 195n
Hollinger, David, 181n
Huet, Marie-Hélène, 175n
Hugo, Victor, 30n
Hunt, Lynn, 56n, 182n
Husserl, Edmund, 138

Isaac, 167n

James, C.L.R., 187n
Jameson, Fredric, 104n, 116n, 180, 183, 203n
Jardin, André, 91n
Jardine, Alice, 175n
Jay, Martin, 37n, 56n, 132n, 116n; *Downcast Eyes: The Denigration of Vision in Twentieth-Century French Thought*, 37n; 'Of Plots, Witnesses, and Judgments,' 132n; 'Should Intellectual History Take a Linguistic Turn? Reflections on the Habermas-Gadamer Debate,' 56n; 'Two Cheers for Paraphrase: The Confessons of a Synoptic Intellectual Historian,' 37n
Jenkins, Keith, 39n
Jones, Gareth Stedman, 116
Joyce, James, 36
Judt, Tony, 36n

Kant, Immanuel, 67, 133, 164n
Kaplan, Alice, 175n
Kaplan, Steven L., 31n, 56n, 82n, 117n, 175n; *Adieu '89*, 31n, 82n; *Bread, Politics, and Political Economy in the Reign of Louis XV*, 117n
Kedward, H.R., 195n
Kellner, Hans, 23n, 181
Khatabi, Abdelkebir, 224
Kierkegaard, Sören, 149, 167
Klein, Richard, 170–1n, 175–6n; *Doing French Studies*, 170–1n; 'The Object of French Studies – *Gebrauchkunst*,' 170–1n
Kloppenberg, James, 39n
Kristeva, Julia, 58–9n, 180, 200–1, 223; *Black Sun: Depression and Melancholia*, 59n; *Powers of Horror: An Essay on Abjection*, 200–1; *Revolution in Poetic Language*, 58–9n
Kritzman, Lawrence D., 175n, 195n
Kuisel, Richard, 179n

Lacan, Jacques, 192, 196, 200, 207, 214, 223
LaCapra, Dominick, 3n, 10n, 18n, 22n, 26n, 39n, 40n, 48n,

50n, 55n, 63n, 71n, 87n, 88n, 120, 132n, 140n, 178n, 182n, 190n, 200n, 209n, 211n, 217n; *Emile Durkheim: Sociologist and Philosopher*, 120; 'European History and the Post-traumatic State,' 63n; *History and Criticism*, 48n, 182n; *History and Memory after Auschwitz*, 3n, 140n, 200n; 'History and Psychoanalysis,' 22n; *History, Politics, and the Novel*, 10n, 87n; 'Ideology and Critique in Dickens's *Bleak House*,' 10n; *Madame Bovary on Trial*, 88n; *A Preface to Sartre*, 39n, 190n; *Representing the Holocaust: History, Theory, Trauma*, 18n, 22n, 26n, 40n, 48n, 50n, 55n, 63n, 140n, 200n, 209n; *Rethinking Intellectual History: Texts, Contexts, Language*, 39n, 48n, 71n, 182n; *Soundings in Critical Theory*, 39n; 'Trauma, Absence, Loss,' 211n; 'The University in Ruins?,' 178n; 'Violence, Justice, and the Force of Law,' 217n; *Writing History, Writing Trauma*, 132n, 182n, 200
LaClau, Ernesto, 5–6n, 183
Lacoue-Labarthe, Philippe, 140n, 183
Lanzmann, Claude, 3n, 180
Latour, Bruno, 116n
Laub, Dori, 52n
Leadbelly (Huddie Ledbetter), 187n
Lefebvre, Georges, 114n

Leroy-Ladurie, Emmanuel, 31n
Levinas, Emmanuel, 167n
Lévi-Strauss, Claude, 188n, 200, 223
Leys, Ruth, 185n
Lilla, Mark, 8, 115n
Lionnet, Françoise, 175n, 190n, 225n; *Postcolonial Representations: Women, Literature, Identity*, 225n; 'Reframing Baudelaire: Literary History, Biography, Postcolonial Theory and Vernacular Languages,' 190n
Loewenberg, Peter, 70n
Lukács, Georg, 36n
Lukács, John, 36n
Lyotard, Jean-François, 51n, 61–2, 140n, 200, 205–8, 223; *The Differend: Phrases in Dispute*, 51n, 61–2n, 140n, 206–7; *Heidegger and 'the jews,'* 51n, 207–8; *The Postmodern Condition: A Report on Knowledge*, 51n
Maistre, Joseph de, 74–6, 79, 106, 114
Mancini, Matthew, 73, 75, 76n, 78n, 95n, 109n
Marx, Karl, 6–7n, 82, 84–5, 93, 111–12, 121, 164n
Megill, Allan, 124n, 181n
Mehlman, Jeffrey, 175n
Meltzer, Françoise, 175n
Midelfort, Erik, 150
Mieszkowski, Jan, 195n
Mill, John Stuart, 93, 110
Miller, D.A., 10n
Miller, Nancy K., 175n
Mink, Louis, 23n

Moi, Toril, 175n, 191n
Montesquieu, Charles-Louis de Secondat, Baron de, 84
Morelly, M., 117
Morris, Meaghan, 116n
Mouffe, Chantal, 5–6n, 183
Mudimbe, Valentin, 175n

Nealon, Jeffrey T., 40n
Nelson, Cary, 194n
Nerval, Gérard de, 142
Nichols, Stephen, 175n
Nietzsche, Friedrich, 6–7n, 14, 35–6n, 124n, 126, 137, 139–40, 142, 145–7, 149, 161, 201, 204n, 212–13; *The Birth of Tragedy from the Spirit of Music*, 146–7; 'On the Future of our Educational Institutions,' 213
Noiriel, Gérard, 174–5n, 184n; 'Foucault and History: The Lessons of a Disillusion,' 184n; *Sur la 'crise' de l'histoire*, 174–5n
Nora, Pierre, 63n, 172n, 226
Novick, Peter, 21, 116n, 181n

Orr, Linda, 175n, 183

Palmer, Bryan D., 24n
Pascal, Blaise, 151
Patterson, Annabel, 57n
Petrey, Sandy, 171n, 175–6n, 187n; 'When Did Literature Stop Being Cultural?' 171n, 187n; 'French Studies/Cultural Studies: Reciprocal Invigoration or Mutual Destruction?' 187n

Pierce, Christine, 190n
Pierson, George Wilson, 111n
Pinel, Philippe, 157–8
Plato, 58n, 146
Pocock, J.G.A., 33–4n, 90
Poster, Mark, 7n
Postone, Moishe, 199n
Prince, Gerald, 175n

Rabinow, Paul, 127n, 128
Readings, Bill, 178n
Reeve, Henry, 93n
Renaut, Alain, 6–7n, 8, 9n, 115n, 138–9n, 214n
Representations, 9, 10n
Richter, Melvin, 92, 92–3n
Ricoeur, Paul, 104n, 116n
Riffaterre, Michael, 175n
Robeson, Paul, 187n
Robespierre, Maximilien, 156
Rooney, Ellen, 60n
Rorty, Richard, 174n
Rose, Gillian, 200n
Ross, Dorothy, 181n
Ross, Kristin, 175n, 178n, 179n
Roth, Michael, 116n
Rousseau, Jean-Jacques, 156
Rousso, Henry, 18n, 226

Sade, Donatien Alphonse François, Marquis de, 161
Sadowsky, Jonathan, 37n
Said, Edward, 184n, 190n, 203n
Saint Simon, Claude Henri de Rouvroy, Comte de, 112
Sakai, Naoki, 178n
Santner, Eric L., 18n, 56n, 62–3n, 164–5n, 197n; 'History

beyond the Pleasure Principle: Some Thoughts on the Representation of Trauma,' 56n, 197n; *My Own Private Germany: Daniel Paul Schreber's Secret History of Modernity*, 164–5n; *Stranded Objects: Mourning, Melancholia, and Film in Postwar Germany,* 18n, 62–3n
Sartre, Jean-Paul, 141, 188n, 190, 199, 207n, 225
Saussure, Ferdinand de, 58
Schmitt, Carl, 217n
Scholes, Robert, 57n
Schorske, Carl, 36n
Schreber, Daniel Paul, 164–5n
Scott, Joan Wallach, 39n, 60–1n, 116n; 'Experience,' 60–1n; *Gender and the Politics of History,* 39n
Shakespeare, William, 149
Shumway, David R., 124n
Singer, Peter, 128n
Socrates, 146–7
Sorel, Julien, 87n
Spence, Jonathan D., 182n
Spiegel, Gabrielle, 116n, 185n; 'History and Postmodernism,' 185n; 'History, Historicism, and the Social Logic of the Text in the Middle Ages,' 185n
Spitzer, Leo, 171n, 176n
Spivak, Gayatri Chakravorty, 183
Starr, Peter, 199n
Stendhal, 83, 87–8
Stone, Lawrence, 185n
Stromberg, Roland N., 36n
Sue, Eugène, 30n

Suleiman, Ezra, 175n
Suleiman, Susan Rubin, 175n
Swain, Gladys, 8

Taylor, A.J.P., 36–7n
Taylor, Charles, 7n, 55–6, 62; 'Foucault on Freedom and Truth,' 7n; *Sources of the Self: The Making of Modern Identity,* 55–6, 62
Terdiman, Richard, 175n, 190n
Thomas, Brooke, 56n
Thompson, E.P., 85, 194n
Thrasymachus, 146
Tocqueville, Alexis de, 3–9, 11–13, 15–20, 73–121, 123, 129n, 165, 167, 182–4, 191n, 199, 214n; *Democracy in America,* 74, 76–8, 81n, 83n, 94–101, 109–11; *The Old Régime and the French Revolution,* 3, 11–12, 73–5, 78–80, 81n, 83–91, 93n, 94, 102–7, 111–18, 123; *Recollections of the French Revolution,* 91
Toews, John, 'Intellectual History after the Linguistic Turn: The Autonomy of Meaning and the Irreducibility of Experience,' 21, 56–60, 64
Treichler, Paula, 194n
Tuke, Samuel, 157–8
Turgot, Anne-Robert, 117

Ungar, Steven, 198n

Van Gogh, Vincent, 204n
Veeser, H. Aram, 56n
Volosinov, V.N., 58n

Index

Voltaire, François-Marie Arouet de, 117

Walzer, Michael, 7n, 126n
Weber, Max, 76n, 77, 84, 101, 156, 158, 164n
West, Cornel, 180
White, Hayden, 23n, 38, 80n, 83n, 88n, 109n, 132n, 180–1, 182n; *The Content of the Form: Narrative Discourse and Historical Representation*, 23n; 'Historical Emplotment and the Problem of Truth,' 132n; *Metahistory: The Historical Imagination in Nineteenth-Century Europe*, 23n, 38, 80n, 83n, 88n, 109n; *Tropics of Discourse: Essays in Cultural Criticism*, 23n, 182n

Williams, Raymond, 194n
Wills, David, 175n
Windschuttle, Keith, 115–16n, 181n
Wood, Nancy, 195n
Wood, Philip R., 195n
Woolf, Virginia, 36, 36–7n
Wright, Richard, 207n

Yates, Frances, 153
Young, James E., 63n

Zammito, John, 21n
Žižek, Slavoj, 51n, 205, 211n; *Enjoy Your Symptom!*, 51n; *Looking Awry*, 51n; *The Sublime Object of Ideology*, 51n, 211n